Little Musicals for Little Theatres

Little Musicals for Little Theatres

A Reference Guide to the Musicals
That Don't Need Chandeliers
or Helicopters to Succeed

Denny Martin Flinn

LIMELIGHT EDITIONS

Published in 2006 by Limelight Editions (an imprint of Amadeus Press, LLC) 512 Newark Pompton Turnpike, Pompton Plains, New Jersey 07444, USA Website: *www.limelighteditions.com*

Book design by Lisa A. Jones

All photographs in this book are used courtesy of the respective theatres and/or photographers.

Printed in the United States of America

Library of Congress Cataloging-in-Publication Data

Flinn, Denny Martin.
  Little musicals for little theatres : a reference guide to the musicals that don't need chandeliers or helicopters to succeed / by Denny Martin Flinn.-- 1st ed.
     p. cm.
  Includes index.
  ISBN-13: 978-0-87910-321-7
  1. Musicals--Production and direction. 2. Musicals--Stories, plots, etc. 3. Musicals--Stage guides. I. Title.
  MT955.F55 2006
  792.6'45--dc22
                    2005037925

For all their hard work in keeping the theatre alive,
this book is dedicated
to amateur thespians everywhere.

Table of Contents

Part Two: The Themed Revues

Part Three: The Composer/Lyricist Revues

Prologue

Off-Broadway's principal reputation began with drama. The first productions of Eugene O'Neill's plays by the Provincetown Players in Greenwich Village in the 1920s and revivals of his plays at the downtown Circle in the Square Theatre in the 1950s marked the beginning of two eras that brought great theatre to small auditoriums. Off-Broadway became a place for theatre that relied on the strength of its drama and ideas, not its sets and costumes.

Musicals, on the other hand, were for uptown, for the tired businessman who, Max Gordon once said, referring to the legs of chorus girls, "could judge a musical before the curtain was halfway up."

But "necessity is the mother of invention" (*Love in a Wood* by William Wycherly, act III, scene 3, 1672). The Princess Theatre musicals of Guy Bolton, P. G. Wodehouse, and Jerome Kern established the "integrated" musical, because the little Princess Theatre, three blocks south of 42nd Street and encompassing only 299 seats, couldn't afford Broadway stars, large ensembles, or orchestras, and had to rely more on character and story. Revues, too, began to be scaled down when the Depression curtailed the lavish spectacles of Ziegfeld and his imitators.

It wasn't until 1955, however—when Lucille Lortel, an actress, acquired the Theatre de Lys on Christopher Street in the West Village (renamed the Lucille Lortel Theatre in 1999) and helped produce an English-language revival of *The Threepenny Opera*—that writers and producers of musicals and revues really began to see the potential in off-Broadway theatres. This "little" production of the German musical created in Berlin during Germany's Weimar era had failed on Broadway in the spring of 1933, where it closed after only twelve performances. At the 299-seat Theatre de Lys, it ran for seven years, and the off-Broadway musical was born.

Thank goodness. For throughout the world there are more small theatres than large ones—that's an unsubstantiated but practical guess, I think—and they deserve musicals.

So the purpose of this book is severalfold: to browse through that small, exotic corner of American art known as the off-Broadway musical; to demonstrate that there are plenty of musicals even the smallest and poorest of theatres can mount successfully; and to encourage theatres that have already performed *Fiddler on the Roof* too many times to strike out in new and different directions.

This book, then, is a reference guide to small musicals: those shows that are unique, intimate, and individual, their success relying more on substance than style, more on charm than spectacle, more on drama than sets and costumes, more on character than chorus girls. All the musicals catalogued here can be produced under almost any circumstances. Their casts run from two to a dozen, although some can be augmented with an optional chorus. Their sets and costumes are inexpensive. The revues in particular are very flexible, give everyone a chance to stop the show, and feature design elements that require more creativity than money.

Off-Broadway has been host to a number of big Broadway musicals revived in smaller circumstances—including *Leave It to Jane,* whose 1959 revival at the Sheridan Square Playhouse had a long run, bringing the early Bolton, Wodehouse, and Kern musicals back into public view; the Brothers Gershwin's *Oh! Kay,* with a book also by Bolton and Wodehouse (1960, East 74th Street Theatre); and Cole Porter's *Gay Divorce* (1960, at the Cherry Lane). This wonderful idea—old Broadway musicals revived off-Broadway—soon faded out, however, as the cost of producing musicals rose to more than the minimal seating could sustain. For that matter, revivals of the now-classic *Threepenny Opera*—the grandfather of off-Broadway musicals—have all been on Broadway, its large cast no longer economically viable in a small theatre. These shows fall outside the giant theatrical shadow cast by *The Fantasticks* (eight actors, two musicians, one set), the quintessential off-Broadway musical, and thus are not catalogued here, because of the resources required to produce them.

On the other hand, I've thrown in a few Broadway shows, if their casts are small enough and their sets manageable by little theatres. *I Do! I Do!*—to take the most remarkable example—premiered in Broadway's venerable 46th Street Theatre (since renamed the Richard Rodgers) starring Robert Preston and Mary Martin, but its two characters and one four-poster bed will sit comfortably in almost any theatre.

A few notes:

Musicals generally undergo a long gestation period, developing in one regional theatre, redeveloping in another, slowly wending their way to New York. The theatres, opening dates, and number of performances listed here are generally for the ultimate New York production, unless otherwise noted, as is the "original" cast. The reason for this is simple: despite long runs in the hinterlands or way-off-Broadway success, the true test is often the commercial New York audience, so the number of performances, where available, might give you an additional barometer with which to ponder that musical's power.

Don't go betting on the precise "number of performances" listed, however. It's amazing how different sources differ. I have tried to suss out the truth, so you can see just how successful the ultimate production was, but am sure there are some errors. That's usually because previews are sometimes counted and sometimes not, and when a production moves from one theatre to another, accountants lose count.

The date is, as often as possible, the official critical opening, not the first public performance.

Regarding the musical numbers, those too may have some variations. The original program might say one thing, but the authors (sometimes wisely, sometimes just out of fretting) often alter the show for future productions and give that version to the licensing house. Many of the revues are virtually constant works-in-progress.

You will, of course, want to investigate further before deciding which shows to put your energy behind. If they are not published, you can usually read the full manuscripts via the licensing company for a small refundable deposit or just postage.

Entries are organized into three sections. First, the book musicals. They have a plot (however lame) and characters. Then, the revues built around a theme (an era, relationships, New York). Finally, the composer compendiums. Although you could always seek permission from the music publishers to put together your own collection of songs, these tried-and-tested revues come complete with organization, arrangements, and orchestrations, and sometimes even a working concept.

Finally, if I've left out a few good, small musicals that you should consider, and I'm sure I have, my apologies. While not all the musicals here are recommended, some that should be aren't here. Time and my insufficient knowledge of them are my only excuses.

So curtains up on the small musicals that either began or belong in the intimate theatres of America, where everyone has a good seat, the voices are hot off the vocal chords, the orchestra is a combo, the chorus doesn't come trampling on like a passel of peacocks for the big numbers, and the spotlight operator has to climb over the last row of seats to access his platform.

Little Musicals for Little Theatres

Part One: The Book Musicals

Love the great American book musical but don't have the resources for Hello, Dolly!*? Here's a collection of shows your theatre can produce with a minimum of resources. Most require only a single or unit set and not too many costumes per performer. A few are internationally famous, but many have languished in the marginalized corner known as "off-Broadway musicals" and deserve a hearing. After your audience has seen* The Fantasticks *and* You're a Good Man, Charlie Brown, *don't worry. There are plenty more where they came from.*

3hree

The New Musical

Well, not *the* new musical, exactly. Three one-act musicals—a tragic romance, a ghost story, and a flight of fancy—each by different authors, done together in their premiere but depending upon each other not a whit. All three were developed and produced in 1999 at the Prince Music Theatre in Philadelphia, then played a brief run at the Ahmanson Theatre in LA, but haven't yet made it to Broadway.

The Mice

Book by Julia Jordan
Music by Laurence O'Keefe
Lyrics by Nell Dunbar Banjamin

Inspired by a short story by Sinclair Lewis.

Time and Place: Winter 1947. Chippewa Falls, Minnesota.

Synopsis: Allan is an exterminator, who requires that his clients leave their home for several hours while he works. In fact, Virga comes over, and that's where and when they frequently consummate their affair, since both are unhappily married. As divorce is out of the question, the doomed lovers finally decide to inhale the rodent poison as they dance their final dance.

Directed by Brad Rouse.

Album Cast:

Virga Vay…Valerie Wright
Orio Vay…Herndon Lackey
Francis…Roger E. Dewitt
The Town…Donna Lynne Champlin,
 Will Gartshore, Rachel Ulanet

Allan Cedar…John Scherer
Bertha Cedar…Jessica Molaskey
Moseley…Christopher Fitzgerald

Musical Numbers:

Mice!…Town, Orlo, Bertha
Two Hours Here…Virga, Allan
What If…Allan, Bertha, Virga, Orlo
That's All I Need…Allan, Virga, Town
If You'd Be Mine…Allan, Virga

Difficulties/Advantages: Romantic but very dark. Will anyone in your audience understand a legal time when: "She wouldn't give me a divorce"?

Lavender Girl

Book by James D. Waedekin
Music and Lyrics by John Bucchino

Time and Place: 1927. The woods outside Montgomery, Alabama.

Synopsis: Colin, on his way to a high-society party on "the hill," runs into (and almost over) Emily, nicknamed Lavender, and takes her to the party, where she draws much attention from the men and envy from the women and dances away the night. Afterwards Colin, clearly in love, loses her in the woods. Following her to her mother's house, he discovers the reason her dress was old fashioned. She died some time ago. At the finale, however, he finds her once more in the moonlight.

Directed by Scott Schwartz.

Original Cast:

Colin...Will Garthshore
Mitch...Christopher Fitzgerald
Louise...Donna Lynne Champlin
Partygoer...Roger E. Dewitt

Lavender...Rachel Ulanet
Leroy...John Scherer
Rita...Valerie Wright
Mama Sayer...Jessica Molaskey

Musical Numbers:

Leavin' Town...Colin
We've Got Time...Colin, Lavender, Company
Dancing...Lavender
Foolish Dreamin'/Something Beautiful...Mama Sayer, Colin, Lavender
Real Enough to Change My Mind...Colin, Lavender

Difficulties/Advantages: The old ghost story (with Cinderella as the ghost), romantic music, and a Charleston thrown in.

Flight of the Lawnchair Man

Book by Peter Ullian
Music and Lyrics by Robert Lindsey Nassif
Based on a concept by Robert Lindsey Nassif.

Time and Place: Today. New Jersey and the air above it.

Synopsis: True: a man in New Jersey attached multiple helium balloons to his lawn chair and floated way up into the sky, whereupon the local police arrested him and the F.A.A. fined him. Undoubtedly inspired by that news story, the authors here have added the (macho) pilot who saw him; his (brave) girlfriend; and Leonardo da Vinci, Charles Lindbergh, and Amelia Earhart—the latter three he meets as they are flying by in their own inventions.

Directed by Harold Prince.

Original Cast:

Big Jack Preston...John Scherer
Gracie...Donna Lynne Champlin
FAA Agent/Mother...Jessica Molaskey
Leonardo da Vinci/Voice of Alex Trebek
   ...Roger E. Dewitt
Amelia Earhart...Rachel Ulanet

Blaire...Valerie Wright
Jerry...Christopher Fitzgerald
Reporter...Will Gartshore
Charles Lindberg/F.A.A.
   Official...Herndon Lackey

Musical Numbers:

To Tame the Sky...Big Jack, Jerry, Gracie, Company
What Is That?...Big Jack, Blaire

3

Tiny…Jerry
Genius…Leonardo da Vinci
The Air Is Free…Gracie
Never Finish Before You Are Finished…Charles Lindbergh, Company
Creature of the Air…Amelia Earhart
Finale…Company

Difficulties/Advantages: While the first two one-acts are darkly romantic, this one is the opposite. Although all the one-acts in this catalogue could be performed alone, the first two here are brief and do go together very well. The third is being expanded into a full-lengther, and it should be a terrific musical if the writers have enough good ideas.

The Amorous Flea

The Amorous Flea at TheatreCNU, Christopher Newport University, Newport News, VA.

Book by Jerry Devine
Music and Lyrics by Bruce Montgomery

Based on Molière's *L'Ecole des Femmes (School for Wives)*.

Of all the classic playwrights, Molière stands as one whose work cries out for music (which in fact he utilized often, in combination with the father of classic ballet, Jean Baptiste Lully). Intrigue among his classic characters, all drawn from commedia dell'arte but revolving around a man with one outsized characteristic—a theatrical technique he pioneered on the heels of Ben Jonson's *Volpone*—lends itself to burlesque sketch humor, and here the adaptors of *School for Wives* have mined that vein well.

Time and Place: The 18th century. Paris.

4

Synopsis: Arnolphe has created every man's dream: a perfectly innocent, beautiful young woman whom he has kept to himself since she was four years old and is about to marry. Just as she has reached the age of her majority, however, she falls in love with a young man who happens by. Arnolphe befriends the young man without exposing his role as the young woman's lecherous fiancé. This leads to any number of takes and double takes as he listens without giving himself away to descriptions of the young man's success in wooing her. By the end of act 2, he's caused the young man to hide in her bedroom, and as he insists she remain in her bed all night, we see four arms close the shutters.

By the next morning, it ought to be clear to even the most naïve of audiences that she's no longer a virgin, a plot twist that wouldn't have passed the Hayes Office in the twentieth century but was probably riotous in the eighteenth. Act 3 brings her original father back to town, insisting that she follow through on a previously arranged marriage. When everyone discovers (long after the audience) that the earlier betrothed is the young man himself, all are satisfied except Arnolphe. Today Hollywood would probably tell the playwright to make the lead more sympathetic, but that wasn't Molière's way, and this Arnolphe is a classic Molière character.

East 78th Street Playhouse; February 17, 1964; 93 performances.

Staged by Jack Sydow.

Original Cast:

Arnolphe…Lew Parker	Chrysalde…David C. Jones
Alain…Jack Fletcher	Georgette…Ann Mitchell
Agnes…Imelda De Martin	Horace…Philip Proctor
Oronte…Ted Tiller	Enrique…Bryce Holman

Musical Numbers:

ACT I	All About Me…Arnolphe
	All About Me (reprise)…Arnolphe
	All About He…Agnes
	All About Him…Alain, Georgette
	Learning Love…Horace
	There Goes a Mad Old Man…Alain, Georgette
	Dialogue on Dalliance…Arnolphe, Agnes
ACT II	March of the Vigilant Vassals…Arnolphe, Alain, Georgette
	Lessons on Life…Arnolphe, Agnes
	Man Is a Man's Best Friend..Arnolphe, Horace
	The Other Side of the Wall…Agnes
	Closeness Begets Closeness…Agnes, Horace
ACT III	It's a Stretchy Day…Arnolphe, Agnes, Alain, Georgette
	When Time Takes Your Hand…Chrysalde
	The Amorous Flea…Arnolphe
	Learning Love (reprise)…Agnes, Horace
	Finale Act III…Full Company

Licensing: Samuel French

Difficulties/Advantages: Five wonderful commedia-style roles, topped by a classic comic who could, in this version, mug to his heart's delight, makes this ideal for a small theatrical company, though all have to sing well.

Angry Housewives

Book by A. M. Collins
Music and Lyrics by Chad Henry

Synopsis: When a makeup party fails to garner enough cash for a broke divorcée with a teenage son, four housewives form a punk band to compete in a talent contest for $2,000. Act 1 ends on their song "Eat Your F*&king Cornflakes." It's a hit.

Act 2 pits the housewives against their men. One has a son who is embarrassed that his mom is in a band; another has a boyfriend who wants her to sail to Hawaii before the band gets a chance to compete in the finals; a third has a husband who wants his wife at home, mixing his martinis. And one husband (for some unscripted reason) wants her to drop out. One by one, the men are reconciled to the idea. In fact, each of them shows up in drag for the finale, pretending to be the missing drummer, so the show can go on. (Then the drummer changes her mind and reappears.) Although they lose the contest to Big Dick and His Privates, they're offered a recording contract, and everyone is happy and not so angry anymore.

Minetta Lane Theatre; September 7, 1986; 15 previews, 137 performances.

Directed by Mitchell Maxwell. Choreographed by Wayne Cilento.

Original Cast:

Bev…Carolyn Casanave	Tim…Michael Manasseri
Wendy…Lorna Patterson	Jetta…Vicki Lewis
Carol…Carmille Saviola	Larry…Nicholas Wyman
Wallace…Michael Lembeck	Lewd Fingers…Lee Wilcoff

Musical Numbers:

ACT I
Hell School…Tim
Think Positive…Bev
Betty Jean…The Housewives
It's Gonna Be Fun…The Housewives
Generic Woman…The Housewives
Not at Home…Jetta
Betsy Moberly…Lewd, Wallace
Eat Your F*&king Cornflakes…The Housewives

ACT II
First Kid on the Block…Tim, the Housewives
Love O Meter…Lewd, Carol
Saturday Night…Wallace, the Housewives
Nobody Loves Me…Larry
Stalling for Time…All
Man from Glad…All
Finale…All

Licensing: Samuel French

Difficulties/Advantages: A punk band means punk music, not theatre music. To each his Dulcinea.

The Apple Tree

Book, Music, and Lyrics by Jerry Bock and Sheldon Harnick
Additional Book by Jerome Coopersmith

This wonderful, underappreciated musical is actually three one-act plays, barely related. Act 1 is based on Mark Twain's "The Diary of Adam and Eve." Act 2 is Frank Stockton's infamous short story "The Lady and the Tiger," read in hundreds of English classes, in which our hero has to decide which door has the lady and which the tiger, and we have to decide for ourselves. Act 3 is a Jules Feiffer take on Cinderella, called "Passionella," with a cleaning lady becoming a movie star. The latter two, besides being slick but weak, require a chorus and thus are not really little musicals. But act 1 is highly recommended as a wonderful small musical, running almost an hour.

The Diary of Adam and Eve

Based on the story by Mark Twain.

Synopsis: Adam, in a garden, is awakened by a voice (guess who) and told to stay away from the apple tree. A pain in his rib reveals Eve. Adam has both curiosity and reservations about Eve. They argue but make it to the sixth day, by which time Adam has built a shelter and, due to her crying, allowed Eve to join him in it when it rains. On Sunday Eve discovers the apple tree and meets the snake, who sings about the charms of forbidden fruit. She tries it. Although this changes things—a lion consumes a lamb and a thunderstorm comes up—she convinces Adam to take a taste. The rain then drives them out of the garden. Time passes, and we find them in a better shelter, now with two children, though Adam thinks they're fish. More time passes, Eve dies, and Adam decides that leaving the garden didn't really matter, because all along it was Eve who brought him happiness.

Shubert Theatre; October 18, 1966; 463 performances.

Directed by Mike Nichols. Choreographed by Herbert Ross and Lee Theodore.

Cast:

Adam...Alan Alda   Snake...Larry Blyden   Eve...Barbara Harris

Musical Numbers:

Eden Prelude...Orchestra
Here in Eden...Eve
Feelings...Eve
Eve...Adam
Friends...Eve
Forbidden Fruit...Snake
Adams's Reprise...Adam
It's a Fish...Adam
Lullaby...Eve
What Makes Me Love Him?...Eve

Licensing: Music Theatre International

Difficulties/Advantages: Requires four actors if you want to impersonate God, only three if you just use a recording, as the original did. The simplicity of the sets and costumes, few props, and the easy singability of the songs make this a simple show to produce. Bear in mind, however, that the three actors ought to be very good, and not just because they're impersonating the original Homo sapiens but because they have substantial parts that need charm and substance to beguile us for an hour.

Avenue X

The A Cappella Musical

Avenue X at the Dallas Theater Center, TX.

Book and Lyrics by John Jiler
Music by Ray Leslee

Blacks versus Italians as a Brooklyn neighborhood changes is the book for a series of original songs in the 1950s and '60s style of a capella doo-wop, with melodies ranging from rock 'n' roll to gospel, blues, jazz, and rap.

Time and Place: 1963. Gravesend, Brooklyn.

Synopsis: Italians Pasquale, Chuck, and Ubazz are going to enter a contest that could start their singing career, but Chuck is so in love with Barbara, Pasquale's sister, that he can't get to rehearsal. Pasquale, singing in a sewer where the reverb is great, meets Milton, also a singer and black, from the projects on the other side of the avenue. Pasquale asks Milton to fill in with them, which he'd love to do, except for Roscoe, who is one mean stepfather and who warns Milton against crossing the avenue. One scene after another

8

develops the racial tension between them, but Pasquale and Milton decide to sing a duet for the contest. When Chuck shows up, however, he's distraught over both Barbara's rejection and the fact that his best friend is going to sing with a black. This escalates, and Milton ends up killed by a subway car. "Where Is Love?" Not here.

Playwright's Horizons; February 21, 1994; 77 performances.

Directed by Mark Brokaw. Choreographed by Ken Roberson.

Original Cast:

The Italians:

Pasquale...Ted Brunetti	Chuck...John Leone
Ubazz...Roger Mazzeo	Barbara...Colette Hawley

The Blacks:

Milton...Harold Perrineau	Roscoe...Chuck Cooper
Julia...Alvaleta Guess	Winston...Keith Johnston

Musical Numbers:

Prologue...Company
A Thousand Summer Nights...Chuck, Pasquale, Ubazz, Company
Scat...Pasquale, Milton
Serves You Right...Pasquale, Milton
Waitin'...Roscoe, Julia
Io Sono Cosi Stanco...Ubazz, Barbara
Santa Cecilia...Barbara, Ubazz
Woman of the World...Barbara, Pasquale, Milton, Ubazz
She's Fifteen...Pasquale, Chuck, Ubazz
Stay...Roscoe, Milton, Winston, Pasquale, Ubazz
Where Are You Tonight?...Chuck, Men
Big Lucy...Roscoe, Milton, Winston, Pasquale, Ubazz
Why?...Milton, Men
Follow Me...Milton, Pasquale, Company
Follow Me (reprise)...Milton, Chorus
Moonlight on Old Sicily...Pasquale, Barbara, Company
Palermo...Chuck
Africa...Winston, Milton, Company
Gloria...Company (without Pasquale)
Command Me...Roscoe, Julia, Winston, Milton (optional), Ubazz
Roscoe's Rap (spoken)...Roscoe
Go There...Roscoe
'Til the End of Time...Roscoe, Chuck, Winston, Ubazz
Where Is Love?...Milton, Pasquale
Epilogue/Where Is Love?...Company

Licensing: Samuel French

Difficulties/Advantages: It takes great singers to sing a cappella, good actors to pull off the rich characters here, and a real authenticity in both the doo-wop style and the ethnicity to realize this unique ninety-minute musical. And with lead-in lines such as "Hey, remember this one" and "Listen to this," the songs don't extend the story or the characters but suspend them. Finally, there's a strange dichotomy between the traditionally ebullient song style and the vicious racial tension of the story. All that said, if you can pull this one off, your audience will be very happy.

9

Baby

Photo: Roger Jones

Baby at the Warehouse Theatre, Stephens College, Columbia, MO.

> Book by Sybille Pearson
> Music by David Shire
> Lyrics by Richard Maltby Jr.
>
> Based on a story developed with Susan Yankowitz.

Time and Place: Now. A New England College Town.

Synopsis: Three women are—or want to be—pregnant, but Danny, who tours with a second-rate punk-rock band (if that's not an oxymoron) and Lizzie are not sure they're ready; Nick has a low sperm count, frustrating Pam; and Alan and Arlene think they're too old to have another kid—don't tell Warren Beatty that—and after raising three children to adulthood, they might rather have some life left of their own. All three go through the trials and tribulations of the infamous nine months, and for a grand finale, a baby is born.

Ethel Barrymore Theatre; December 4, 1983; 241 performances.

Directed by Richard Maltby Jr. Musical Staging by Wayne Cilento.

Original Cast:

Lizzie Fields…Liz Callaway	Alan MacNally…James Congdon
Pam Sakarian…Catherine Cox	Arlene MacNally…Beth Fowler
Danny Hooper…Todd Graff	Nick Sakarian…Martin Vidnovic
Nurse/Ensemble…Barbara Gilbert	Mr. Weiss/Ensemble…Phillip Hoffman

Intern/Ensemble...Lon Hoyt
Dean Webber/Mr. Hart/Ensemble
...Dennis Waring

Doctor/Ensemble...John Jellison
Ensemble...Kirsti Carnahan, Kim Criswell,
Lisa Robinson, Judith Thiergaard

Musical Numbers:

ACT I   We Start Today...Principals, Ensemble
What Could Be Better...Lizzie, Danny
The Plaza...Alan, Arlene
Baby, Baby, Baby...Nick and Pam, Danny and Lizzie, Alan and Arlene
I Want It All...Lizzie, Pam, Arlene
At Night She Comes Home to Me...Nick, Danny
What Could Be Better (reprise)...Lizzie, Danny
Fatherhood Blues.. Danny, Alan, Nick, Dean Webber, Professor Weiss
Romance—Part I...Pam, Nick
I Know I Chose Right.. Danny
The Story Goes On...Lizzie

ACT II   The Ladies Singing Their Song...Lizzie, Ladies
What Is a Woman?...Arlene
Romance (reprise)...Pam, Nick
Romance—Part III...Pam, Nick
Easier to Love...Alan
Two People in Love...Danny, Lizzie, Ensemble
With You.. Pam, Nick
And What If We Had Loved Like That?...Alan, Arlene
Birth Sequence...Principals, Ensemble

Licensing: Music Theatre International

Difficulties/Advantages: The moderate fame of this show is based on the score, which is strong pop. An advantage is that the show will not date soon, allowing for contemporary sets (simple or even unit) and costumes. The disadvantage is that it's not a theatre score and thus has little atmosphere or style. The dull, nondescript original Broadway production compounded this problem. It also featured an utterly useless chorus, when you really need only three couples in three age groups—twenties, thirties, and forties—and five small roles that could be doubled.

One problem with the book is known as the "Ninety-nine Bottles of Beer" problem in dramatic literature. Every time the book develops an idea or theme of sorts, it has to be repeated three times from three points of view. We just know that we've got two more scenes or choruses coming on the same subject before we can move on. Still, it covers nine months that feature numerous emotions many women will either be familiar with or want to be. Perhaps tightened up and in a more intimate theatre, it could even touch a man's cynical heart.

Ballad for a Firing Squad

Book by Jerome Coopersmith
Music by Edward Thomas
Lyrics by Martin Charnin

The 1967–68 Broadway season almost featured a musical based on the World War II spy Mata Hari. It is more or less legendary for having closed in Washington about twenty minutes into the first act during its pre-Broadway tryout. That's when David Merrick, its producer, walked out and decided not to throw good money after bad. "I can tell about a musical in the first twenty minutes," Merrick once said.

But the ever inventive and ambitious Martin Charnin—its lyricist and instigator—reconfigured the show for off-Broadway, and it opened again, at the Theatre de Lys, where it ran somewhat longer. (Not to worry about Martin Charnin. A few years later, he created the musical *Annie*.)

Time and Place: World War I, 1917. On the battlefields, in the salons, and in the offices of the French Intelligence Service in Paris, France.

Synopsis: (By Jerome Coopersmith.) "Captain Henri LaFarge, a zealous slave-driving officer of French military intelligence, is obsessed with tracking down the person he believes to be Germany's number one spy in France—the exotic dancer Mata Hari. Taking personal charge of her surveillance, LaFarge becomes attracted to the woman and, against his better judgment, has an affair with her. To satisfy his newly formed doubts about her loyalty to France, LaFarge sets up a trap into which the dancer falls. She is tried before a military tribunal and sentenced to death, after which LaFarge learns that Mata Hari may have been framed by his superiors who were eager to find a scapegoat for their military losses. LaFarge attempts to stop the execution but fails to do so. Our last vision of him is that of a broken man, ironically applauded by the citizens of France for capturing the spy.

"A parallel story line involves a young boy of seventeen who is seduced into joining the army by recruiters singing praises of the glories of war. In a series of short scenes interwoven with the Mata Hari story, the boy is gradually hardened to the realities of death and of killing. The stories converge when the boy is seen as a member of Mata Hari's execution squad."

Theatre de Lys; December 11, 1968; 15 performances.

Directed by Martin Charnin. Choreographed by Alan Johnson.

Original Cast (off-Broadway):

The Young Soldier…Bruce Scott
LaFarge…James Hurst
Mata Hari…Renata Vaselle
General Delacorte…Elliott Savage
Pistolette…Vi Velasco
Philipe…George Marcy
Mme. Dupre…Irma Rogers
1st American Soldier…Peter Shawn
Old French Soldier…Dominic Chianese

Major Bonnard…Stanley Church
Countess…Liz Sheridan
Paulette…Adelle Rasey
Duvalier…George Marcy
Michele…Neva Small
Claudine…Liz Sheridan
Maurice…Dominic Chianese
2nd American Soldier…Joseph Corby

Musical Numbers:

ACT I   Ballad for a Firing Squad…Young Soldier
Is This Fact?…LaFarge, Major Bonnard
Dance at the Salon…Mata Hari
There Is Only One Thing to Be Sure Of…Mata Hara, Company
How Young You Were Tonight…LaFarge, Paulette
I'm Saving Myself for a Soldier…Duvalier, Pistolette, Company
Everyone Has Something to Hide…Mata Hari
Fritzie…Young Soldier
The Choice Is Yours…Mata Hari, LaFarge

Sextet…Paulette, Claudine, Mme. Dupre, Philipe, Michele, Maurice
Maman…Young Soldier
Not Now, Not Here…Mata Hari
Is This Fact? (reprise)…LaFarge
Maman (reprise)…Young Soldier

ACT II   I Did Not Sleep Last Night…Mata Hari
Hello Yank…Young Soldier, Old Soldier, Two American Soldiers
I Don't See Him Very Much Anymore…Paulette
Sextet (reprise)…Paulette, Claudine, Mme. Dupre, Philipe, Michele, Maurice
What Then?…LaFarge
What Might Have Been…Mata Hari
Ballad for a Firing Squad…Young Soldier

Licensing: The authors; contact Edward Thomas at Somat Publishing, 162 West 56th Street, Suite 503, New York, New York 10019; 212-581-0910

Difficulties/Advantages: That second paragraph of the synopsis doesn't do justice to the soldier's song "Maman," one of the most powerful antiwar songs ever written and on whose basis alone I have included this seventeen-role off-Broadway musical. With doubling and possibly some rewrites, you could perhaps bring the cast down. As it was done at the Theatre de Lys (now Lucille Lortel), it ought to be manageable for small theatres, and it deserves a rehearing.

Bat Boy

Story and Book by Keythe Farley and Brian Flemming
Music and Lyrics by Laurence O'Keefe

Cross *Pygmalion* with *Beauty and the Beast*, throw in a touch of *Jekyll and Hyde*, and you've got *Bat Boy*. It's a show chock-full of high camp, but isn't that what off-Broadway does best?

Time and Place: The present. Hope Falls, West Virginia, population 500.

Synopsis: The Bat Boy—half boy, half bat—is discovered in a cave (where else) by the Taylor children. He bites Little Ruthie but is civilized by the wife of the town's veterinarian, Dr. Parker (in a hilarious take on a "Rain in Spain" type number). Unfortunately, not unlike the plant in *Little Shop of Horrors,* he's addicted to blood. (But he's working on a twelve-step program.) When the wife appears to care more for the Bat Boy than for her husband, the vet murders Ruthie in the hospital and plans to get the Bat Boy blamed.

Act 2 opens on the town's revival meeting. The Bat Boy—you can now call him Edgar—appears to ask for acceptance (now in elegant garb and with BBC accent), but Dr. Parker announces that Ruthie has died by the Bat Boy's bite. Chaos. Edgar flees to the forest. Mom and daughter Shelley find him first. Shelley confesses her love and Edgar returns it. This upsets Mom because—you must have got it by now—Edgar and Shelley are brother and sister! The whole town arrives and the climax ensues, in which Dr. Parker and his wife explain, in a clever flashback sequence, just why the Bat Boy is their son Edgar. (Those darn science experiments.) In a finish worthy of *Hamlet,* Mom, Dad, and Bat Boy all die, the carnage an inevitable result of the beast in all of us.

Union Square Theatre; March 21, 2001; 278 performances.

Directed by Scott Schwartz. Musical staging by Christopher Gatelli.

Bat Boy at the Actor's Theatre of Charlotte, NC.

Original Off-Broadway Cast:

Bat Boy...Deven May
Dr. Thomas Parker...Sean McCourt
Sheriff Reynolds...Richard Pruitt
Taylor, Ned...Daria Hardeman
Mrs. Taylor, Roy, Rev. Billy Hightower,
   Institute Man...Trent Armand Kendall

Meredith Parker...Kaitlin Hopkins
Shelley Parker...Kerry Butler
Rick Taylor, Lorraine, Doctor, Mr. Dillon
   ...Doug Storm
Bud, Daisy, Pan...Jim Price

Musical Numbers:

ACT I   Hold Me, Bat Boy...Company
           Christian Charity...Sheriff, Shelley, Meredith
           Ugly Boy...Shelley, Meredith
           Whatcha Wanna Do?...Shelley, Rick
           A Home for You...Meredith, Bat Boy
           Another Dead Cow...Bud, Ned, Roy, Lorraine, Maggie
           Dance with Me, Darling...Parker
           Mrs. Taylor's Lullaby...Mrs. Taylor
           Show You a Thing or Two...Bat Boy, Meredith, Shelley, Parker
           Christian Charity (reprise)...Cheriff, Parker, Ned, Bud, Lorraine, Townsperson #2,
             Maggie
           A Home for You (reprise)...Bat Boy
           Comfort and Joy...Parker, Voice, Meredith, Shelley, Town
ACT II   A Joyful Noise...Hightower, Ned, Bud, Maggie, Lorraine, Sheriff, Choir
           Let Me Walk Among You...Bat Boy
           Find the Bat Boy...Rick, Townfolk

Three Bedroom House…Meredith, Shelley
Children, Children…Pan, Animals, Baby Boy, Shelley
Inside Your Heart…Baby Boy, Shelley
Apology to a Cow…Bat Boy
Finale: I Imagine You're Upset…Bat Boy, Shelley, Meredith, Parker, Sheriff, Townfolk
Finale: Hold Me, Bat Boy (reprise)…Shelley, Chorus

Licensing: Dramatists Play Service

Difficulties/Advantages: Here's a quote from the authors: "There are many ways to stage this show. A cast of ten is possible (see the New York credits), as is a cast of one hundred and ten. A spare set is fine, an elaborate set can work, too. Intense blood effects, no blood at all—it's up to you, your taste, and your budget." This is followed, however, by the usual—and important—caveat for satires: play it straight. If you laugh at yourself, the audience won't. Truth works. Or, as Neil Simon once said, "Never try to make comedy funny."

This should be a ball to play, given that its salient entertainment is that it "sends up" show business genres, and the score, according to the composer, is "eclectic" (read pastiche), with influences as wide as Stephen Sondheim, Bernard Herrmann, Miklos Rozsa, Frank Loesser, Kurt Weill, Gilbert and Sullivan, Led Zeppelin, Bad Company, Boston, and Queen. It didn't find much of a New York audience but is finding a larger, less fickle one worldwide. A whole bunch of juicy roles, much funnier and hipper than *Beauty and the Beast,* and the old "tolerance" theme is always nice.

Birds of Paradise

Book by Winnie Holzman and David Evans
Music by David Evans
Lyrics by Winnie Holzman

That rare thing, a genuine musical comedy farce, without stooping to spoof.

Time and Place: The present. The meeting hall of the oldest church on Harbor Island, a small fictional island somewhere on the eastern seaboard.

Synopsis: An amateur theatre company is about to rehearse Dave's musical in front of a well-known actor who left the island two decades ago for fame and fortune, and is home visiting his brother. Suddenly the actor likes Homer's musical, not Dave's, and wants to play the lead and direct, which he does. He cuts and reinterprets Homer's masterpiece, undertakes an affair with an actress, and avoids calls from his agent…

Until he hears it's a bona fide offer for a role in a Broadway play, which he badly needs, because his career isn't going all that well, to tell the truth. All this precipitates angst among the amateurs, as well as within the marriage of his brother and his sister-in-law. When the actor quits the day before opening, he reveals himself to be a cad (as far as anyone sympathizing with real people is concerned), which causes a new togetherness among the previously bickering cast, and the show goes on without him anyway.

Promenade Theatre; October 2, 1987; 29 previews, 24 performances.

Directed by Arthur Laurents. Musical staging by Linda Haberman.

Original Cast:

Stella...Barbara Walsh
Dave...Andrew Hill Newman
Hope...Donna Murphy
Lawrence Wood...John Cunningham

Marjorie...Mary Beth Peil
Andy...J. K. Simmons
Homer...Todd Graff
Julia...Crista Moore

Musical Numbers:

ACT I   So Many Nights...Homer, Marjorie, Stella, Andy, Hope, Dave
         Diva...Hope, Dave, Andy
         Every Day Is Night...Julia
         Somebody...Wood, Company
         Coming True...Homer, Julia
         It's Only a Play...Homer, Company
         She's Out There...Andy
         Birds of Paradise...Marjorie, Stella, Hope
         Imagining You...Company
ACT II   Penguins Must Sing...Dave, Hope, Andy
         You're Mine...Marjorie
         Things I Can't Forget...Homer, Marjorie
         After Opening Night...Homer, Marjorie
         Chekhov...Company
         Something New...Company

Licensing: Samuel French

Difficulties/Advantages: Being believable and wacky at the same time is the trick to farce characters. These four male and four female roles have plenty of opportunity to be both, and
putting on a bad musical can lead to plenty of laughs. (See the films *Waiting for Guffman*
and *The Tall Guy.*) This tight comedy has a few moments of real honesty and a wonderful theme too. Author: "I think one ought to annoy the audience, make them squirm,
shock them out of their complacency!" Experienced actor: "But isn't it relatively safe to
shock people? The real risk is revealing yourself." If only all those writers and directors
still stuck in the sixties avant-garde theatre movement had learned that by now.

Boy Meets Boy

Book by Bill Solly and Donald Ward
Music and Lyrics by Bill Solly

When, in the early going, the premise turns out to be that homosexuality is normal and
accepted, you know you're not in a musical about gays, but in a gay musical. Not a bad
idea, if only the plot were better.

Time and Place: December 1936. London and Paris.

Synopsis: We begin with the news that there's going to be a fabulous party at the Savoy, because
notorious gay American newspaperman Casey O'Brien is in town. We don't get to see
the party, but the next morning, Casey is hung over and has missed the big story: The
King has abdicated for Wally Simpson. Off to find another story to make it up to his
editors, Casey comes upon the fact that American millionaire Clarence and young
schlub Guy were going to be married—groom to groom—but Guy jilted him, ending

up the night at Casey's party, where Casey doesn't believe he's Guy, so Guy pretends he knows Guy and gets an evening on the town by elaborating on Guy to Casey. Later, alone, the schlub turns himself into a handsome young man, with just his confidence (and a song). This Guy Casey falls in love with. They plan to run off to Paris, and Clarence tries to stop them but fails, but at the train station, handsome Guy becomes schlub Guy again and says that handsome Guy has jilted Casey. It's a noble move, because he has been convinced that he'd ruin Guy's career. The first-act curtain falls on boy-loses-boy, and Casey still doesn't seem to spot that schlub Guy and handsome guy are one and the same.

In Paris, we get the obligatory French nightclub number, performed by Guy's aunt. Casey arrives and, with Clarence's help, manages to convince Guy that his career won't be ruined—yes, this is all as inane as it sounds—and boy gets boy "in the end" (which they sing, in the only decent double entendre in the libretto).

Actors' Playhouse; September 17, 1975; 463 performances.

Directed by Ron Troutman. Musical numbers staged by Robin Reseen.

Original Cast:

Casey O'Brien…Joe Barrett	Andrew…Paul Ratkevich
Guy Rose…David Gallegly	Bellboy…Bobby Bowen
Reporters…Richard King, Bobby Reed, Dan Rounds	
Photographers…Jan Crean, Monica Grignon	
The Van Wagners…Bobby Bowen, Kathy Willinger	
Clarence Cutler…Raymond Wood	
Lady Rose…Rita Gordon	Bruce…Bobby Reed
Assistant Hotel Manager…Richard King	Porter…Richard King
Rosita…Kathy Willinger	Lolita…Mary-Ellen Hanlon
Pepita…Jan Crean	Jane…Monica Grignon
Josephine La Rose…Rita Gordon	Alphonse…Bobby Bowen

Musical Numbers:

ACT I Prologue: Boy Meets Boy/Party in Room 203…Chorus
Giving It Up for Love…Casey, Andrew
Me…Clarence, Chorus
The English Rose…Reporters, Photographers
Marry an American…Chorus
It's a Boy's Life…Casey, Guy
Does Anybody Love You?…Guy
You're Beautiful…Guy
Let's!…Casey, Chorus
Let's! (dance)…Casey, Guy
Giving It Up for Love (reprise)…Casey
Finaletto…Clarence, Chorus

ACT II Just My Luck…Casey, Clarence, Girls
It's a Dolly…Josephine, Boys
What Do I Care?…Guy
Clarence's Turn…Clarence
Does Anybody Love You (reprise)…Casey, Guy
Finale…Company

Licensing: Unknown

Difficulties/Advantages: Unlike the uptown *La Cage aux Folles*, there are no homosexual issues here. The whole thing is simply a romantic comedy of the oldest style, with a handsome leading man and…a handsome leading man. That's what makes it interesting, if a bit silly. But then, so were the Princess Theatre Musicals, and we revere them. There are twenty-two roles, but the script will show you how to do it with thirteen performers.

Brownstone

By Josh Rubins, Peter Larson, and Andrew Cadiff

Although *Brownstone* is about "city living in general, about relationships and feelings that could affect people living anywhere," it really is a quintessentially New York piece, particularly considering the architecture. A cantata for urban thirtysomethings, its various themes, popular in the eighties, seem quaint today, even on the verge of cliché. (Or having lived through them all, am I just blasé?)

Time and Place: The entire action takes place during the course of one year, from autumn to autumn, in and around a brownstone apartment building in New York City.

Synopsis: Three singles and a couple live in a brownstone walk-up. Stuart moves to the big city and is stymied by his attempts to make friends—especially with Howard, a reclusive writer married to Mary, a schoolteacher eager to have children but not getting along with her husband. Stuart finally manages a tryst with Joan, a single woman dreaming of living in the country. Howard moves out because his wife hates his unfinished Russian thriller. His nightmare—in song and dance, of course—is the babies she wants. Joan's is living in a co-op, which the building is becoming, so everyone has to decide whether to buy in or get out. Howard moves back in—with the beginnings of the serious fiction he was once noted for. Joan moves to the country, and at the curtain, Stuart finally meets Claudia, who has been dying to meet someone since her last breakup, but in a series of carefully staged comings and goings equal to a French farce (without the sex), they haven't run into each other all year, despite living in the same cramped apartment house. They smile at each other as the lights fade out, and the audience is left with the mistaken impression that ordinary young singles can afford a brownstone apartment in Manhattan.

Hudson Guild Theatre, May 23–June 24, 1984.

Directed by Andrew Cadiff. Choreographed by Cheryl Carty.

Original Cast:

Howard…Lenny Wolpe	Mary…Maureen McGovern
Claudia…Loni Ackerman	Stuart…Ralph Bruneau
Joan…Kimberly Farr	

Licensing: Broadway Play Publishing

Difficulties/Advantages: Five good roles, no doubling or expansion possible. Four apartments, front and rear on first and second floors, with staircases, hallways, small lobby/mailbox area, outside stoop, and trash-can well are required. According to the authors, this can be done very realistically or just with platforms and indications. In fact, without all four apartment sets, well-dressed for the characters who inhabit them, this would be a pretty dull musical.

Celebration

A Musical Fable
Words by Tom Jones
Music by Harvey Schmidt

This is included here for three reasons. One, it's by Jones and Schmidt, they of *The Fantasticks*, the quintessential small musical. Two, there are only four principals. The chorus numbered twelve on Broadway, but that's a very flexible number. Three, Jones himself admits that "When we moved it into the Ambassador Theatre (from off-Broadway), it didn't feel as good. It seemed somewhat silly up there, not because it was less effective than a Broadway musical, but because it wasn't a Broadway musical."

Time and Place: New Year's Eve, during a total eclipse of the sun. A city and a garden.

Synopsis: But time and place are irrelevant here. *Celebration*—like *The Fantasticks*—is a fable about young love and the obstacles to retaining it. We start with a total eclipse of the sun and our narrator Potemkin and the Revelers celebrating the winter solstice, although already there's an ominous tone, for we are reminded that ancient civilizations, not understanding the relationship of sun and earth, worried that spring might never come again. A total eclipse must have really terrified them. An orphan shows up and is befriended by our narrator and introduced to the evil ways of the city. He meets a girl, an angel. There's an attraction, but he's nobody and she wants to be somebody. Enter a rich man, too glutinous to enter the kingdom of God. But he's bored: hasn't had a good laugh, good cry, or good erection in twenty-five years. The boy sings about the beauty of his garden, and this helps. In fact, the boy reminds him of himself years ago. Mr. Rich meets the girl too. Finally, there's that erection. (Not to worry, all done in metaphor.) He has more to offer the girl, and she accepts. Plans for a big celebration bring down the act 1 curtain.

The girl is now loaded down with diamonds. But the boy has his garden. The rich man is joyous over how young the girl makes him feel. He has himself done over by beauticians and sees himself as young and handsome as the boy—whose garden he's going to tear up (artificial flowers last longer)but he promises him Knowledge and Experience of the world instead: better stuff. Potemkin arranges a bacchanal, and the rich man has a great time, but the rich man can't stay young, and the boy decides to stay and fight the rich man for the garden. In the end, time moves inexorably on. Summer battles winter. Youth battles age. Inevitably there is only one winner. And seeds will sprout in the garden again.

Ambassador Theatre; January 22, 1969; 109 performances.

Directed by Tom Jones. Musical numbers staged and choreographed by Vernon Lusby.

Original Cast:

Potemkin...Keith Charles
Angel...Susan Watson
Orphan...Michael Glenn-Smith
Rich...Ted Thurston
The Revelers...Glenn Bastion, Cindi Bulak, Stephen de Ghelder, Leah Horen, Patricia Lens, Norman Mathews, Frank Newell, Pamela Peadon, Felix Rice, Sally Riggs, Gary Wales, Hal Watters

Musical Numbers:

ACT I   Celebration...Potemkin, the Revelers
Orphan in the Storm...Orphan, the Revelers

Survive…Potemkin, the Revelers
Somebody…Angel, the Devil Girls
Bored…Rich
My Garden…Orphan, the Revelers
Love Song…Angel, Potemkin, Rich, Orphan, the Revelers
To the Garden…Everyone

ACT II I'm Glad to See You've Got What You Want…Angel, Orphan
It's You Who Makes Me Young…Rich, the Revelers
Not My Problem…Potemkin, the Dancing Machines
Fifty Million Years Ago…Orphan
The Beautician Ballet…Potemkin, the Revelers
Saturnalia…Potemkin, the Revelers
Under the Tree…Angel, the Girls
Winter and Summer…Everyone
Celebration (finale)…Everyone

Licensing: Music Theatre International

Difficulties/Advantages: To each his own interpretation of a fable, but here's mine: Capitalism run amuck gets its comeuppance. Okay, I'm prejudiced. Love keeps us young? If so, time's momentum is a dark and awful thing, for seasons won't stop changing, and boy and girl will grow old too. More to the point, *Celebration* is a wonderful piece for its score (although Jones and Schmidt are notorious for writing many songs for a single show, it's hard to believe they could ever write a bad one), its language (much of the dialogue is in verse), and its provoking story. The sets are a rough platform, the costumes are simple, the props are drawn on signs, and the masks can be crude—all in all ideal to get the perfect look on limited circumstances with good creativity. *Celebration* belongs in any open space where it can have the impact and audience it deserves, not in an elegant theatre. Not that there's only one way to produce it. A few years later, Bob Fosse staged the same kind of thing with all the panache of slick show-business musicals, and the result was a five-year run for *Pippin,* another young man who has to learn that life is no musical comedy.

A Class Act

Book by Linda Kline and Lonny Price
Music and Lyrics by Edward Kleban

A posthumous *musical à clef* of the life of Edward Kleban—record producer, composer of numerous unproduced Broadway scores, lyricist of *A Chorus Line,* and galloping neurotic—using his own catalogue.

Time and Place: From 1958 to 1988. The stage of the Shubert Theatre and other locations.

Synopsis: Framed as a memorial for Ed Kleban, whose ghost is there, *A Class Act* is the story of a man who wanted all his adult life to write songs for Broadway musicals but, with one extraordinary exception, did not succeed. Ed has his first of several mental breakdowns during college. After college he works for Columbia Records, producing many fine cast albums. His temperament is his own worst enemy, but he finds solace in writing songs and safety in the famous Lehman Engle/BMI Writer's workshop, where he writes more and more unproduced musicals. He also stumbles through an on-again, off-again romance with childhood friend Sophie. He is hired to write additional lyrics for the revival of *Irene* starring Debbie Reynolds but is fired out of town, precipitating an almost-third breakdown.

Act 2 finds him resigning his position at Columbia to write full time, and revisiting Sophie, only to discover that he's too late, she has a boyfriend. Then Michael Bennett asks him to write the lyrics—and only the lyrics—for Bennett's latest project. Agreeing to do so, he embarks on a collaboration, which, while rocky in the beginning, results in one of the most successful musicals of all time, both commercially and artistically: *A Chorus Line*. Although he wins the Tony, Kleban finds it very difficult to keep writing, refuses to do lyrics only, and never gets another show on. He dies of cancer—he was a lifetime smoker—an intensely frustrated artist, but in a grand gesture, leaves his *Chorus Line* fortune to a foundation for promising songwriters and his songs to his friends.

Off-Broadway: Manhattan Theatre Club, October 30, 2000, 42 previews, 38 performances. Broadway: Ambassador Theatre, March 11, 2001, 30 previews, 105 performances.

Directed by Lonny Price. Choreographed by Scott Wise (off-Broadway) and Marguerite Derricks (Broadway).

Original Broadway Cast:

Lucy…Donna Bullock	Bobby et al.…David Hibbard
Ed…Lonny Price	Felicia…Sara Ramirez
Lehman…Patrick Quinn	Charley et al.…Jeff Blumenkrantz
Mona…Nancy Anderson	Sophie…Randy Graff

Musical Numbers:

ACT I   Light on My Feet…Ed, Lucy, Bobby, Felicia, Charley, Lehman, Mona
Fountain in the Garden…Mona, Lucy, Lehman, Bobby, Felicia, Charley
One More Beautiful Song. . .Ed, Sophie
Friday at Four/Bobby's Song…Ed, Mona, Felicia, Bobby, Lucy, Charley/Bobby
Charm Song…Lehman, Mona, Lucy, Bobby, Felicia, Ed, Charley
Paris Through the Window. . .Ed, Bobby, Charley
Mona…Mona with Ed
Making Up Ways…Ed
Under Separate Cover…Lucy, Ed, Sophie
Gauguin's Shoes…Ed, Company
Follow Your Star…Sophie, Ed

ACT II   Better…Ed, Felicia, Mona, Lucy, Lehman, Charley, Bobby
Scintillating Sophie…Ed
Next Best Thing to Love. . .Sophie
Broadway Boogie Woogie…Lucy, Bobby
One (excerpt from *A Chorus Line*)…Bobby, Sophie, Lucy, Mona, Lehman, Charley, Felicia
Better (reprise)…Ed, Bobby, Lehman, Felicia, Mona, Lucy, Sophie, Charley
I Choose You…Ed, Lucy
Light on My Feet (reprise)…Bobby, Ed, Lehman, Mona, Charley
Say Something Funny…Lucy, Lehman, Sophie, Felicia, Bobby, Mona, Charley
When the Dawn Breaks…Ed
Self Portrait…Ed, Company

Licensing: Rodgers and Hammerstein Theatre Library

Difficulties/Advantages: Four men and four women, some real, some fictional. When the character of Michael Bennett says to the character of Ed Kleban, "I made Hepburn look good in *Coco,*" you know you're in a show-biz musical, and although you can't beat death for a tear-stained ending, this is one that few civilians west of the Hudson River will appreciate. If character is destiny, Kleban's failure to see his own musicals produced on Broadway would have to be attributed to his personality—conflicted, phobic, neurotic, and difficult to work with. Indeed, those who heard many of his songs at various BMI workshops can only wonder what other reason there could be, for they were, for several years running, the highlight of the annual showcase: charming and popular. It's just as true, however, that the Great White Way is Blood Alley where ambitious hearts are concerned, and the business of Broadway is fatefully fickle.

In any case, this biographical musical doesn't have much of a story, unless your audience is the type to want a Woody Allen movie without the humor. A simple revue of his many unsung songs—an idea the writers/owners of Kleban's trunk rejected—framed with "One More Beautiful Song" would probably be far more entertaining and spread his reputation much farther.

The Club

A Musical Diversion

By Eve Merriam

The music is authentic, from the period 1894–1905.

Time and Place: Late Victorian era. An exclusive men's club.

Synopsis: There is no plot, really, but four gentlemen and the club's employees gather, sing and dance a great deal (including putting on the "Spring Frolic"), and tell very corny jokes ("His wife just turned forty, and he'd sure like to exchange her for a couple of twenties") and bawdy limericks. And get progressively drunker. It's a wonderful collage of condescending male-chauvinist behavior and a neat look at a bygone era—more authentic I'd think than Wodehouse's young men in spats—but the concept is what makes for a very entertaining evening: all the men are played by women. That's right: Algy, Bertie, and the rest are male impersonators. Think of Julie Andrews as Victor. If the actresses are good, it takes a moment to catch on—the program, see below, is nicely mysterious—but in a minute or two, the audience is in on it, something comes over them, and they're with you all the way. Tommy Tune made a confident, imaginative directing debut with the original off-Broadway production.

Circle in the Square Downtown; October 14, 1976; 674 performances.

Directed by T.(a.k.a Tommy) Tune.

Original Cast:

Messrs.

Johnny…M. Dell	Bertie…G. Hodes
Algy…J. Beretta	Freddie…C. Monferdini
Bobby…J. J. Hafner	Maestro…M. Innerarity
Henry…T. White	

Musical Numbers:

Come to the Club Tonight…Members in Good Standing

The Juice of the Grape...Imbibers
To the Ladies...Gentlemen Songbirds and Steppers
String of Pearls...Freddie and Friends
Coquin de Printemps...Monsieur Algy
Ticker Tape...Johnny and Co.
A Good Cigar...Bertie with Puffers
Pinky Panky Poo...Sporting Players
If Money Talks ("It Ain't on Speakin' Terms with Me")...Henry
New Shoes...Ragtime Tappers
A Little Valise...Maestro
He Reminds Her of His Father...Bobby
Following in Father's Footsteps...Dad and the Sonnyboy
Dreams of a Rarebit Fiend...Cane Dancer
Bertie's Annual Aria...Bertie
Spring Frolic: Rose Garden...Entire Company
Juice of the Grape (reprise)...Imbibers
Come to the Club Tonight (reprise)...Entire Company

Licensing: Samuel French

Difficulties/Advantages: An all-female show is gold to many schools, where the problem is fewer boys than girls joining the drama club. This one offers seven women a terrific opportunity to perform unusual roles, while singing and dancing in a turn-of-the-century music-hall style.

Clue—The Musical

Based on the Board Game by Parker Brothers

Book by Peter DePietro
Music by Galen Blum, Wayne Barker, and Vinnie Martucci
Lyrics by Tom Chiodo

Fortunately, Clue sails on as the world's second-most popular board game (Monopoly is the first) with no diminution of interest (since 1944), no thanks to either the film-version flop or this silly musical incarnation.

Time and Place: Timeless as the game.

Synopsis: Our host, Mr. Boddy, explains the incomprehensible instructions in which the audience, having been given paper and pencil, is to guess the murderer, the room, and the weapon. (If you needed to know that, you're missing out on one of the best board games in history. Go immediately to Toys R Us and purchase.) We then meet the usual suspects. They sing their stories and interact with each other, someone murders Mr. Boddy, a detective appears, there are clues in rhyme you'll need to make note of, and you turn in your guesses. When the detective sorts things out, those members of the audience who guessed correctly get to stand up and take a bow.

Players Theatre; December 3, 1997; 17 previews, 29 performances.

Directed by Peter DePietro.

Original Cast:

Mr. Boddy...Robert Bartley   Mrs. Peacock...Wysandria Woolsey

Professor Plum...Ian Knaur
Colonel Mustard...Michael Kostroff
Mr. Green...Marc Robman

Miss Scarlet...Tiffany Taylor
Mrs. White...Daniel Leroy McDonald
Detective...Denny Dillon

Musical Numbers:

ACT I   The Game...Mr. Boddy, Suspects
Life Is a Bowl of Pits...Mrs. White
Everyday Devices...Miss Scarlet and Mr. Green, with Colonel Mustard, Professor
      Plum, Mrs. White, Mrs. Peacock
Once a Widow...Mrs. Peacock
Corridors and Halls...Mr. Boddy, Suspects
The Murder...Mr. Boddy, Suspects
After the Murder (the game reprise)...Suspects
She Hasn't Got a Clue...Suspects
Everyday Devices (reprise)...Suspects
Seduction Deduction...Professor Plum, Detective
Foul Weather Friend...Suspects
Don't Blame Me...Entire Cast
The Final Clue...Mr. Boddy, Suspects
The Game (finale)...Mr. Boddy, Suspects
She Hasn't Got a Clue (reprise)/Bows...Entire Cast

Licensing: Samuel French

Difficulties/Advantages: The characters in this ensemble piece might be fun to portray, and having to memorize a bunch of different endings, depending on that night's results, is always a challenge, but the result is not much more than confusion for the audience.

Colette Collage

Book and Lyrics by Tom Jones
Music by Harvey Schmidt
Book Revisions by Michael Stewart and Ralph Allen

Although subtitled "Two Musicals About Colette," the work is really two acts, meant to be performed one right after the other and constituting no more than one normal-length musical evening. This ingenuous description, along with the "collage" business, is no more than a warning to audiences that the form isn't quite linear or traditional.

A musical bio of the famous French journalist, beauty shop operator, nude music-hall performer, and author of more than seventy books, plays, operas, and films, including the stories of *Cheri* and *Gigi,* the latter becoming the classic MGM musical film by Lerner and Loewe. Her lively, promiscuous (she was refused burial in consecrated ground due to her lifestyle), and well-chronicled life is now a model for feminists and a natural for a musical. This one took a circuitous route and should still be considered unfinished, although brimming with melody and wit.

After writing three songs for a play about Colette starring Zoe Caldwell, Jones and Schmidt decided to pen a full-fledged Broadway musical. It was a little *too* fledged, I suppose, as numerous problems beset the original Seattle and Denver tryouts starring Diana Rigg in 1982, and the musical was withdrawn. Rewritten as a lighter, more delicate production, it reappeared at the York Theatre Company in New York City starring Jana Robbins, then for a 1991 run at Music Theatre Works starring Betsy Joslyn.

Colette Collage at the Conservatory of Theatre Arts, Leigh Gerdine College of Fine Arts, Webster University, St. Louis, MO.

From the authors: "The title is carefully chosen, not just for its alliteration but as some indication for the concept of the show: a collage, a colorful assembly of many elements arranged in an abstract pattern to create a unified work. Scenes shift in a wistful way. Time and place are telescoped here and there. There is no slavish adherence to plot progression or development from scene to scene. The form is free and contemplative. The performers often ruminate aloud or confront the audience directly."

Time and Place: 1890 to 1953. France.

Synopsis: Colette, eighty years old, indulges in memories that begin with her seventeen-year-old self.

ACT I "Willy"
She marries Willy, pen name of an author twice her age, with as many ghost writers as young women to seduce. To keep him interested in her, she dresses as a school girl and pretends innocence. She tells him stories of her childhood, which he publishes, after encouraging her to include sexual sequences. Published under Willy's name, "Claudine" is a huge success, and Colette writes many more of Claudine's—often sexual—adventures. Upset that she doesn't share in the fame, she runs off to be in vaudeville. She performs, and takes up with a lesbian, but returns to her writing when Willy offers her money and credit. Now thirty, she finally finds the courage to go out on her own.

ACT II "Maurice"
Successful and famous, with a daughter, Colette meets a young merchant with whom she has an affair, although twenty years separate them. Maurice is Jewish and is taken prisoner during WWII, but Colette bribes the Germans, and he returns to her as the war ends. The musical ends with the eighty-year-old Colette celebrating the joys of her life.

York Theatre; March 31, 1983; 17 performances.

Directed by Fran Soeder. Choreographed by Janet Watson and Scott Harris.

Cast:

Maurice...Steven F. Hall
Sido...Joanne Beretta
Colette...Jana Robbins
Nita and Fluff...Susan J. Baum
Dr. Dutrate and Stage Manager...Dan Shaheen
Ida...Terry Baughan

Jacques...George Hall
Willy...Timothy Jerome
Captain...Howard Pinhasik
Aimee...Mayla McKeehan
Claudine...Suzanne Bedford
Cheri...Tim Ewing

Musical Numbers:

Joy
Come to Life
A Simple Country Wedding
Do It for Willy
Willy Will Grow Cold
The Claudines
Why Can't I Walk Through That Door
The Music Hall
I Miss You
La Vagabonde
Love Is Not a Sentiment Worthy of Respect
Now I Must Walk Through That Door
Autumn Afternoon
Ooh-La-La
Something for the Summer
Madame Colette
Be My Lady
The Room Is Filled with You
Growing Older

Licensing: Music Theatre International

Difficulties/Advantages: One of those musicals that never gelled, but filled with strong scenes and music. Slides help, as does an actress who can play from fifteen to eighty, although it might be better to have two—or even three—women essay the lead role.

Company

A Musical Comedy

Book by George Furth
Music and Lyrics by Stephen Sondheim

Company is anything but a "little musical," so I'm really stretching things here, but this groundbreaking, still-hip musical with a Sondheim score requires only fourteen people, contemporary costumes, and a unit set, and is a real gem open to various design interpretations, so here it is.

Producer/director Harold Prince took to Sondheim what was originally a compendium of eleven short one-act plays about couples, and the result is the apotheosis of the concept musical. They added a single male who functions as a guide through five disparate Big Apple relationships, is a bachelor with three of his own, and gets to sing

Company at the School of Theatre and Dance, Northern Illinois University, DeKalb, IL.

Photo: George Tarbay

the penultimate theme: that it's better to be married than single, an idea that the show belies for two hours, then embraces in the final song, which was actually written out of town in a desperate attempt to make the show a little less dark. It worked, and the result is a musical that celebrates the Sturm und Drang of relationships (among neurotic New Yorkers) with great comedy and a sizzling score that will never date, but is as classic a Manhattan melody as any by Rodgers and Hart.

Time and Place: Now. New York City. (The musical opened in the spring of 1970, but there seems no reason in the world to do it as a period piece. Relationships between men and women haven't changed much in a hundred years, much less a few generations, and Sondheim's driving urban score will surely be as rich and heartstopping one hundred years from now.)

Synopsis: Robert (Bob, Bobby, Bubi) enters to find a surprise party for his thirty-fifth birthday. Then, in a seamless series of musical numbers and vignettes, we visit with five couples and meet three girls he is dating. There isn't a plot or story, and none is needed, so rich are the little scenes and brilliant the big songs. After he draws the conclusion that "alone is alone, not alive" he fails to show up at his own party—deciding, we suppose, that being a third wheel with all his "couple" friends isn't worth much—and although the curtain descends on this rather dark note for anyone who has been a single friend to a couple, perhaps he's headed out to find someone for himself.

Alvin Theatre; April 26, 1970; 7 previews, 705 performances.

Production directed by Harold Prince. Musical numbers staged by Michael Bennett.

Original Cast:

Robert...Dean Jones
(who dropped out within a matter of weeks and was replaced with Larry Kert)

Sarah...Barbara Barrie	Harry...Charles Kimbrough
Susan...Alice Cannon	Peter...John Cunningham
Jenny...Teri Ralston	David...George Coe
Amy...Beth Howland	Paul...Steve Elmore
Joanne...Elaine Stritch	Larry...Charles Braswell

Marta…Pamela Myers   Kathy…Donna McKechnie
April…Susan Browning

Musical Numbers:

ACT I   Company…Robert, Company
The Little Things You Do Together…Joanne, Company
Sorry-Grateful…Harry, David, Larry
You Could Drive a Person Crazy…Kathy, April, Marta
Have I Got a Girl for You?…Larry, Peter, Paul, David, Harry
Someone Is Waiting…Robert
Another Hundred People…Marta
Getting Married Today…Amy, Paul, Jenny, Company

ACT II   Side by Side by Side…Robert, Couples
What Would We Do Without You?…Robert, Couples
Poor Baby…Sarah, Jenny, Susan, Amy, Joanne
Love Dance…Kathy
Barcelona…Robert, April
The Ladies Who Lunch…Joanne
Being Alive…Robert

Licensing: Music Theatre International (Apparently you can't sing "Happy Birthday" without paying royalties to someone named Mildred Hill, which is why in the original show the song was done in monotone.)

Difficulties/Advantages: All fourteen roles require adults. That plus the sophisticated material really puts *Company* out of reach of high schools, although not colleges or community theatres. One woman has to dance a sexy solo—although it's been done effectively as a pas de deux, and it's been cut—and everyone has to sing, with varying abilities. The original unit set was structural, with several levels (and an elevator in between) backed by projections of New York City and furniture coming and going as needed. But here again creativity is all, so while the original gleaming steel and glass look was great, it's not the only way to go. The only obstacle for little theatres: eleven performers are all on stage at once several times—dancing and singing two big numbers—so you've got to have a fairly wide proscenium. It's hard to imagine Sondheim without an orchestra, although it's possible a jazz combo could give a nice interpretation of his smallest show.

The Contrast

Adapted by Anthony Stimac
Music by Don Pippin
Lyrics by Steve Brown

Based on the first American comedy, written in 1787 by Royall Tyler.

Apparently "eleven years after the signing of the Declaration of Independence the first play written by an American 'citizen' was produced in New York City, April 16, 1787." Whether or not it deserves to be exhumed we'll leave to one of those "classic" theatres. It certainly is based on English Restoration comedy, although with a good deal of Marx Brothers thrown in, at least in the musical version.

Time and Place: 1787. New York.

Synopsis: Maria is betrothed by her father to Mr. Dimple, because he knows the value of a money match, but her heart isn't in the engagement. No wonder, since Mr. Dimple's behavior is odious on purpose. Unable to break the engagement, he hopes that Maria will, so that he can marry Letitia, because she's rich, although he'll dally with Charlotte on the side. Manly, Charlotte's brother, is the real catch. He and his servant, Jonathan, are rough-hewn Americans, so Dimple's servant, Jessamy, attempts to teach Jonathan proper courting manners, then introduces him to Jenny, where the manners prove useless. In other words, by the end of act 1, we should be aghast at how duplicitous these "Continentals" are, while the country-bred "Americans" are handsome and not at all hypocritical, if clumsy at courting.

Dimple contrives to meet Manly, as well as make assignations with both Charlotte and Letitia. But his debts and his intrigues prove his undoing, leaving Maria available for Manly, so true love triumphs. In any event, what we have been introduced to, and laughed at, is the hypocrisy of those wishing to emulate European manners, in "contrast" to the new "Americans," devoted to the simple virtues. Thus a most patriotic first American comedy.

Eastside Playhouse; November 27, 1972; 24 performances.

Directed by Anthony Stimac. Choreographed by Bill Guske.

Original Cast:

Charlotte…Connie Danese   Letitia…Elaine Kerr
Frank…Gene Kelton   Maria…Patti Perkins
Van Rough…Gene Kelton   Colonel Manly…Robert G. Denison
Jonathan…Philip MacKenzie   Jessamy…Grady Clarkson
Dimple…Ty McConnell   Jenny…Pamela Adams

Musical Numbers:

ACT I   Prologue…Company
         A Woman Rarely Ever…Charlotte, Letitia
         A House Full of People…Maria
         Keep Your Little Eye upon the Main Chance, Mary…Van Rough
         So They Call It New York…Jonathan, Jessamy
         Dear Lord Chesterfield…Dimple
         Dear Lord Chesterfield (reprise)…Jessamy
         A Sort of Courting Song…Jenny, Jonathan
         So Far…Company
ACT II   She Can't Really Be…Dimple, Manly
         That Little Monosyllable…Charlotte, Maria
         It's Too Much…Dimple, Charlotte, Maria, Manly, Letitia
         Keep Your Little Eye upon the Main Chance, Mary (reprise)…Van Rough
         Wouldn't I…Maria, Manly
         A Hundred Thousand Ways…Jessamy, Jonathan
         The Contrast…Company
         So Far (reprise)…Company

Licensing: Samuel French

Difficulties/Advantages: A few pieces of period furniture are all that is required, although there is apparently a difference between the rougher "Americans" and the "Continentals" in style, which might take some researching. Period costumes—wigs, petticoats, corsets—will be harder. "Chorus may be added if desired." A note from the authors claims this to be "the only American Restoration Play in existence." Probably true, since the English alone fielded Restoration plays. Thus, you're pretty well encouraged to find your own freewheeling style. Best lines: Question: "Sir, do you ever attend the theatre?" Answer: "I was tortured there once."

Cowgirls

Photo: La Verne Jones

Cowgirls at Murphy's Auditorium, New Harmony, IN.

Book by Betsy Howie
Conception, Music, and Lyrics by Mary Murfitt

"The higher my hair," one character says, "the closer I am to God," and you know you're in a country-western musical. This one has a pretty obvious setup, just enough to keep the story going until the talented performers in the original—who played, in aggregate, piano, guitar, mandolin, violin, cello, harmonica, and washtub—can perform the finale medley. Like many off-Broadway musicals with slim books whose purpose is to showcase a bunch of songs, this one too depends on the musical performances. A subtle theme about the strength of women peers through the honky-tonk, making this a mildly feminist musical as well.

Time and Place: The present, a Friday and Saturday night. Hiram Hall, a country music club in Rexford, Kansas.

Synopsis: Hiram Hall, a country music club in Rexford, Kansas, has mistakenly booked a classical trio, the Coghills, thinking they were a country-western trio, the Cowgirls. The owner is a daughter who has inherited an eviction notice from her deceased father. She's also a good singer, but she refuses to perform because her mother, who taught her "cookin', singin', and poker," walked out on the family years ago, and she doesn't want to emulate her. There are also two employees hoping for their big break. The members of the trio, at the end of a three-month tour that's been a disaster already, all have their own back stories to tell. Between the six women, there's more than enough talent to put on the show, and of course, by the second act, they do.

Minetta Lane Theatre; March 19,1996; 16 previews, 321 performances.

Directed and choreographed by Eleanor Reissa.

Original Cast:

Jo Carlson...Rhonda Coullet   Rita...Mary Ehlinger
Lee.. Lori Fischer   Mary Lou...Mary Murfitt
Mo...Betsy Howie   Mickey...Jackie Sanders

Musical Numbers:

ACT I   Overture: Beethoven's Sonata Pathetique, Opus 13...The Trio: Rita, Lee, Mary Lou
            Three Little Maids (Gilbert and Sullivan)...The Trio
            Jesse's Lullaby...Rita with Lee, Mary Lou
            Ode to Connie Carlson...Mickey, Mo
            Sigma Alpha Iota...Rita, Lee, Mary Lou
            Ode to Jo...Mickey, Mo
            From Chopin to Country...Rita, Lee, Mary Lou
            Kingdom of Country...Jo, Trio
            Songs My Mama Sang...Jo, May Lou
            Heads or Tails...Lee, Rita
            Love's Sorrow...Jo, Rita, Lee
            Looking for a Miracle...Mary Lou, Jo, Company
ACT II   Don't Call Me Trailer Trash...Mickey, Mo
            Honky Tonky Girl...Rita
            Every Saturday Night...Jo, Trio
            Don't Look Down...Lee with Rita
            They're All Cowgirls to Me...Jo, Trio
            Saddle Tramp Blues...Mary Lou with Rita, Lee
            It's Time to Come Home...Jo
            We're a Travelin' Trio...The Trio
            Sunflower...The Trio
            Concert Medley...Company
            House Rules...Jo, Company
            Cowgirls...The Trio

Licensing: Dramatists Play Service

Difficulties/Advantages: This show couldn't really be done without the six girls themselves playing their own accompaniment. This saves you a band but requires some strong country-western playing and singing on stage.

Curley McDimple

Book by Mary Boyland and Robert Dahdah
Music and Lyrics by Robert Dahdah

The spoof and the satire are perennial off-Broadway styles, and an outsized number of the shows in this book take their lineage from popular genres. The movie musical in its many epochs, the operetta, sci-fi, gothic, and pulp fiction—all have been delightfully lambasted by off-Broadway musicals. This one is a "musical valentine to the thirties"—specifically, Shirley Temple musicals.

Time and Place: The early to mid 1930s. Sarah's Boarding House, a shabby brownstone in the West 40s in Manhattan.

Synopsis: Jimmy is a starving tap dancer, Alice equally as far down on her luck, when little orphan Curley McDimple is found on the doorstep of their boarding house (run by Sarah, but the mortgage is due, and mean old Mr. Gillingwater intends to foreclose). Of course they put on a show to raise the money, but Curley is taken to an orphanage by mean old Miss Hamilton. The show goes on when Miss Hamilton is offered a part she can't refuse, and when it ends, a photo in Curley's locket identifies her as Mr. Gillingwater's granddaughter. With Sarah marrying Mr. Gillingwater and Jimmy marrying Alice, Curley gets a mother and father and grandmother and grandfather, not so mean any longer, all at once…and top billing with Jimmy and Alice at the Palace, because J. J. Shubert was in the audience.

Bert Wheeler Theatre; November 22, 1967; 96 performances.

Directed by Robert Dahdah. Dance directors: Lonnie Evans, Kathy Harris, and George Hillman.

Original Cast:

Jimmy…Paul Cahill	Sarah.. Helen Blount
Alice…Bernadette Peters	Curley McDimple…Bayn Johnson
Bill…George Hillman	Miss Hamilton…Norma Bigree
Mr. Gillingwater…Gene Galin	

Hattie…Butterfly McQueen (a role added during the run, almost certainly because the unique McQueen, she of "Miss Scarlett! Miss Scarlett!" became available)

Musical Numbers:

ACT I   Overture
A Cup of Coffee…Jimmy
I Try…Jimmy, Alice
Curley McDimple…Curley, Jimmy, Sarah, Alice, Bill
Love Is the Loveliest Love Song…Alice
Are There Any More Rosie O'Gradys?…Sarah, Jimmy, Alice, Curley, Bill
Dancing in the Rain…Curley, Bill, Company
At the Playland Jamboree…Curley, Company
I've Got a Secret…Jimmy, Curley

ACT II   Stars and Lovers…Alice, Jimmy, Company
The Meanest Man in Town…Alice, Jimmy, Company
I Try (reprise)…Jimmy, Alice
Something Nice Is Going to Happen…Curley
Swing-a-Ding-a-Ling…Curley

Hi De Hi De Hi, Hi De Hi De Ho...Sarah, Alice, Jimmy, Bill, Mr. Gillingwater, Miss Hamilton
Swing-a-Ding-a-Ling (reprise)...Curley, Company
Something Nice Is Going to Happen (reprise)...Miss Hamilton
Love Is the Loveliest Love Song (reprise)...Jimmy, Company
Finale...Company

Licensing: Samuel French

Difficulties/Advantages: As always, the key to a spoof is to take it very seriously, not easy to do with the hee-haw dialogue here, a book so broad it takes a Herculean effort to put it over. There's plenty of opportunity to expand the production numbers with a large chorus, depending on the size of the stage and the number of tap dancers you can recruit, but the original seven will do just as well. One gimmick that might make it a real blockbuster would be to do the show all in black and white and the show-within-the-show in color—altogether a real possibility if you've already put on *42nd Street*, it was a big success, and you're looking for a sequel. Or if you have only seven performers, a small space, and your public is clamoring for another *Dames at Sea*.

Dames at Sea

Dames at Sea at the William Paterson University Theatre, Wayne, NJ.

Book and Lyrics by George Haimsohn and Robin Miller
Music by Jim Wise

Among the most successful of off-Broadway musicals, *Dames at Sea* spawned little yachts all over the world for the knowing laughs it received with its all-talking, all-singing, all-dancing cast of six spoofing the movie musicals of the 1930s. (You can tell by the character names: "Dick" and "Ruby.") In fact, its original success was almost entirely based on the introduction of Bernadette Peters, she of the Kewpie-doll lips and nasal soprano, and managed a television-film version before it disappeared into that great graveyard in the sky where spoofs seem to go when the cultural zeitgeist passes out of silly mode.

In fact, three years after *Dames* captivated New York's off-Broadway audiences, *No, No, Nanette* was revived with the real Ruby Keeler, and audiences responded so enthusiastically that the era of the spoof was all but dead. Why laugh at an over-the-top version when you can still enjoy the real thing?

Time and Place: The early 1930s. Any 42nd Street Theatre. Act II: on the battleship.

Synopsis: The show opens at—where else?—rehearsal for a new Broadway musical with seven tons of costumes and scenery (all offstage, fortunately). Ruby, just off the bus from Centerville, Utah, gets a job in the show and meets a would-be songwriter currently in the Navy, all during her first day in the Big Apple. But Mona, the show's star, has other plans for Dick the Songwriter. And, as if the producer didn't have enough trouble with the demanding Mona, the theatre is being torn down. Act 1 closes with Dick and his sailor friend Lucky offering to open the show that night on their battleship.

Naturally, act 2 is on the battleship. Ruby takes over the lead role when the opening number makes Mona seasick. She becomes the toast of the Navy and marries Dick, while Mona gets the Captain and Joan gets Lucky.

Bouwerie Lane Theatre; December 20, 1968; 575 performances.

Directed and choreographed by Neal Kenyon.

Original Cast:

Mona Kent…Tamara Long	Joan…Sally Stark
Hennesey…Steve Elmore	Ruby…Bernadette Peters
Dick…David Christmas	Lucky…Joseph R. Sicari
The Captain…Steve Elmore	

Musical Numbers:

ACT I   Wall Street…Mona
It's You…Dick and Ruby
Broadway Baby…Dick
That Mister Man of Mine…Mona, Chorus
Choo-Choo Honeymoon…Joan, Lucky
The Sailor of My Dreams…Ruby
Singapore Sue…Lucky, Company
Broadway Baby (reprise)
Good Times Are Here to Stay…Joan, Company

ACT II   Dames at Sea…Company
The Beguine…Mona, Captain
Raining in My Heart…Ruby, Chorus
There's Something About You…Dick, Ruby
Raining in My Heart (reprise)…Ruby
The Echo Waltz…Mona, Joan, Ruby, Company
The Tar Star…Ruby, Chorus
Let's Have a Simple Wedding…Company

Licensing: Samuel French

Difficulties/Advantages: Only six performers, or seven if Hennessey and the Captain are not doubled, but a chorus of almost any size can be added to many of the production routines if you've got the performers.

With the availability of the full-sized real thing—*42nd Street*—this little show has really fallen into a marginal corner of the American musical. Still, wouldn't it be great to run them in rep, one on your main stage and one in your little theatre?

Das Barbecü

Book and Lyrics by Jim Luigs
Music by Scott Warrender

Wagner's famous *Ring* cycle, spoofed in country-western Texas.

Time and Place: The Present. Texas.

Synopsis: Wotan expects his son Siegfried to marry Brünhilde, but Siegfried wakes up engaged to Gutrune and Brünhilde to Gunther. A flashback shows us how (a Mickey Finn at a honky-tonk). It all has to do with control of the Ring of Power, but since I could barely follow Wagner's version, I'm not going to try to parse this one.

In act 2, Brünhilde and Siegfried figure out that they were drugged, the Rhinemaidens make a musical appearance, and various relatives connive over the Ring, but Siegfried gets shot dead and Brünhilde immolates herself in a Texas-size barbecue. And at the bottom of a river, there's still "A Ring of Gold in Texas."

Minetta Lane Theatre; October 25, 1994; 30 performances.

Directed by Christopher Ashley. Musical Staging By Stephen Terrell.

Original Cast:

Narrator…Julie Johnson
Wotan…J. K. Simmons
Fricka…Julie Johnson
Siegfried…Jerry McGarty
Gutrune…Carolee Carmello
Brünhilde…Sally Mayes
Gunther…J. K. Simmons
Erda…Julie Johnson
The Norn Triplets…Carolee Carmello, Sally Mayes, Jerry McGarity
Needa Troutt…Julie Johnson
Milam Lamar…Jerry McGarity
Hagen…J. K. Simmons
Back-up Singer…Julie Johnson

The Dwarves…Carolee Carmello, Sally Mayes, J. K. Simmons
Alberich…Jerry McGarrity
Freia…Carolee Carmello
The Giants…Jerry McGarity, J. K. Simmons
Y-Vonne Duvall…Carolee Carmello
Katsy Snapp…Julie Johnson
The Rhinemaidens…Carolee Carmello, Julie Johnson, Sally Mayes
The Valkyries…Carolee Carmello, Julie Johnson
Tambourine Girl…Carolee Carmello

Musical Numbers:

ACT I   A Ring of Gold in Texas…Company
What I Had in Mind…Brünhilde, Siegfried, Gutrune, Gunther
Hog Tie Your Man…The Norn Triplets
Makin' Guacamole…Needa Troutt, Milam Lamar, Gutrune
Rodeo Romeo…Siegfried, Back-up Singer, Gutrune
County Fair…Brünhilde

Public Enemy Number One…The Texas Rangers, Alberich
A Ring of Gold in Texas (coda)…Actor One, Actor Two, Actor Three

ACT II   A Little House for Me…Fricka, Freia
River of Fire…Wotan
If Not fer You…Wotan, Alberich
Slide a Little Closer…Siegfried, Brünhilde
Barbecue for Two…Brünhilde, Gutrune
After the Gold is Gone…The Rivermaidens
Wanderin' Man…Siegfried, Fricka
Turn the Tide…Brünhilde, Erda, Wotan
Closing…Company

Licensing: Samuel French

Difficulties/Advantages: If you look closely at the cast list, you'll see that in fact it only requires two men and three women to play twenty-eight parts. There's a number of locations around Texas (and if you've got trap doors in your stage, they'd be very useful here), but the style is much more humorous than realistic. The characters are caricatures and, with all the doubling, have their hands full. Why anyone bothered to set Wagner's *Ring* in Texas and ham it up, I don't know, but I suppose there have been worse productions of the real thing.

A Day in Hollywood, A Night in the Ukraine

A Musical Double Feature

Photo: Savannah Seamann

A Day in Hollywood, A Night in the Ukraine at Central Community College, Columbus, NE.

Book and Lyrics by Dick Vosburgh
Music by Frank Lazarus
Additional Music and Lyrics by Jerry Herman

36

Originally produced in England in 1979 as a Fringe theatre production, this musical was brought over by the impresario/producer Alexander Cohen and, with the help of Tommy Tune, spiffed up for Broadway. The two acts really have nothing much to do with each other, unless you count that act 1 is a revue of songs from 1930s films and the Marx Brothers made movies in the 1930s. However, they do go well together, and the final number of the revue introduces the Marx Brothers "movie" we're about to see.

John Golden Theatre, May 1, 1980; then moved to the Royale for a total of 9 previews, 588 performances.

Directed and Choreographed by Tommy Tune. Co-choreographed by Thommie Walsh.

Act I: "A Day in Hollywood"

Time and Place: Tonight. The lobby of Grauman's Chinese Theatre, with an "inner above" (a stage where we see only the legs of the performers, a very clever idea which you can use or not, depending on your own approach to the staging).

A musical revue celebrating the songs of the Hollywood musicals of the 1930s. We begin with three Jerry Herman originals, one more by the authors that allows for a lot of clever choreography, three true stories about how certain songs came to be written, then a medley of Richard Whiting tunes (he who wrote "Hooray for Hollywood," which unaccountably is not included). There follows a classic Tommy Tune tap number based on the production code of the period ("The effect of nudity on the average audience is immoral"), the same number he staged for *Seesaw* ("Chapter 54, Number 1909"), and finally the cast as ushers invites us to see…act 2.

Musical Numbers:

Just Go to the Movies (Jerry Herman)
Famous Feet (Lazarus and Vosburgh)
Nelson (Jerry Herman)
The Best in the World (Jerry Herman)
Cocktails for Two (Sam Coslow and Arthur Johnston)
Two Sleepy People (Hoagy Carmichael and Frank Loesser)
Over the Rainbow (E. Y. Harburg and Harold Arlen)
It All Comes Out of the Piano (Lazarus and Vosburgh)
Ain't We Got Fun (Richard A. Whiting. Gus Kahn and Raymond Egan)
Too Marvelous for Words (Johnny Mercer and Richard A. Whiting)
Japanese Sandman (Raymond Egan and Richard A. Whiting)
On the Good Ship Lollipop (Sidney Clare and Richard A. Whiting)
Double Trouble (Richard A. Whiting, Leo Robin and Ralph Rainger)
Louise (Leo Robin and Richard A. Whiting)
Sleepy Time Gal (Joseph R. Alden, Raymond B. Egan, Ange Lorenzo and Richard A. Whiting)
Beyond the Blue Horizon (Frank Harling, Leo Robin and Richard A. Whiting)
Thanks for the Memory (Leo Robin and Ralph Rainger)
Doin' the Production Code (Lazarus and Vosburgh)
A Night in the Ukraine (Lazarus and Vosburgh)

Act II: "A Night in the Ukraine"

Time and Place: Before the Revolution. The morning room of the Pavlenko residence in the Ukraine.

A "new" Marx Brothers musical. The appropriately inane plot is very loosely based on Chekhov's one act-play, *The Bear*, but who cares about plot when it's the Marx Brothers. (Supposedly George Kauffman, standing in the back of the theatre watching them perform his *Cocoanuts*, said to a companion, "Wait a minute, I think I just heard one of my original lines.")

Musical Numbers (all songs by Lazarus and Vosburgh):

> A Night in the Ukraine (entr'acte)
> A Night in the Ukraine
> Carlo's Piano Solo (melody in F)
> Samovar the Lawyer
> Just Like That
> Again
> Gino's Harp Solo
> Natasha
> A Night in the Ukraine (finale)

For Broadway, all the actors performed the revue, then played:

> Mrs. Pavlenko, a Rich Widow...Peggy Hewett (in the Margaret Dumont role)
> Carlo, Mrs. Pavlenko's Italian Footman...Frank Lazarus (as Chico)
> Gino, Mrs. Pavlenko's Gardener...Priscilla Lopez (as Harpo)
> Serge B. Samovar, a Moscow Lawyer...David Garrison (as Groucho)
> Nina, Mrs. Pavlenko's Daughter...Kate Draper
> Constantine, a Coachman...Stephen James
> Masha, the Maid...Niki Harris
> Sascha, a Manservant...Albert Stephenson (as Zeppo)

Licensing: Samuel French

Difficulties/Advantages: A minimum of eight actors, two sets. For act 1 you'll need an ensemble of singers and dancers, configured however you like. The material is bookless, although there's some narration. The original staging was Herculean in its efforts to make a series of old songs entertaining, so you can follow the "acting edition" for help. For act 2, you'll need Groucho, Harpo, Chico, and even Margaret Dumont—not easy to cast. On Broadway the same cast did both acts, but as already stated, these two one-act musicals—although they go together well—don't have to be done in tandem. If you do have three clever actors who can do the impersonations, you can perform some of the funniest comedy ever written or, in this case, mimicked. The Marx Brothers routines were, for my money, hysterical, and this pastiche is very accurate. But then, it's not my money, it's yours.

Diamond Studs

The Life of Jesse James: A Horse Opera in Two Acts,
a.k.a. A Saloon Musical

Book by Jim Wann
Music and Lyrics by Bland Simpson and Jim Wann

A number of off-Broadway shows were "performed" by the band. Or perhaps we should say, the actors played the instruments. This one featured many of the already-well-known-in-North-Carolina Red Clay Ramblers, whose show, with the Southern

Diamond Studs, off-Broadway cast at the Westside Theatre, Chelsea Theatre Center in Brooklyn, NY.

States Fidelity Choir, more or less about Jesse James, came to New York with a whoop and a holler and succeeded. The Red Clay Ramblers are a great string band, but the show has been performed successfully by many others, so your theatre can do it too.

Time and Place: Wide-ranging, but generally the Old West, when Jesse James was infamous.

Synopsis: The authors don't make any bones about their version of James's notorious life being any more accurate than any others. Here Jesse and his brother ride with Quantrill's raiders during the Civil War, then rob banks and move on to trains; some get caught and some get killed; Frank James retires and Jesse keeps going until, due to a large "dead or alive" reward, an associate kills him when he ain't lookin'. Suffice it to say, it's the rompin', stompin' music that makes the show, which, in the original, turned the entire theatre into a saloon, with a stage at one end and the audience at tables and chairs and invited to dance along with some of the numbers.

Westside Theater, Chelsea Theater Center of Brooklyn; January 14, 1975; 232 performances.

Directed by John L. Haber. Choreographed by Patricia Birch.

Original Cast:

Jesse James...Jim Wann
C. C. Porkbarrel...Bland Simpson
Bob Ford...John Foley
Allen Pinkerton...Mike Sheehan
Major Edwards...Jan Davidson
Zerelda James, Cole Younger...Tommy Thompson
Jim Younger...Jim Watson
Bob Younger...Bill Hicks

Berny Greencheese...Mike Craver
William Clark Quantrill...Scott Bradley
Zee James...Joyce Cohen
Belle Starr...Madelyn Smoak
Tourist's Wife...Frances Tamburro
Saloon People...Edith Davis, Anne Gilland, Abigail Lewis, Connie O'Connell, Penny Peyser, Bill Smith

In addition, there are approximately 31 small roles, which can be doubled from the above.

39

Musical Numbers (some of which are authentic, some of which are written by the authors):

ACT I   Jesse James Robbed This Train
             Those Southern States That I Love
             The Year of Jubilo
             The Unreconstructed Rebel
             Mama Fantastic
             Steal Away
             I Don't Need a Man to Know I'm Good
             Northfield Minnesota
             King Cole
             New Prisoner's Song
             K. C. Line
             Cakewalk into Kansas City

ACT II   When I Was a Cowboy
             Pancho Villa
             Put It Where the Moon Don't Shine
             Sleep Time Down South
             Jesse James Robbed This Train (reprise)
             Bright Morning Star
             When I Get the Call
             Cakewalk into Kansas City (encore)

Licensing: Samuel French

Difficulties/Advantages: Twelve to fourteen players are recommended, but this is a wildly flexible show, with performers changing "hats" for frequent changes of character. And although the cast played their own instruments, there's plenty of flexibility there too. It all takes place on the saloon's stage, and the scenes are hardly more than brief vignettes to set up the theme of the songs. Played fast and broadly in the vaudeville style, it should be a great deal of fun for the cast and the audience.

Dracula: The Musical?

Book, Music, and Lyrics by Rick Abbot

To date, the only successful staged *Dracula*s are the ones without song and dance—and the films, of course. This attempt skirts the issue by spoofing it, very much like a Hollywood sketch from the old Carol Burnett show—you remember the days when Tim Conway would have played Renfield; Harvey Korman, the Doctor; Lyle Waggoner, the Count; Vickie Lawrence, Mina; and Carol, probably the maid. And there was always the moment when they would crack each other up.

Time and Place: The mid 1800s. The Seward family madhouse, a short gallop from London.

Synopsis: Do I really need to outline the most famous horror story in literature? In this version, by the end of act 1, Mina has been taken off by Count Dracula, and when she returns in act 2, she's pretty pale, with three puncture marks (two from the usual source, and the castle has mosquitoes). At the finale, sunrise manages to kill the Count, which is a good thing, because the best this cast can do is to threaten him with a garlic-covered pot roast. Lines such as: "Nelly: Can I offer you a drink? / Dracula: I was hoping you'd say that," and "Van: The third assault on Mina will turn her into the same dreaded thing that he himself must forever be! / Sophie: Hungarian?" should give you the idea. Other comic bits will be harder to pull off, including an inane and frequent musical diversion when Renfield, the madman who eats bugs and worships Dracula, breaks into a gypsy song and dance every time someone mentions the name of an American state.

Required Roles:

Dr. Sam Seward

Sophie Seward

Nelly Norton

Dr. Van Helsing

Jonathan Harker (can double with Dracula)

Mina Seward

Bubu Padoop

Boris Renfield

Count Dracula

Musical Numbers:

Act I   Overture…Accompanist
Vocational Reflection…Sam
I Love the Night…Mina, Bubu
Where Was I?…Boris
Alone!…Dracula
A Wonderful Place to Work…Nelly
How Outrageous!…Van, Mina, Bubu, Nelly, Sophie
Don't Be Afraid!…Dracula
Where Was I? (first reprise)…Boris
Come into My World…Dracula, Mina
Stupid Superstition…Sam, Sophie, Nelly, Bubu

Act II   Entr'acte…Accompanist
The Lady in White…Sophie, Bubu, Nelly
I'd Make a Horrid Husband…Van, Bubu
Where Was I? (second reprise)…Boris
Don't Be Afraid (reprise)…Dracula, Nelly
You Haven't Got a Chance!…Dracula
Where Was I? (final reprise)…Boris
At Last! (finale)…All Survivors

Licensing: Samuel French

Difficulties/Advantages: Could be fun, but you'll have to work hard to turn groans into laughs. Right from the start—when a character says, "The telephone hasn't been invented yet," and everyone freezes while the stage manager walks across the stage and removes the prop telephone—you've got to set the style. Some of the staging—"A huge bat flies out of the smoke" and the mirror that doesn't show a reflection—will require some minor special-effects efforts. But with enough effort—and remembering the dictum that if the actors laugh at themselves the audience won't—this could be much more entertaining than the lugubrious effort recently on the Great White Way.

Eating Raoul

Book by Paul Bartel
Music by Jed Feuer
Lyrics by Boyd Graham
Based on the film by Paul Bartel.

From the cult film, a cult musical.

Time and Place: Late 1960s. Los Angeles, California.

Synopsis: Conservative couple Paul and Mary Bland want to get out of swinging Los Angeles and open a restaurant in a small town, but they need some seed money. When one of the weirdo-swingers from next door, two sheets to the wind, comes into their apartment and begins to molest Mary, Paul knows what to do—with a heavy frying pan. The dead guy's pockets reveal the beginning of their restaurant nest egg, and their path to the restaurant is discovered. But how to get more perverts into their apartment? The solution comes when Donna the Dominatrix comes into their apartment by mistake. They get the idea, take up the sex trade, and bop any number of customers. But what to do with all those bodies? Raoul, the building superintendent and a frustrated night club entertainer (allowing for at least two non—plot numbers) discovers their game—and offers to help.

Act 2 reveals that Raoul is expanding Mary's love life. When Paul discovers that he's making more money than they are by fencing the bodies to a dog-food manufacturer, selling the victims' cars, and playing the hot Latin lover to his wife, he plans revenge, which leads to a struggle between the two men. The frying pan really heats up, and Mary has to choose. They get their restaurant, and—à la *Sweeney Todd*—Raoul ends up on the menu.

Union Square Theatre; April 21, 1992; 24 previews, 14 performances.

Directed by Toni Kotite. Choreographed by Lynne Taylor-Corbett.

Original Cast:

Mary Bland. . .Courtenay Collins	Basketball Player...Cindy Benson
Paul Bland...Eddie Korbich	Tyrone...Cindy Benson
Mr. Kray...Jonathan Brody	Yolanda...Cindy Benson
Fat Man...Jonathan Brody	Raoul...Adrian Zmed
Mr. Leech...David Masenheimer	Cop...Lovette George
Bobby...David Masenheimer	Inez (Raoulette)...Lovette George
Howard...David Masenheimer	Gladys (Raoulette)...Susan Wood
Donna's Boys...M. W. Reid, Jonathan Brody	Dr. Doberman...M. W. Reid
	Ginger...M. W. Reid
Donna the Dominatrix...Cindy Benson	Tourist/Swinger, etc...Allen Hidalgo

Musical Numbers:

ACT I   Meet the Blands...Chorus
A Small Restaurant...Paul, Mary
La La Land...Chorus
Swing, Swing, Swing...Chorus
A Small Restaurant (reprise)...Paul, Mary
Happy Birthday Harry...The Boys
You Gotta Take Pains...Donna and Her Boys

A Thought Occurs...Paul, Mary
Victim Update #1...Howard
Sexperts...The Girls
Basketball...Basketball Player
Empty Bed...Junior
Victim Update #2...Chorus
Tool for You...Raoul and the Raoulettes
A Thought Occurs (reprise)...Raoul, Paul, Mary
Think About Tomorrow...Raoul, Paul, Mary

ACT II Entr'acte Victim Update #3...Chorus
Hot Monkey Love...Raoul and the Raoulettes
A Small Restaurant (reprise)...Paul, Mary
Momma Said...Ginger, Paul, Mary, Raoul
Lovers in Love...Raoul, Mary
Mary...Paul
Victim Update # 4...Chorus
Eating Raoul...Raoul and the Raoulettes, Chorus
Trio...Raoul, Paul, Mary
Eating Raoul (reprise)...Raoul
I've Got to Stop Him...Paul
Swing, Swing, Swing (reprise)...Donna, Mr. Leeche, Chorus
One Last Bop...Mary
Finale...Chorus

Licensing: Samuel French

Difficulties/Advantages: High camp of the John Waters variety, including an S & M song and dance, and dead people singing. Thus not for the faint of heart or Bible Belt audiences. Nine to seventeen actors, and you can always throw in a few more Raoulettes. A phrase that should warm the hearts of small theatre producers is this one from the first page of the script: "It is recommended that the various settings in the play be indicated by projections or the sparsest possible scenery."

Evelyn and the Polka King

A Play by John Olive
Music by Carl Finch and Bob Lucas
Lyrics by Bob Lucas

A strong play with a dozen great polkas interwoven. Don't laugh until you read it. It's a powerful and wonderfully entertaining piece.

Time and Place: Contemporary. A cemetery; a small apartment; lobby and stairwell of the Palmer House, Chicago; Lincoln Park Zoo; rehearsal studio; farmyard; soybean field; roof of a barn; state and greenroom of a nightclub; old Roman Catholic church; small-town Sheriff's office; clump of woods; park in Millerville, Wisconsin; recording studio; and other locales.

Synopsis: Henry was the Polka King but so bad an alcoholic that now, after twenty-five years of drinking, he doesn't remember much. That's the situation when eighteen-year-old Evelyn shows up with a suitcase full of money and says that he's her biological father, and she needs help finding her biological mother, a woman about whom Henry can only recall a first name, Wanda, and the address "Kraut Valley," not on any map. They travel around the country, Henry resuscitating his career with the Vibra-Tones (hence the songs) and Evelyn giving away the money to good causes. All the while, Henry tries to remember more of Wanda and Kraut Valley, even trying hypnosis, and Evelyn, we shortly discover, is being chased by a lawyer and the police, because the money was under the desk of her adopted father, whose business may have been shady. Evelyn is finally caught, but while she waits in a Sheriff's office, Henry busts her out (literally, the band's van chains itself to the bars on the window and pulls). Together they find Wanda, who is a bit ragged but with Evelyn's help pulls herself together. Evelyn moves on to college—her stepfather, being in jail, no longer a threat—and Henry gets his recording career back.

Actors Theatre of Louisville; March 3–28, 1992.

Directed by Jeff Hooper.

Original Cast:

> Henry Czermiak...Tom Ligon
> Evelyn Starkweather...Seana Kofoed
> Margaret O'Reilly, Bunny Ann Hoffmocken, Laura Watson, Eleanor Masters, Wanda
> > Stoliewski...Margo Skinner

Musical Numbers:

ACT I   Overture
There's Something Happening Waltz
The Oyez Polka (on tape)
The Audition Polka
The Zosia Polka
The Anniversary/Psychotherapy Waltz (instrumental)
The I Hate Polka Polka
ACT II   The Oyez Polka
The Kielbasa, Beer and Sauerkraut Polka (or Kiss My Ass, I'm Polish)
Where Do I Go from Here Waltz
The Polka from Hell
Love Polka Number Nine
The Jailbreak Oberek
The Ozone Polka

Licensing: Susan Schulman Literary Agency, 454 West 44th Street, New York, New York 10036; 212-713-1633

Difficulties/Advantages: Two of the richest and quirkiest characters you'll find in a small musical. More of a play really, with the polkas terrific as interludes and commentary. One woman played a number of others, so three is the minimum, but there's an additional five good minor roles if you expand. The set must be inventive, because it covers as much ground as a film, and your band—five in the original—should play a mean polka, but this unusual piece offers great roles; creative directing, drama, and humor; and a new appreciation of the wonderful buoyancy of polka music for your audience.

F. Jasmine Addams

Book by Carson McCullers, G. Wood, and Theodore Mann
Music and Lyrics by G. Wood

Based on *The Member of the Wedding* by Carson McCullers.

A good example of the old adage: If it isn't broken, don't fix it. But then if Jerry Herman felt that way about *The Matchmaker,* we wouldn't have *Hello, Dolly!* Although the novel, the play (featuring a transcendent Ethel Waters), and the film version (featuring a sparkling young Julie Harris) all succeeded, this musical version did not, despite staying very close to the original. A musical was perhaps inevitable, and although the score was charming and jazz-influenced, the songs just didn't rise to the occasion—that is, to the dramatic power of the story and dialogue.

Time and Place: August to November, 1945. The kitchen and backyard of the Addams household in a small Southern town.

Synopsis: Frankie Addams, a twelve-year-old tomboy, is mothered by the family's black cook in the wake of her mother's earlier death. Scorned by the girls in the neighborhood and worshipful of her older brother, Frankie assumes that she will go with her brother and his new wife on their honeymoon and live with them.

Circle in the Square, Downtown; October 27, 1971; 6 performances.

Directed by Theodore Mann. Musical numbers staged by Patricia Birch.

Original Cast:

Bernice Sadie Brown…Theresa Merritt
John Henry West…Johnny Doran
T. T. Williams.. Robert Kya-Hill
Sis Laura…Alicia Marcelo
Janice…Erika Petersen
Mary Littlejohn…Carol Anne Ziske
Doris Mackey…Merry Fiershem

Frankie Addams…Neva Small
Honey Camden…Northern J. Calloway
Mr. Addams…William LeMassena
Jarvis…Bill Biskup
Barney MacKean…Edmund Gaynes
Helen Fletcher…Page Miller

Musical Numbers:

How About You and Me
If I Had a…
Miss Pinhead
Baby, That's Love
Did I Make a Good Impression?
Good as Anybody
The We of Me
Travelin' On
Sunshine Tomorrow
F. Jasmine Addams
How Sweet Is Peach Ice Cream
Do Me a Favor
Another Day
Quite Suddenly

Licensing: Unknown

Difficulties/Advantages: It must be said that if you have the actors for it, a production of this classic play would probably be stronger than the musical version. Both Frankie and Bernice are among the greatest dramatic roles ever written, and either can steal the show. Nevertheless, while the short run of the musical precluded further productions, possibly the estate of Carson McCullers wouldn't mind another attempt. It's a powerful play with, here, a well-integrated score, but the thrust stage of the original production disallowed the audience's suspension of disbelief. Perhaps in a proscenium theatre?

Falsettos

Photo: Cliff Simon

Falsettos at the University of Alabama at Birmingham, AL.

Falsettos began as a trilogy of one-act plays.

In Trousers

Book, Music, and Lyrics by William Finn

Time and Place: Late 1970s. Certainly a city, probably New York.

Synopsis: A fourteen-year-old Marvin attempts to rape his teacher, Miss Goldberg; grows up; marries; has a son; dreams of "kissing men"; and finally takes up with Whizzer Brown, a man—all in songs with whiny, shallow, repetitive lyrics.

Originally workshopped and produced at Playwrights Horizon in 1979, the musical was rewritten and opened off-Broadway at the Promenade Theatre; March 26, 1985; 16 previews, 16 performances.

Directed by Matt Casella.

Cast:

Marvin...Stephen Bogardus His Wife...Catherine Cox
His High School Sweetheart... His Teacher, Miss Goldberg...
    Sherry Hursey   Kathy Garrick

Musical Numbers (latest version):

In Trousers...All
I Can't Sleep...Marvin, Ladies
A Helluva Day...Trina
I Have a Family...Marvin
How Marvin Eats His Breakfast...Marvin, Ladies
Marvin's Giddy Seizures...Ladies
My High School Sweetheart...Sweetheart, All
Set Those Sails...Miss Goldberg
I Swear I Won't Ever Again (part 1)...Marvin
High School Ladies at 5 O'Clock...Ladies, Marvin
I Swear I Won't Ever Again (part 2)...Marvin
The Rape of Miss Goldberg...Marvin, Miss Goldberg
I Swear I Won't Ever Again (part 3)...Marvin
Love Me for What I Am...Trina, All
I Am Wearing a Hat...Ladies
Wedding Song...All
3 Seconds...Marvin
Wedding Song (part 2)...All
How the Body Falls Apart...Ladies
I Felt Him Slipping Away...Trina
Whizzer Going Down...Trina
Marvin's Giddy Seizures (part 2)...Ladies
I'm Breaking Down...Trina
Packing Up...Marvin
Breakfast over Sugar...Marvin, Trina
How America Got Its Name...All
Been a Helluva Day (reprise)...Trina
Another Sleepless Night...All
Goodnight (No Hard Feelings) or In Trousers (reprise) The Dream...All

Licensing: Samuel French

Disadvantages/Advantages: You can't possibly do a more leaden production than the original.

March of the Falsettos

Book, Music, and Lyrics by William Finn

Time and Place: 1979. Certainly a city, probably New York.

Synopsis: Marvin has left his wife for a man; his son Jason sees a shrink, who subsequently marries his mom; and all bitch at each other for a number of songs. In the final song, there is, at long last, a rich and respectful note: that a father and son's love should transcend the father's sexual preference (and the son's, one would hope).

Playwrights Horizon; March 27, 1981; 298 performances.

Directed by James Lapine.

Original Cast:

Marvin...Michael Rupert
Jason, His Son...James Kushner
Mendel, His Psychiatrist...Chip Zien

Trina, His Ex-Wife...Alison Fraser
Whizzer Brown, His Lover...Stephen Bogardus

Musical Numbers:

Four Jews in a Room Bitching...Men
A Tight-Knit Family...Marvin
Love Is Blind...Trina, Mendel, Everybody
Thrill of First Love...Marvin, Whizzer
Marvin at the Psychiatrist...Marvin, Mendel, Jason
My Father's a Homo...Jason
Everyone Tells Jason to See a Psychiatrist...Marvin, Trina, Jason, Whizzer
This Had Better Come to a Stop...All
I'm Breaking Down...Trina
Please Come to My House...Trina, Mendel, Jason
Jason's Therapy...Jason, Mendel, Everybody
A Marriage Proposal...Mendel
A Tight-Knit Family (reprise)...Marvin, Mendel
Trina's Song...Trina
March of the Falsettos...Marvin, Whizzer, Jason, Mendel
Trina's Song (reprise)...Trina
The Chess Game...Marvin, Whizzer
Making a Home...Mendel, Trina
The Games I Play...Whizzer
Marvin Hits Trina...Everybody
I Never Wanted to Love You...Everybody
Father to Son...Marvin, Jason

Licensing: Samuel French

Disadvantages /Advantages: Look for a very sympathetic gay audience.

Falsettoland

By William Finn and James Lapine
Music and Lyrics by William Finn

Time and Place: 1981. Certainly a city, probably New York.

Synopsis: The final act in the Marvin Songs Trilogy introduces—in case there haven't been enough sad oddballs for you—two lesbians. Jason is about to be bar mitzvahed, Marvin breaks up with and reunites with Whizzer, Mendel the Shrink and Marvin's ex-wife Trina are ambivalent about their marriage, and the two lesbians are Jason's godparents. Whizzer is stricken with AIDS, but life is affirmed when Jason opts to hold his bar mitzvah in Whizzer's hospital room. The theme seems to be that "family values" can be a great tent for all, although with all the bitching shouted at the audience in these three plays, you wouldn't rush into a relationship after the final curtain.

Originally produced at Playwrights Horizons, the musical subsequently opened off-Broadway at the Lucille Lortel Theatre; September 16, 1990; 4 previews, 161 performances.

Directed by James Lapine.

Cast:

Marvin...Michael Rupert
Trina...Faith Prince
Jason...Danny Gerard
Whizzer...Stephen Bogardus
Dr. Charlotte...Heather MacRae

Cordelia...Janet Metz
Mendel...Chip Zien (replaced by Lonny Price when the show moved to off-Broadway)

Musical Numbers:

Welcome to Falsettoland...Everybody
About Time...Marvin
The Year of the Child...Everybody but Whizzer
Miracle of Judaism...Jason
Sitting Watching Jason Play Baseball...Everybody
A Day in Falsettoland...Everybody
Racquetball...Marvin, Whizzer
The Fight...Marvin, Trina, Mendel, Jason
Everyone Hates His Parents...Mendel, Jason
What More Can I Say...Marvin
Something Bad Is Happening...Marvin
Second Racquetball...Marvin, Whizzer
Holding to the Ground...Trina
Days Like This...Everybody
Cancelling the Bar Mitzvah...Trina, Mendel, Jason
Unlikely Lovers...Marvin, Whizzer, Charlotte, Cordelia
Another Miracle of Judaism...Jason
Something Bad Is Happening (reprise)...Charlotte
You Gotta Die Sometime...Whizzer
Jason's Bar Mitzvah...Everybody
What Would I Do?...Marvin, Whizzer

Licensing: Samuel French

Difficulties/Advantages: These three heterophobic and nearly anti-Semitic one-acts might at first glance, on their own, seem charming, but together they give away the fact that they add up to very little. The third act alone wouldn't really make much sense without the second, and if you did all three in one night, you'd risk driving your audience insane with four hours of relentlessly unmelodic shouting. Shallow poetry that seems only thin as theatre lyrics and music unrelated to time, place, or character anchor this "chamber" work. Marvin is a wishy-washy nebbish, his lover alternates between fickle and sadistic, and the wife feels sorry for herself for three long acts. Only the son is a fleshed-out, interesting character: a normal teenager worried that his father's sexual preference might be genetic, and unwilling to accept his mom's new husband as a member of the family. Nevertheless, in 1992, the second and third of the three musicals were finally produced as a full evening, entitled:

Falsettos

Book by William Finn and James Lapine
Music and Lyrics by William Finn

John Golden Theatre; April 29, 1992; 33 previews, 487 performances.
Directed by James Lapine.

Cast:

Marvin...Michael Rupert
Whizzer...Stephen Bogardus
Mendel...Chip Zien
Jason...Jonathan Kaplan
Jason (Wednesday and Saturday
    matinees)...Harrison Leeds

Trina...Barbara Walsh
Charlotte...Heather MacRae
Cordelia...Carolee Carmello

Licensing: Samuel French

Difficulties/Advantages: According to the script: "All the furniture is on wheels. Locations change in the blink of an eye." Unfortunately, this doesn't help the fact that there are difficulties with all-singing musicals. They allow for very little variety in the show's dynamics. They're relentless. They force even the smallest ideas into overblown crescendos. Unless the songs are true dialogues (e.g., "Barcelona" in *Company*) the entire show ends up in a presentational mode with the audience harangued for hours, which was my impression of this one.

Included here because of its popularity and because it requires only eight actors, I personally find this an example of a cult musical that exhibits little skill and few ideas but found a gay audience to champion it into acceptance. With lyrics such as "It's romance, he bewares," characters who seem to feel much sorrier for themselves than we ever could for them, and the endless shouting of feelings at the audience, you'd better have very charming actors and a very sympathetic audience to take this one on.

The Fantasticks

Book and Lyrics by Tom Jones
Music by Harvey Schmidt

Based on *Les Romanesques* by Edmond Rostand.

This is the mother of all off-Broadway musicals and still the best for its utter guilessness, supremely melodic and humorous score, theatrical setting and style, and timeless story of young love—and romance. Which, it turns out by act 2, is something quite different.

Never was "less is more" better proved than with the success of *The Fantasticks* at the 153-seat Sullivan Street Playhouse. It didn't start out that way, however. The little-known Edmund Rostand play *Les Romanesques* (1894)—which was followed by his more successful *Cyrano de Bergerac* three years later—was first to be the source of a big Broadway musical, set in two adjoining ranches in the Southwest, one Anglo and one Spanish. "We had cowboys, Mexican bandits, and even a half-breed villain. We worked it out, very haphazardly, over a period of several years, trying to take the story and force it into a Rodgers and Hammerstein mold, which is what everybody did in those days" (Jones). "I always imagined everybody on real horses on the stage of the Winter

The Fantasticks at the School of Theatre and Dance, Northern Illinois University, DeKalb, IL.

Garden" (Schmidt). "Eventually the whole project collapsed, our treatment was too heavy, too inflated for the simple little Rostand piece. It seemed hopeless" (Jones).

In the summer of 1959, however, Word Baker, a friend from college, reappeared, having been asked by actress-turned-temporary-producer Mildred Dunnock to direct three one-act plays at Barnard College during the summer. Baker wanted one of them to be a musical, and he invited Jones and Schmidt to try out what they were working on, provided it could be reduced to the modest circumstances offered, and be ready to go into rehearsal in three weeks. The writers threw out everything they had done except the song "Try to Remember." Then, under the influence of Bergman's film *The Seventh Seal* (featuring a small band of actors traveling in a wagon during medieval times) and a then-current City Center production by the Piccolo Theatro di Milano of Carlo Goldoni's *Servant of Two Masters* (done on a platform as if by a troupe of itinerant commedia players), the authors completely rewrote their sprawling Southwestern musical (although it was a milieu they would return to for *110 in the Shade*). Here the circumstances of way-off-Broadway played an important part, for the simplicity they derived by going back to the original play, the experimental nature of mixing the presentational form with musical comedy, the use of a narrator (El Gallo) to help tell the story, a property man (The Mute) from the Chinese Theatre, and the verse-with-rhyming-couplets-dialogue would have been far too experimental for Broadway producers.

The summer production charmed Lore Noto, who had been attracted to discover more when he heard several of Jones's opening speeches in a Jones-directed acting class. Noto got the jump on other impresarios by attending a dress rehearsal, whereupon he committed to producing a commercial run and raised the $16,500 necessary.

Overnight reviews were not positive. (Walter Kerr: "Averages out a little less than satisfactory.") Weeklies were better, and the producer was encouraged by word of

51

mouth, particularly inside the theatre industry, many of whose practitioners were charmed by the theatricality and freshness of the show. The producer bet his savings to keep the show running, for which the original cast members, receiving $45 a week, were probably grateful. It weathered the hot summer, and since then, the Little Musical That Could has played in 12,000 productions in 2,000 American cities and 700 productions in sixty-seven foreign countries (and counting) and become the world's longest-running musical, and the longest running show in American theatre history. In 1964 there was a Hallmark Hall of Fame television version that was truncated but faithful. In 1970 the producer took over the role of the Boy's Father and played it for sixteen years. (No wonder he kept the show running.) Only London's *The Mousetrap* has lasted longer. And, oh yes, the original forty-four investors have received a 19,465 percent return on their investment.

Time and Place: Act 1 is "in the moonlight." Act 2 is "in the sunlight." Aside from that, however, this fable is usually—and probably best—performed in timeless costumes and on a theatrical set.

Synopsis: A compendium of a musical's score played by a single piano or small trio while the audience grows restless staring at a small stage is probably the most deadening of all openings for an off-Broadway musical. *The Fantasticks* avoids this trap with a clever pantomime—the cast preparing to do the play, setting out the props, taking down a curtain—all carried out during the sparkling piano and harp overture.

We are introduced to all the principal characters: the young lovers, Matt and Luisa; their fathers, Hucklebee and Bellomy, who have encouraged the match with the devious plot of building a fence between their houses and pretending to a Capulets vs. Montagues feud between their families; and El Gallo, who is hired to effect a reconciliation now that the match has been made, and does so—with the help of the old actor (who recites Shakespeare) and the Indian (who does death scenes)—by pretending to abduct the young lady and allowing the young man to save her and vanquish him. This brings the families together in a pleasant tableau that, El Gallo warns us as he announces an intermission, won't be easy to hold. Thus the classic happy ending is effected by the end of act 1, and—in a neat theatrical structure utilized some years later by the Sondheim/Lapine Broadway musical *Into the Woods*—leaves us wondering just what is left for the rest of the play.

Plenty. Act 2 begins with the tableau, but they can't hold it, as El Gallo predicted. It's a hot day, and the lovers and the fathers give in to bickering, whereupon the fathers admit to their ploy, showing Matt the bill for Luisa's abduction. The lovers break up, the fathers rebuild the wall, and El Gallo sends the boy off to see the real world with Henry and Mortimer while he romances Luisa. She agrees to go away with him, but he steals her precious necklace and deserts her instead. Thus are both young people introduced to the harsh realities of the real world, and they grow wiser for it. The boy returns, and they reconcile, aware now that, as we were warned in the opening song, "Without a hurt, the heart is hollow."

Sullivan Street Playhouse; May 3, 1960; 17,162 performances (42 years, 9 Presidents, 6 mayors).

Directed by Word Baker. Musical direction and arrangements by Julian Stein. Production designed by Ed Wittstein.

Original Cast:

The Mute…Richard Stauffer	El Gallo…Jerry Orbach
Luisa…Rita Gardner	Matt…Kenneth Nelson

Hucklebee...William Larsen
Henry...Thomas Bruce
(a *nom de acteur* for the author Tom Jones)
The Harpist...Beverly Mann

Bellomy...Hugh Thomas
Mortimer...George Curley
The Pianist...Julian Stein

Musical Numbers:

ACT I Overture...Company
Try to Remember...El Gallo
Much More...Luisa
Metaphor...Matt, Luisa
Never Say "No"...Hucklebee, Bellomy
It Depends on What You Pay...El Gallo, Bellomy, Hucklebee (this song, featuring an obligato on the word *rape,* was replaced with "The Abduction" later in the run, when the author's consciousness was tweaked by the rise of feminism)
Soon It's Gonna Rain...Matt, Luisa
The Rape Ballet...Company
Happy Ending...Matt, Luisa, Hucklebee, Bellomy
ACT II The Plum Is Too Ripe...Matt, Luisa, Hucklebee, Bellomy
I Can See It...El Gallo, Matt
Plant a Radish...Hucklebee, Bellomy
Round and Round...El Gallo, Luisa, Company
They Were You...Matt, Luisa
Try to Remember (reprise)...El Gallo

Licensing: Music Theatre International

Difficulties/Advantages: A cast of eight with only one female (although the Mute and the Indian have been played by women in past productions). The piano and harp accompaniment is brilliant, and the score is not helped by larger orchestrations, only overshadowed. The theatrical conceits must be played with rigor and commitment, the young lovers cannot be saccharine, and your El Gallo must reek of masculinity (while still being able to sing). Achieve that, and everyone else can chew the scenery; the production will work. Be careful of overly imaginative designers. The piece nearly always succeeds—and is timeless—because of the raw, theatrical, commedia dell'arte style from which it evolved.

A film made and barely released doesn't do the stage version justice—nothing on celluloid could—but does have a beautiful production design and moderately faithful screenplay. The casting is a nightmare of hits and misses, with Joel Grey and Brad Sullivan as the fathers (Grey all show-biz pizzazz and Sullivan a nonmusical method actor), Jean Louisa Kelly and Joseph McIntyre as the lovers (she a Victorian wedding cake, he right out of a contemporary pop boy-group), and Jonathon Morris playing El Gallo like a fop in *The Scarlet Pimpernel.* All told, however, it's not nearly as bad as its reputation, and the DVD, while no replacement for seeing it live, is worth perusing.

As I was preparing this book, *The Fantasticks'* one and only producer passed away. Born and raised in Brooklyn, he received the Purple Heart at the Battle of the Bulge in World War II before returning to New York. His first and only theatre project had to weather rough handling by the critics, but his perseverance and stewardship gave it the nudge it needed to catch on. Without his passion for the show, both off-Broadway's seminal little musical and the subsequent melodious careers of Jones and Schmidt might have been a footnote in theatre history instead of a shining beacon. Lore Noto, 1923–2002. Remember him in the light.

Fashion

By Anna Cora Mowatt
Adapted by Anthony Stimac
Music by Don Pippin
Lyrics by Steve Brown

With this dialogue, "Fashion! And pray what is fashion, Madam? An agreement between certain parties to live without their souls! To substitute etiquette for virtue—decorum for purity—manners for morals!—to affect a shame for the works of their Creator! and expend all their rapture upon the works of their tailors and dressmakers," you can see that the original 1845 play's theme probably would be more in fashion today than ever. Unfortunately, this musical's lugubrious book and uninspiring score wouldn't be.

Time and Place: Today. A high-fashion living room on Long Island, headquarters of the Long Island Masque and Wig Society, an organization devoted to the ideal of the preservation of early American drama.

Synopsis: The Ladies of the Long Island Masque and Wig Society put on a play, the first American comedy to be written by a woman. The play:

Mr. Tiffany had a successful business until he married a woman who wanted badly to be fashionable. She spends every penny he makes; now he's on the verge of bankruptcy and about to go to jail. Plus, a worker is blackmailing him. A cook from Europe passes himself off as a count, and the daughter vamps him, hoping to gain a title. But the maid knows that the count is a fraud. Other plot lines of mistaken identity complicate matters, rising to a climax at the end of act 1 but resolving themselves ("As I pressed that child in my arms, I swore that my wealth should never curse her as it cursed her mother") by the end of act 2. In other words, this is Roman comedy structure in early American theatre dialogue, to which the director of the Masque and Wig Society has added songs.

McAlpin Rooftop Theatre; February 18, 1974; 62 performances (plus 32 more at the Little Hippodrome).

Directed by Anthony Stimac. Additional choreography by Gene Kelton.

Original Cast:

Kim/Colonel Howard…Holland Taylor	Jean/Millinette…Sydney Blake
Edwina/Frankson…Susan Romann	Richard/Count Jolimaitre…Ty McConnell
Evelyn/Mrs. Tiffany…Mary Jo Catlett	Rita/Seraphina Tiffany…Sandra Thornton
Nan/Adam Trueman…Henrietta Valor	Pat/Mr. Anthony Tiffany…Jan Buttram
Suzanne/Joseph Snobson…Rhoda Butler	Marion/Gertrude…Joanne Gibson

Musical Numbers:

ACT I   Rococo Rag…Mrs. Tiffany, Company
You're Out of Fashion…Count, Mrs. Tiffany, Seraphina
The Good Old American Way…Trueman, Mr. Tiffany
What Kind of Man Is He?…Gertrude
My Daughter the Countess…Mrs. Tiffany
Take Me…Seraphina, Snobson, Count, Mr. and Mrs. Tiffany
What Do They Know About Paris?…Count, Millinette
I Must Devise a Plan…Company

Act II　Meet Me Tonight…Company
　　　　　My Title Song…Mrs. Tiffany, Company
　　　　　A Life Without Her…Trueman
　　　　　What Kind of Man Is He? (reprise)…Gertrude, Colonel Howard
　　　　　My Daughter the Countess (reprise)…Mrs. Tiffany
　　　　　My Title Song (reprise)…Trueman, Company

Licensing: Samuel French

Difficulties/Advantages: The set is singular, in spite of the various locales. The idea is for the cast to turn the typical contempo living room into various sets by rearranging the furniture. As for the cast, of the ten roles, only the director was played by a man in the original, the Masque and Wig Society—at least in Long Island—being made up only of women, thereby allowing at least the one simple theatrical device: all the roles in this adaptation of Ms. Mowatt's original play being played by women, a twist on the Elizabethan theatre in which all roles are played by men. So although one male to nine females is just about the ratio that most community theatres and drama departments feature, the play actually could support six men and four women if everyone stuck to their gender.

　　A more straightforward musical version of Ms. Mowatt's play, titled *Yankee Ingenuity,* is also available.

Festival

Book and Lyrics by Stephen Downs and Randal Martin
Music by Stephen Downs
Additional Book and Special Material by Bruce Vilanch

Based on the chantefable "Aucassin and Nicolette."

This is another "company of actors" musical, in which the emphasis is on vaudeville and burlesque more than realism. Story-theatre technique and narration carry the plot, but it's the musical numbers, contemporary (for the seventies), that provide the bulk of the entertainment.

Time and Place: The contemporary company acts out what is a French medieval fable.

Synopsis: The actors enter with trunks of clothes and props, and announce their plan to present the French version of the classic plot—used from the Hatfields and the McCoys to the Capulets and the Montagues, or, as they announce, "like *Romeo and Juliet,* only fewer people die." Beaucaire, the stern father, promises his son Aucassin in marriage to a veritable crone for the dowry, but Aucassin is in love with the lovely Nicolette, whose adopted father is wiser, although ineffective when Beaucaire imprisons his son and sends his henchman to kill Nicolette. Of course the henchman can't do it and releases her, and Nicolette flees to the forest, where encounters with an oxherd and shepherds promote singing and dancing. Aucassin escapes and follows, and they undertake life in a lowly hut, but before long, Beaucaire and the pirates he has hired capture them, returning Aucassin home. Nicolette makes it to Carthage, where she turns out to be the daughter of the King. Gypsies help disguise her as a man, a ploy that allows her to return to visit Aucassin and question his love, which he loyally expounds upon. Beaucaire, thought to be dead in a shipwreck, returns (thanks to the troubadour/narrator, who is rewriting the story even as they speak), and she, turning out to be born a princess, blesses their marriage, which is celebrated in a song and dance, appropriately titled "The Ceremony."

Downstairs at City Center; May 17, 1979.

Directed by Wayne Bryan. Choreographed by Stan Mazin.

Original Cast:

Prologue
    Troubadour...Michael Rupert
Beaucaire
    Aucassin...Bill Hutton
    Count Garin de Beaucaire...Michael Magnusen
    The Would-be Bride...Robin Taylor
    Viscount Bougars de Valence...John Windsor
    Viscountess...Roxann Parker
    Nicolette...Maureen McNamara
    Pirates...Lindy Nisbet, Leon Stewart
The War
    Aucassin's Warrior...Robin Taylor   Valence's Warrior...Lindy Nisbet
The Prison
    Henchman...Michael Rupert
The Forest
    Oxherd...Leon Stewart   Shepherdess...Robin Taylor
    Shepherd...John Windsor
Beaucaire
    The Minstrel...Michael Rupert
Pirates
    Captain...Michael Rupert
    Pirates...Lindy Nisbet, Roxann Parker, Leon Stewart, Robin Taylor, John Windsor
Carthage
    King of Carthage...Michael Rupert
    Sons of King...John Windsor, Leon Stewart, Michael Magnusen
    Harem Dancer...Robin Taylor
    Gypsies...Roxann Parker, Robin Taylor
    Gypsy Queen...Lindy Nisbet
Beaucaire
    Messenger...Robin Taylor

Musical Numbers:

Overture...Orchestra
Our Song...Troubadour, Company
The Ballad of Oh and For the Love...Troubadour, Company
Beata, Biax (Beautiful, Beautiful)...Aucassin
The War...Warriors
Just Like You...Beaucaire, Aucassin, Henchman
Special Day...Nicolette, Aucassin
The Time Is Come...Henchman, Nicolette. Aucassin
Roger the Ox...Oxherd
Why Do You Weep?...Minstrel
When the Lady Passes...Aucassin, Shepherds, Company
Gifts to You...Nicolette, Aucassin
The Escape (quintet)...Company
Pirates Song...Pirate Captain, Company
I Can't Remember...King, Sons, Nicolette

One Step Further…Gypsies, Nicolette, Gypsy Queen
Through Love's Eyes…Beaucaire, Aucassin
Let Him Love You…Viscountess, Nicolette
The Ceremony…Company
I Speak of Love…Troubadour
Finale (Our Song: reprise)…Company
(The original was in one act, but the script suggests an intermission, for those theatres looking to sell things.)

Licensing: Samuel French

Difficulties/Advantages: If you've already done *The Fantasticks* and *Godspell* and they were well received, this one becomes a possibility. A note in the script: "It is important that musical values be emphasized, with good singing-actors on stage and good musicians accompanying." (Gee, and we thought we'd use lousy performers.) The original New York production featured nine actors, but as you can see by the cast list, there are plenty of roles. Its set was an amusement park, but you can invent just about anything, and frankly you'll want to keep the designs simple and humorous so as not to overshadow the rather simple show. (I believe it was a Broadway musical-comedy designer who once said, "If they leave the theatre humming the scenery, you're in trouble.") Contemporary music and contemporary humor (of the ba-da-bump variety) carry the day, while story theatre technique moves the plot along swiftly enough.

A Fine and Private Place

"A New Musical-in-Progress"

Book and Lyrics by Erik Haagensen
Music by Richard Isen

Based on the book by Peter S. Beagle.

A "musical-in-progress"? Call back when you're ready.

Time and Place: Early summer. Yorkchester Cemetery, a vernal oasis in the Bronx.

Synopsis: Rebeck is a man with a special talent. He can communicate with ghosts—which, upon burial, apparently everyone is, until they're ready to move on. Rebeck lives at the cemetery to give them someone to talk to and work through their issues. As we begin, he meets Michael, a very successful writer whose death is something of a mystery. Either his wife killed him—the tabloids think so—or he committed suicide because he was blocked. Either way, he blames his wife. Michael meets a woman ghost, but her story is something of a secret also. Rebeck meets the widow Klapper, who drops by to visit her husband's grave but doesn't know why Rebeck is there. That all four have a secret ends the first act.

　　Curtain up, and Rebeck has admitted to the widow that he lives in the cemetery. She offers to take him in, but he's not, in fact, homeless. It takes him most of the act to admit to her that he talks to ghosts. Michael and Laura confess they love each other (not much of a revelation), but Michael admits that he did commit suicide and was a failure as a writer. In the meantime, the police have found his suicide note, so the wife is off the hook. And he has to be reburied in another cemetery, because this one is Catholic and doesn't accept suicides. The cemetery guard, who all along could see the ghosts and knew what Rebeck was up to, helps Rebeck and the widow dig up and rebury Laura's body so she can go to the new cemetery with Michael. Then Rebeck gets the courage to leave the cemetery for good and move in with the widow.

Goodspeed Opera House/Norma Terris Theatre; August 3–20, 1989.

Directed by Robert Kalfin.

Original Cast:

Jonathan Rebeck...Charles Goff
Michael Morgan...Brian Sutherland
Campos...Larri Rebbega (apparently Gabriel Barre, as Raven and Campos are intended to double)

Raven...Gabriel Barre
Gertrude Klapper...Evalyn Baron
Laura Durand...Maureen Silliman

Musical Numbers:

ACT I   Prelude...Orchestra
Prologue...Rebeck
I'm Not Going Gently...Michael
Much More Alive...Rebeck
You Know What I Mean...Klapper
A Fine and Private Place...Laura, Michael
As Long as I Can...Michael
Stop Kidding Yourself...Rebeck, Klapper
The Telepathetique...Michael, Laura, Klapper
What Did You Expect?/Let Me Explain...Laura, Michael
It's None of My Business...Klapper, Rebeck
Quartet...Michael, Laura, Rebeck, Klapper

ACT II   What Should I Do?...Klapper, Laura Rebeck, Michael
Close Your Eyes...Laura
Argument...Rebeck, Klapper
No One Ever Knows...Klapper
Because of Them All...Michael, Laura
Much More Alive (reprise)...Rebeck
Do Something...Laura, Michael, Rebeck
How Can I Leave Here?...Rebeck
Finale...Orchestra

Licensing: Samuel French

Difficulties/Advantages: "Lay off the Shirley Maclaine books" is a comic line the authors might have done better by taking to heart. Lame jokes by a hip blackbird who follows the proceedings, a nonsensical plot line, and insensate lyrics don't make this one very appealing.

First Lady Suite

By Michael John LaChiusa
Four one-act "chamber" musicals.
New York Shakespeare Festival; November 30, 1993; 32 performances.
Directed by Kirsten Sanderson. Choreographed by Janet Bogardus.

Over Texas

Time and Place: November 22, 1963. On board Air Force One, en route from Fort Worth to Love Field, Dallas, Texas.

Synopsis: Evelyn, personal secretary for President Kennedy, and Mary, personal secretary for Jackie Kennedy (if you're under sixty, you'll know her as Jackie Onassis), complain about being overworked. Mary falls asleep and dreams of Mrs. Kennedy and Lady Bird Johnson. All very surreal.

Original Cast:

Evely Lincoln...Carolann Page   Mary Gallagher...Debra Stricklin
A Presidential Aide...David Wasson   The First Lady (Jacqueline Bouvier
Lady Bird Johnson...Alice Playten   Kennedy)...Maureen Moore

Where's Mamie?

Time and Place: 1957. Ike and Mamie Eisenhower's bedroom, the White House.

Mamie complains about being left alone on her birthday. Marian Anderson, the black opera star, appears, attempting to get Mamie to speak to her husband about sending the troops to Little Rock to protect black school-children integrating a school. Mamie and Marian travel back in time to World War II, Algiers, where Mamie discovers Ike's affair with his chauffeur. She and Marian tie the chauffeur up and dump her in the back seat of a jeep. Ike professes his love for Mamie and sends the ladies home on a B-52. It wasn't such a bad birthday for Mamie after all.

Original Cast:

Mamie Eisenhower...Alice Playten   Marian Anderson...Priscilla Baskerville
Ike (Dwight D. Eisenhower)...David Wasson   Ike's Chauffeur...Debra Stricklin

Olio

Time and Place: 1950. A luncheon for Christian Democratic mothers and daughters.

Synopsis: Daughter Margaret Truman, as a child, sings for the Christian Democratic Mothers and Daughters, while her mother, Bess, does about everything annoying an audience member can do. At the end of the song, Margaret runs off crying.

Original Cast:

Bess Truman...David Wasson   Margaret Truman...Debra Stricklin

Eleanor Sleeps Here

Time and Place: 1936. Interior of Amelia Earhart's Lockheed Electra, night.

Synopsis: Amelia Earhart is taking Eleanor Roosevelt and her friend Lorena flying. For most of the trip, Lorena, once a rising journalist, complains about coming under Eleanor's spell and giving up her objective career.

Original Cast:

Eleanor Roosevelt...Carolann Page   Hick (Lorena Hickok)...Carol Woods
Amelia Earhart...Maureen Moore

Licensing: Dramatists Play Service

Difficulties/Advantages: Fourteen roles can be played by seven. Four different musical styles and much surrealism. For all the boundary stretching, there's very little there.

Flora, the Red Menace

Book by David Thompson
Music by John Kander
Lyrics by Fred Ebb
Originally Adapted by George Abbott
Based on the novel *Love Is Just Around the Corner* by Lester Atwell.

It's hard for older folks to envision anyone but Liza Minnelli as Flora, so permanently did the eighteen year old implant her personality in the entertainment cosmos with her debut musical in 1965. But Minnelli no longer holds sway, and your cast could make this early Kander and Ebb musical—it's their score that makes it worthwhile—come alive in spite of an "early musical" book. (Flora sublets space in her studio to a dance act so we can get in a number.) An off-Broadway revival brought the cast down to little-musical size—nine—and capitalism is still running rampant over labor, so this classic also-ran musical bears considering in your hometown.

Time and Place: 1935. New York City.

Synopsis: Flora graduates college with optimism but has trouble finding a job until she is hired to sketch clothes for a department store. She also meets Harry, who is a committed Communist—it's 1935 and the Depression is emboldening the labor class—and he signs her up for the cause. She likes Harry, even steals some valentine candy for him, but is competing with Comrade Charlotte, a vamp with activist fervor and her eyes on Harry too.

But Harry expects Flora to toe the party line, and when she has to cross a picket line in front of the department store—not for selfish reasons but to save the jobs of thirty-three fellow employees who want to unionize—she does. The jobs are saved—all but hers. The dance act gets a booking, but Harry breaks up with her. When the curtain goes down, she still needs a good break.

Alvin Theatre; May 11, 1965; 7 previews, 87 performances.

Directed by George Abbott. Musical staging by Lee Theodore.

The original Broadway cast numbered forty performers, but the show was revived at the Vineyard Theatre where it featured a more manageable nine: November 20, 1987 to January 23, 1988; 46 performances.

Revival directed by Scott Ellis. Choreographed by Susan Stroman.

Revival Cast

Flora Meszaros...Veanne Cox
Charlotte...Lyn Greene
Mr. Weiss and Others...Ray DeMattis
Kenny and Others...Dirk Lumbard
Mr. Stanley and Others...David Ossian

Harry Toukarian...Peter Frechette
Willy and Others...Eddie Korbich
Elsa and Others...B.J. Jefferson
Maggie and Others...Maggy Gorrill

Musical Numbers (from the revised book):

ACT I   Opening/Graduation Song...Company
The Kid Herself...Flora, Artists
All I Need Is One Good Break...Artists
It's Not Every Day of the Week...Flora, Harry
Sign Here...Harry
Quiet Thing...Flora
The Flame...Charlotte, Communists
It's Not Every Day of the Week (reprise)...Flora, Harry
Dear Love...Flora, Company

ACT II   Keeping It Hot...Kenny, Maggie
Express Yourself...Charlotte
Where Did Everybody Go?...Harry, Flora, Charlotte
You Are You...Mr. Weiss, Elsa, Flora
The Joke...Harry, Company
Quiet Thing (reprise)...Willy
Sing Happy...Flora

Licensing Agent: Samuel French

Difficulties/Advantages: Kander and Ebb (music and lyrics) and Liza Minnelli (Liza Minnelli) are certainly a trio of Broadway babies, but the small-cast revival, designed with a simple set and a few pieces of furniture coming and going compliments of the cast, makes this an ideal small musical—although one which, not uncommonly for musicals of the period, features a strong score with simplistic book. Although the revival features Brechtian transitions—our narrator reprises "Mister Just Give Me a Job" several times—there is very little material actually reflecting the McCarthy era blacklisting and red-baiting that took place fifteen years after the story but fifteen years before the musical. The heroine requires a sad-sack-with-spine character—the kind Minnelli later triumphed with in *Cabaret*—who can get your sympathy just by belting songs, and the hero requires an Austin Pendelton—type actor with a natural inferiority complex (Bob Dishey played the original). Nevertheless, it's a tight libretto with fresh, unique songs by Kander and Ebb at the very beginning of their illustrious careers, and plenty of opportunity for your cast to "Sing Happy."

The Gift of the Magi

Adaptation, Music, and Lyrics by Peter Ekstrom

From the short story by O. Henry.

A very brief one-act version of the classic O. Henry short story.

Time and Place: 1905, the morning of Christmas Eve and that night. A one-room flat in New York City.

Synopsis: Surely you know the plot: Too poor for Christmas presents, she sells her beloved hair for a watch chain, and he pawns his ancestral watch for tortoise-shell combs. But love is better than even our most prized possessions.

Actors Theatre of Louisville; 17-plus Christmas seasons in Louisville.

Directed by Larry Deckel.

Original Cast:

Della…Beverly Lambert   Jim…Peter Boynton

Musical Numbers:

Overture/Opening Song…Della, Jim
Tomorrow Is Christmas…Jim, Della
Now I've Got You!…Jim, Della
Jim and the Queen of Sheba…Jim, Della
If We Had Money…Jim, Della
Look at My Watch…Jim
What Can I Give Him?…Della
I Shall Let My Hair Down/Madame Sofronie…Della
Entre Scene/Della Returns…Della
Your Hair Is Gone!…Jim, Della
Jim and Della Open Their Gifts/By the Way/Finale…Jim, Della

Licensing: Samuel French

Difficulties/Advantages: There are only two characters and one set in this version, so it would make a good Christmastime one-act or curtain raiser for a more substantial holiday show, or you could pair it with the following one-act that was written as a companion piece.

The New Leaf

Adaptation, Music, and Lyrics by Peter Ekstrom

From the short story by O. Henry.

Even more sentimental than *Magi.*

Time and Place: 1905. A studio in Greenwich Village.

Synopsis: Johnsy and Sue are female artists living and working in a studio, across the hall from Behrman, also an artist, although he seems to spend more time drinking than painting. When Johnsy comes down with pneumonia, the Doctor warns Sue that she isn't expected to survive. Johnsy, looking out the window, watches leaves fall from a tree and predicts that she will die when the last leaf falls. Sue visits Behrman in his studio, only to discover that he hasn't painted in forty-five years; he's a failure. She tells him about Johnsy. That night there's a storm and high winds, but the next morning there is a single leaf still hanging on, and Johnsy, taking the spirit of the leaf, gets better. Behrman, who died in the night, is found in the alley with ladder, lantern, and paint supplies. (He wasn't a failure after all, and that leaf will be there forever.)

Musical Numbers:

What's She Like?...Doctor, Sue, Johnsy
Let's Drink a Toast!...Behrman, Sue, Johnsy
I Want to Paint the Bay of Naples...Johnsy
The Last Leaf...Johnsy, Sue
Tomorrow When You're Feeling Well Again...Sue
Come into My Humble Abode...Behrman
I'm a Failure in Art...Behrman, Sue
Listen to the Wind...Sue
How the Wind Howled...Doctor
The Last Leaf Finale...Johnsy, Sue, Doctor

Licensing: Samuel French

Difficulties/Advantages: Two men, two women, one studio. Both musicals feature operetta-like scores and require coloratura sopranos and well-trained baritones. Both acts are tight and skillful, and O. Henry's delicious stories are never out of date. You'll find both scores on a CD by Harbinger Records, an obscure but invaluable independent.

The Gifts of the Magi

The Gifts of the Magi at the Lamb's Players Theatre, San Diego, CA.

Book by Mark St. Germain
Music by Randy Courts
Lyrics by Mark St. Germain and Randy Courts

Drawn from two short stories by O. Henry.

Time and Place: December 23–25, 1905. New York City.

Synopsis: Okay, for anyone who doesn't know O. Henry's short story about the young married couple who are utterly broke (but of course, deeply in love) and unable to buy each other Christmas gifts, here's the most discussed ending in English literature classes: she sells her long, beloved hair to buy him a chain for his most precious possession, his pocket watch, while he sells his pocket watch to buy her a beautiful set of combs for her hair. In this musical version, the authors have combined that famous story with another, which features a happy-go-lucky, homeless bum named Soapy, who wants to get arrested so he can spend the winter in a warm jail.

Lamb's Theatre; December 3, 1984.

Directed by Christopher Catt. Choreographed by Piper Pickrell.

Original Cast:

Will...Michael Brian	City Her...Lynne Winterstellar
City Him...Brick Hartney	Jim Dillingham...Jeff McCarthy
Della Dillingham...Leslie Hicks	Soapy Smith...Bert Michaels

Musical Numbers:

Star of the Night...City Him and Her
Gifts of the Magi...Willy, Company
Christmas Is to Blame...Willy, City Him and Her
How Much to Buy My Dream?...Jim
The Restaurant...Soapy, City Him and Her
Once More...Jim, Della
Bum Luck...Soapy, Jim
Greed...Company
Pockets...Pockets
The Same Girl...Della
Star of the Night (reprise)...Jim, Della, City Him and Her
Gifts of the Magi (reprise)...Company

(The script was revised for a 1990 revival, and the numbers listed here are from the revised edition.)

Licensing: Dramatists Play Service

Difficulties/Advantages: Although other short stories have been combined to form full-length musicals—notably, James Michener's "Fo' Dolla" and "Our Heroine" make up the plot and subplot of Rodgers and Hammerstein's *South Pacific*—the two classic O. Henry stories here have nothing whatsoever to do with each other, and their being jerry-rigged together weakens them both. It might have been better to write two one-act musicals. However, if it's the holiday season and your audiences already know Dickens's *Christmas Carol* by heart, you're guaranteed to get a romantic tear or two out of them with a stage-musical version of what may be the most sentimental Christmas story ever written. In this version, five performers are needed, but two of them play a number of characters, so it can be expanded to provide more roles if needed.

The Gig

Book, Music, and Lyrics by Douglas J. Cohen

Based on the motion picture by Frank D. Gilroy.

Frank Gilroy's small, wonderful picture about middle-aged men in an amateur Dixieland jazz group that takes a professional gig and learns some life lessons has here been transmuted into a small musical...for no particularly good reason. Not to say it wouldn't be fun to produce and worthwhile to see, but the songs don't really add very much.

Time and Place: August, 1975. New York City and the Catskills.

Synopsis: After playing together every Wednesday night for years, a used car salesman, a stock-broker, a real estate salesman, a clarinet teacher, a dentist, and a delicatessen owner accept a two-week gig as the house band at the Paradise Manor. (In the Catskills, the grander the name, the seedier the bungalows.) But Georgie, the bass player, has to go into the hospital, so a professional is hired to take his place. That the accommodations aren't luxurious and they're treated as "help" is just their first introduction to life on the road. They're forced to play easy-listening music instead of jazz, but they manage to win over their aged audience with their own "Biff-Bam-Bang!" And two of the guys get it on with waitresses (although they shouldn't).

But act 2 introduces us to Rickie Valentine, on a comeback from a canceled TV show and rehab, and her tough-guy manager. When the amateurs can't cut her charts, they're fired and retreat, nursing their wounds, leaving the pro to recruit more pros. To the extent that the story is about male bonding, the group falls apart but, upon hearing that Georgie has died, make amends and resume their friendship. To the extent that the story is meant to show the not-so-glamorous life of real musicians to them and to us, it succeeds. By the end, you'll love the story but won't want your son to take music lessons.

This one has wound its way through numerous readings, workshops and stock productions, but as of this writing, had not made it to off-Broadway. Its first fully staged production was in Sacramento, July 15–21, 1996.

Sacramento Cast:

Marty...William Parry
Georgie/Vince Amati...David Brummel
Gil...Charles Pistone
Marshall Wilson...Don Mayo
Donna.. Catherine Campbell
Miss Ricki Valentine...Michele Pawk

Jack...James Judy
Aaron...Steve Routman
Arthur...Scott Robertson
Abe Mitgang...Freddie Roman
Lucy...Audrey Klinger

Musical Numbers:

AcT I   Opening Sequence/Farewell Mere Existence, Hello Jazz...Marty, Jack, Arthur, Aaron, Gil, Jack
Four Hours Away from Paradise/Time Out...Marty Georgie, Arthur, Aaron, Gil, Jack
Departures...Jack, Marty Arthur, Aaron, Gil
A Real Nice Trip, Part 1...Marshall, Marty Gil, Jack, Aaron, Arthur
A Real Nice Trip, Part 2...Abe with Marty, Jack, Marshall, Aaron, Gil, Arthur
Play Nice...Abe with Marshall, Marty, Jack, Aaron, Gil, Arthur

	Drifting…Marty, Jack, Gil, Marshall, Aaron, Arthur
	Benny Goodman…Aaron with Guys
	Drifting (reprise)…Marty with Aaron, Georgie, Marshall, Gil, Jack, Arthur
ACT II	Biff-Bam-Bang!…Marty with Jack, Arthur, Marshall, Gil, Aaron, Abe
	Beautiful…Arthur, Lucy, Gil, Donna
	Time Out (reprise)…Georgie
	Beautiful (reprise)…Marty
	Ricki Is Back in Town!/Me and Mr. "G"…Ricki Valentine
	Time to Put the Toys Away…Donna, Lucy
	Choices…Marshall
	I Can't Live Without Your Horn…Marty, Jack, Gil, Aaron, Arthur
	Biff-Bam-Bang! (reprise)…Marty, Jack, Gil, Aaron, Arthur

Licensing: Samuel French

Difficulties/Advantages: See the film, read the play, then decide. There are nine men and three women without doubling, which could bring the cast down to ten. A unit set will do, but there's no inherently dramatic reason for it, just budget, and the wonderful ambience of the Catskills in their heyday was part of the film's charm. Either you have seven character actors who can sing and form a Dixieland band, or the actors have to fake their instruments, which takes a good deal of practice too. In the film, the professional musician is black, the others are white. There's no real necessity for this, but the 1985 film, without anything overt, used this angle smoothly.

Godspell

A Musical Based upon the Gospel According to St. Matthew

Music and Lyrics by Stephen Schwartz
Book by John Michael Tebelak

Synopsis: Stephen Schwartz's tuneful pop score, including the hit single "Day by Day," wasn't the only asset that made this freshly-minted-in-college off-Broadway musical endearing and very, very successful. Based on the Gospel According to St. Matthew—the story of the last days of Christ—various parables were hilariously performed by the cast of ten as hippies, utilizing clowning, pantomime, charades, vaudeville, and topical impersonations.

Tried out at LaMama off-off-Broadway; then produced at the Cherry Lane Theatre off-Broadway, opening May 17, 1971; moved to the Promenade Theatre also off-Broadway; then to Broadway at the Broadhurst, then the Plymouth, and finally the Ambassador, for a grand total of 2,124 performances off-Broadway and 527 on Broadway.

Conceived and directed by John Michael Tebelak.

Off-Broadway Cast:

Lamar Alford	Peggy Gordon
David Haskell	Joanne Jonas
Robin Lamont	Sonia Manzano
Gilmer McCormick	Jeffrey Mylett
Stephen Nathan	Herb Simon

66

Godspell at the Amas Musical Theatre, New York, NY.

Musical Numbers:

ACT I   Tower of Babel
         Prepare Ye the Way of the Lord
         Save the People
         Day by Day
         Learn Your Lessons Well
         Bless the Lord
         All for the Best
         All Good Gifts
         Light of the World
ACT II   Turn Back, O Man
         Alas for You
         By My Side (Lyrics by Jay Hamburger, music by Peggy Gordon)
         We Beseech Thee
         On the Willows
         Finale

Licensing: Music Theatre International. For stock and amateur productions, contact Theatre Maximus, 1650 Broadway, Suite 601, New York, New York 10019; 212-765-5913

Difficulties/Advantages: An ideal show for a cast of nearly any size, any age, and any ethnic background, all on stage all the time, with lots of bits to be handed out and a baker's dozen of wonderful songs. *Godspell* can be performed almost anywhere with any kind of production and offers a great challenge to the imagination of directors, choreographers, and designers. The original hippies and clowns needn't be the central motif; a more contemporary group look could be substituted, as the stories are never dated and the songs are lovely and rambunctious in any decade.

The Grass Harp

Book and Lyrics by Kenward Elmslie
Music by Claibe Richardson
Based on the novel by Truman Capote.

Lost in the cavernous Martin Beck theatre on Broadway and with a story too light for razzmatazz, this short-lived but wonderful musical based on the Truman Capote novella deserves a great small theatre production more than any musical I can think of. But assembling a cast equal to the originals—Barbara Cook, Karen Morrow, Max Showalter, Rusty Thacker, and Carol Brice—would be nearly impossible.

Time and Place: The past (the story was written in 1951). The Talbo House, in Joy City, and in River Woods (surely the South).

Synopsis: Dolly makes her Gypsy Dropsy Cure out of plants (and not a little sherry), and it seems to cure just about everything. Her sister, however, has been charmed by a man who wants to patent the recipe and become "Big Rich." Unwilling, Dolly, Catherine, and her young cousin (who dreams about "Floozies" but is in love with Maude) run away to a giant tree house. There, Babylove and her five children come by and put on their "Miracle Show" (which happens to be one of the all-time showstoppers). They all get arrested at big sister's insistence but escape when Dolly's Dropsy Cure gets the sheriff drunk. Before he can rearrest them, the con man runs off with sister's money, and she reunites with Dolly, having learned her lesson. The rousing "Yellow Drum" march has almost nothing to do with anything—their father used to sing it around the house—but is so spirit-lifting you can't leave the theatre without taking it with you.

Martin Beck Theatre; November 2, 1971; 11 performances.

Directed by Ellis Rabb. Choreographed by Rhoda Levine.

Original Cast:

Dolly Talbo…Barbara Cook
Collin Talbo…Russ Thacker
Catherine Creek…Carol Brice
Verena Talbo…Ruth Ford
Dr. Morris Ritz…Max Showalter
Judge Cool…John Baragrey

Maude Riordan…Christine Stabile
Babylove…Karen Morrow
Sheriff Amos Legrand…Harvey Vernon
The Heavenly Pride-n-Joys…Kelly Boa,
    Trudy Bordoff, Collin Duffy,
    Eva Grant, David Craig Moskin

Musical Numbers:

Dropsy Cure Weather…Dolly, Catherine, Collin
Floozies…Collin
Think Big Rich…Dr. Ritz
If There's Love Enough…Catherine
Yellow Drum…Dolly, Catherine, Collin
Marry with Me…Catherine
Chain of Love…Dolly
The One Person in the World…Judge Cool
This One Day…Collin
The Babylove Miracle Show…Babylove, the Pride-n-Joys, Dolly, Catherine, Collin,
    Judge Cool, Maude
Walk into Heaven…Babylove

Something for Nothing...Dr. Ritz

The Indian Blues...Catherine, Babylove, the Pride-n-Joys, Dolly, Collin, Maude, Judge Cool

Take a Little Sip...Collin, Catherine, Dolly, Maude, Judge Cool, Babylove, the Pride-n-Joys

Yellow Drum...Dolly, Catherine, Collin, Maude, Judge Cool, Babylove, the Pride-n-Joys

What Do I Do Now He's Gone...Verena

Pick Yourself a Flower...Babylove, Catherine, Collin, Maude, Judge Cool, Dolly, the Pride-n-Joys

Reach Out...Dolly, Catherine, Babylove, Collin, Maude, Judge Cool, Verena, the Pride-n-Joys, Amos

Yellow Drum...Company

Licensing: Samuel French

Difficulties/Advantages: The cast of nine adults and five children ranging from eight to fourteen years old would stretch the definition of little theatre, but this *Harp* is really a gem. The set could be simple and impressionistic, and with one costume apiece (and a lot of talent), the necessary resources aren't overwhelming. Truly one of the ones-that-got-away when the original production didn't succeed. Listen to the album if you don't believe me, and you'll want to produce this one.

The Great American Backstage Musical

Book by Bill Solly and Donald Ward
Music and Lyrics by Bill Solly

An also-ran in the *Dames at Sea* category, this spoof of Hollywood musicals of the 1940s played San Francisco (where spoofs are always welcome) and Los Angeles (where they don't know the difference), then London, and finally New York, where it died.

Time and Place: 1939–1945. New York, London, and the battlefields of Europe.

Synopsis: The usual cast of Fox musical characters is putting on a show at a dive downtown and hoping to get seen by uptown producers. Kelly loves Johnny, Harry loves Kelly, and Sylvia and Banjo were just made to be played by Comden and Green. When English star Constance vamps Johnny, he turns her down, but the next day, when Kelly is offered a spot in a Shubert musical and turns it down to stay with her Johnny, Johnny opts for Constance just so Kelly won't lose her chance at the big time. On that star-crossed note, World War II gets underway. Johnny and Banjo entertain the troops until they get bombed, literally, while Kelly becomes a big movie star and Harry inherits five million dollars. The war ends and Harry buys the old dive, gets the old gang together, and puts on a show. Kelly gets her Johnny, Harry marries Constance, and with Sylvia and Banjo, they all dance "The End."

Silver Lining, New York; Sept 15, 1983; 5 previews, 18 performances.

Directed and Choreographed by Bob Talmadge.

Original Los Angeles Cast:

Kelly Moran...Gaye Kruger   Banjo...Jerry Clark

Sylvia...Marsha Kramer
Johnny Brash...Tim Bowman

Harry...Joe Barrett
Constance Duquette...Tamara Long

Off-Broadway Cast:

Johnny Brash...Mark Fotopoulos
Harry...Joe Barrett
Banjo...Bob Amaral

Sylvia...Suzanne Dawson
Kelly Moran.. Paige O'Hara
Constance Duquette...Maris Clement

Musical Numbers:

Overture
Opening Number...Kelly, Johnny, Banjo, Sylvia, Harry
I Got the What?...Banjo, Johnny, Kelly, Sylvia
Crumbs in My Bed...Sylvia
On the Avenue...Kelly, Harry
Cheerio...Johnny, Kelly, Company
You Should Be Being Made Love To...Constance
On the Avenue (reprise)...Kelly, Harry
The Star of the Show...Johnny
When the Money Comes In...Kelly, Company
News of You...Constance, Harry
I Could Fall in Love...Constance
Ba-Boom!...Johnny, Banjo
Cheerio (reprise)...Kelly
I'll Wait for Joe...Sylvia
The End...Company

Licensing: Samuel French

Difficulties/Advantages: Enthusiasm is everything here. Produce only if your neighborhood is tired of *Dames at Sea* and just must have another takeoff on the early days of movie musicals. As for the production, this from the authors: "*The Great American Backstage Musical* was originally conceived as an entertainment that could be presented without sets and with a minimum of costumes in any space capable of accommodating six actors, a piano or two, and an audience. It has worked well with more elaborate productions, but the simple approach still remains a valid alternative that can lead to real benefits in maintaining the bright, brisk pace that is absolutely vital to the show's success." In other words, like so many others of its ilk, it's flexible. It occurs to me that *Curley McDimple, Dames at Sea,* and this one could all just as well be lavish, chorus-packed Broadway-size musicals in the vein of *42nd Street,* if you had the notion. (In fact, the television version of *Dames* was just that.) But then, if you're reading this book, you're probably looking for something smaller anyway.

Gunmetal Blues

Book by Scott Wentworth
Music and Lyrics by Craig Bohmler and Marion Adler

The character of Buddy Toupee was inspired by the work of Richard March.

Story-theatre technique, with which a lounge piano player and two actors narrate and act out, nearly simultaneously, a hard-boiled mystery.

Time: Tonight. Pretty late.

Place: The Red Eye Lounge. It's one of those bars in one of those hotels out by an airport.

Synopsis: The Private Eye gets hired by the Rich Man's very attractive Blonde Assistant to find the Rich Man's Daughter, because last night the Rich Man shot himself. The Private Eye takes the case, kisses the Assistant, bribes the Doorman, gets cold-cocked, and is told to lay off by both the Cop and the Mob. Because it was murder. He drinks at the Lounge (where the Rich Man's Girlfriend sings) and passes out.

Lights up, and he's nursing a hangover. But the homeless Princess and the mail give him a few clues. Of course the Blonde isn't really the Assistant. The Princess is dead, but Jenny is still around, thinking she killed her father. She didn't. The Piano Player did.

Theatre Off-Park; March 27, 1992; 271 performances.

Directed by Davis Hall.

Original Cast:

The Piano Player…Daniel Marcus	The Blonde…Marion Adler
The Private Eye…Scott Wentworth	The Barkeep…Michael Knowles

Musical Numbers:

ACT I   Welcome to This Window…Buddy
Don't Know What I Expected…Buddy, Sam, Laura
Facts!…Sam
Loose Change…Princess
Mansion Hill…Sam, Buddy
Shadowplay…Laura
The Blonde Song…Carol
Childhood Days…Buddy, Sam, Carol
Take a Break…Buddy

ACT II   Buddy Toupee—Live…Buddy
Gunmetal Blues…Sam
I'm the One That Got Away…Princess
Don't Know What I Expected (reprise)…Buddy, Sam, Carol
Put It on My Tab…Carol
The Virtuoso…Buddy
Finale…Buddy, Sam, Jenny

Licensing: Samuel French

Difficulties/Advantages: "Evocative of the late forties/early fifties," say the production notes. And the oft-repeated warning to play it straight. But with lines such as "The room smelled of stale cigarette smoke and shattered dreams," you'd have to have an attitude. Great part for a woman—she plays four distinct roles—and Buddy doesn't have to play the piano, someone else could, but it sure adds to the atmosphere. As for the Private Detective, unless you've got a Bogart-type, you're nowhere, kid.

Hark!

A Musical in Two Acts with Epilogue and Prologue
Lyrics by Robert Lorick
Music by Dan Goggin and Marvin Jolley

A song cycle created in and typical of the late sixties, questioning all the traditions and institutions of life in both specific and allegorical forms, and done in a circuslike setting with (very effective) projections for setting the mood for each song.

Time and Place: Now (though pretty much rooted in the ideas of the 1960s). America.

Synopsis: The company of six (in the original, but it's very flexible) introduces themselves and beckons us to listen. ("Hark!") Then they become children playing games; then adolescents, college kids, soldiers, adults. Part 2 finds them in love, heading into middle age. In a long sequence, they portray various American types, and finally death looms.

Mercer Arts Center; May 22, 1972; 152 performances.

Directed by Darwin Knight.

Original Cast:

Dan Goggin	Marvin Solley
Elaine Petricoff	Danny Guerrero
Sharron Miller	Jack Blackton

Musical Numbers:

Prologue...Company

PART I   "The Cycle Begins"

Smart People...Company

Games (dance)...Company

What D'ya Wanna Be?...Company

Six Little Kids...Dan, Marvin

Icarus...Marvin, Elaine, Company

Sun Down...Sharron

Conversation Piece...Elaine, Jack, Dan, Sharron

The Outstanding Member...Danny, Company

How Am I Doin', Dad?...Company

All Good Things...Danny

Molly...Dan, Marvin

Smart People (reprise)...Company

In a Hundred Years...Company

PART II   "The Cycle Continues"

A Difficult Stage...Company

Coffee Morning...Jack

Suburbia Square Dance...Dan, Marvin, Company

I See the People...Jack, Dan, Marvin

Pretty Jack...Sharron

Big Day Tomorrow...Danny

Lullaby...Elaine

Here's to You, Mrs. Rodriguez...Dan, Marvin

Early Sunday...Jack, Company

What's Your Sun Sign, Mr. Simpson?...Company

All Good Things (reprise)...Dan

A Dying Business...Danny, Company

Waltz with Me, Lady...Marvin

Epilogue...Company

In a Hundred Years (reprise)...Company

Licensing: Samuel French

Difficulties/Advantages: Although the original production featured a circuslike area, with lights and projections on a cyclorama, there is enormous room for your own creativity. How much of this sixties artifact is still relevant, however, is probably up to where in America your audience harks from. One crucial issue for shows like these is that all the songs are pretty much presentational. That is, without a book/plot, the songs are generally performed to the audience, with only a moderate amount of interaction between the various characters the company is to portray, as in a revue.

Hedwig and the Angry Inch

Photo: Glenn Raiha

Hedwig and the Angry Inch at the Capital Playhouse, Olympia, WA.

Book by John Cameron Mitchell
Music and Lyrics by Stephen Trask

A glam-punk musical about a man whose botched sex-change operation left him the second half of the title.

Time and Place: The 70s. Kansas (although we're not there any more, you'll say quickly).

Synopsis: There's a plot of sorts: Young Hansel, in love with an American G.I. in Berlin, opts for the sex-change operation in order to marry him and get to America. Left with only that inch, he loses the G.I. but finds love in Kansas City with a sixteen-year-old Jesus freak. The young man is wilier than he is, however, and steals the songs he—now she— writes, using them to become a rock star, leaving Hansel/Hedwig and his band (the

"Angry Inch," of course) to play Ramada Inns. Like many off-Broadway musicals lately, you won't get it unless you see it.

Jane St. Theatre; February 14, 1998; 12 previews, 857 performances.

Directed by Peter Askin.

Original Cast:

Hedwig/Tommy Gnosis...
 John Cameron Mitchell
Yitzak...Miriam Shor

Cheater (The Angry Inch), a Punk
 Band...Stephen Trask, Scott Bilbrey,
 David McKinley, Chris Weilding

Musical Numbers:

Tear Me Down
The Origin of Love
Sugar Daddy
Angry Inch
Wig in a Box
Wicked Little Town
The Long Grift
Hedwig's Lament
Exquisite Corpse
Midnight Radio

Licensing: Dramatists Play Service

Difficulties/Advantages: Not for conservatives. It's not likely that either the story or the music and lyrics will carry well into the hinterlands of stock and amateur theatre, but every major city should see this one, and if yours hasn't yet, give it a try. A film version gives you a rough idea of the show but doesn't boast the theatricality of the stage version.

Hello Again

Words and Music by Michael John LaChiusa

Suggested by the play *La Ronde* by Arthur Schnitzler.

Arthur Schnitzler's 1897 play *Reigen (Hands Around)* is better known as *La Ronde,* the title of Max Ophuls's 1950 film version. It is "a play in ten duologues." Each couple is seen before and after sex. The man in the first scene is the man in the second, the woman in the second is the woman in the third, and so forth. The last man makes love with the first woman to complete the circle. The privately published play caused one of the greatest scandals in the history of German theatre. It provoked anti-Semitic riots in Berlin. A six-day obscenity trial resulted in an acquittal, but the author refused performances of the play until after his death. Since then, a countless number of plays and musicals have been adapted from this source, including David Hare's recent *The Blue Room* and this 1994 musical.

Time and Place: Throughout the 20th century.

Synopsis: In his version, LaChiusa has set each sequence in a different decade—although not in chronological order—and used very little dialogue, lots of singing, and a good deal of dance. (He says it should be thought of as a "ballet with words.") The Whore sleeps with the Soldier, the Soldier with the Nurse, and so forth, until the Senator sleeps with the Whore and everyone sings "Hello Again."

Mitzi E. Newhouse Theatre at Lincoln Center; December 28, 1993; 65 performances.

Directed and choreographed by Graziela Daniele.

Original Cast:

The Whore...Donna Murphy
The Nurse...Judy Blazer
The Young Wife...Carolee Carmello
The Young Thing...John Cameron Mitchell
The Actress...Michele Pawk

The Soldier...David A. White
The College Boy...Michael Park
The Husband...Dennis Parlato
The Writer...Malcolm Gets
The Senator...John Dossett

The various principals play a series of smaller roles as well.

Musical Numbers:

Hello Again...Whore, Soldier
Zei Gezent...Trio
I Gotta Little Time...Soldier, Nurse
We Kiss...Quintet
In Some Other Life...Nurse, College Boy
Story of My Life...College Boy, Young Wife, Patrons
At the Prom...Pop Singer
Ah, Maien Zeit!...Prima Donna
The Greatest of Adventures...Husband, Young Wife
Tom...Young Wife
Listen to the Music...Husband, Young Thing
Montage...Young Thing, Writer
Safe...Young Thing
The One I Love...Young Thing, Writer
Silent Movie...Writer, Actress
Rock with Rock...Soldier
Angel of Mercy...Nurse
Mistress of the Senator...Actress, Senator
The Bed Was Not My Own...Senator
Hello Again...Company

Licensing Agent: Dramatists Play Service

Difficulties/Advantages: Much simulated sex eliminates this one from school drama departments. In Schnitzer's original, a red handkerchief was passed from couple to couple, a symbol of the venereal disease, rampant at the time, which—theme coming—united the various classes in a class-divided society. Here the handkerchief is replaced with a brooch, but the rich scenes are reduced to cliché lyrics such as, "The greatest of adventures which a man and woman share is marriage." It's a very musical piece that is, in the end, a great deal shallower than the more than 100-year-old play. But ten talented musical theatre performers would get a workout with ten songs-as-dialogue sequences.

Hijinks!

By Robert Kalfin, Steve Brown, and John McKinney

Based on an idea by William Bolcom, David Brooks, Robert Kalfin and Arnold Weinstein.

Adapted from *Captain Jinks of the Horse Marines* by Clyde Fitch.

Songs are authentic, ranging through the 19th century from "Auld Lang Syne" (1799) to "Wait 'Till the Sun Shines, Nellie" (1905).

A musical version of Clyde Fitch's successful 1901 play. Fitch was considered to be the Neil Simon of his day, the first American playwright to build a name for himself that drew audiences to the theatre, turning out forty or so melodramas, with four running on Broadway at one time. This musical version features Fitch himself watching the story of Capt. Jinks and Madame Trentoni (really Aurelia Johnson from Trenton, New Jersey, an opera singer come to America with forty-eight pieces of luggage to sing at the Brooklyn Academy), who play out their meeting and romance for Fitch's sake, in the hopes that he'll write a play about it. An upright onstage piano surrounded by the cast and the lyrics of all the songs projected on the set give you an idea of the festivities, in which the audience is requested to sing along with all the classic gay-nineties tunes that have been inserted. Indeed, it's almost as if we were invited into the parlor to gather around the piano, for that's what most of the tunes were intended for in a time prior to radio and television, record players, and films.

Time and Place: 1872. Act I: End of October, the landing dock of the Cunard Steamship Company in New York. Act II: A fortnight later, at Madame Trentoni's in the Brevoort House. Act III: The same night.

Synopsis: At the landing dock of the Cunard Steamship Company, Madame Trentoni disembarks and is interviewed by adoring reporters. Capt. Jinks and his two cohorts bet on which one of them will make love to the lady first. When Jinks meets her, however, he falls instantly in love, as she with him—there's a musical bell tone and a lighting change to make sure you get it—and calls off the bet. Bribing the customs inspector to help her through, however, lands him in jail and leaves the way wide open for his two friends.

Act 2 moves on to Madame Trentoni's suite in the Brevoort House. It's two weeks later, and we find our hero and heroine deeply in love, with his friends anxious to discredit him. They manage to show her uncle, a ballet master, an IOU regarding the bet, and when Aurelia sees it, she is convinced that she was being wooed only for her money. Her unhappiness is played out amidst rehearsals for the ballet, in which several outsized women—of a type never known, even at the time, to be a *corps de*—battle it out for supremacy in a wild waltz.

In act 3 all is resolved, although without any significant plot twists. She receives and believes him, and there you are. Even his mother—who had earlier tried to talk Trentoni out of marriage on the grounds that, as an "actress," she was beneath her son and would ruin his career—saw last night's performance and cried, thereby welcoming her as a daughter-in-law.

Cheryl Crawford Theatre at the Chelsea Theater Center; December 13, 1980; 37 performances.

Directed by Robert Kalfin. Dances and musical staging by Larry Hayden.

Original Cast:

Frau Hochspits/Sailor…Evelyn Baro
Policeman/Sun Reporter…Sal Basile
Sailor…Bruce Conner
Fitch, Times Reporter, Papa
    Belliarti…Michael Connolly
Mrs. Maggitt, Sailor…Elizabeth Devine
Charlie, Herald Reporter…Randall
    Easterbrook
Gussie, Tribune Reporter…Scott Ellis
Peter…Christopher Farr

Capt. Jinks…Joseph Kolinski
Jenny…Sarah Lowman
Musical Director, Pianist,
    Detective…Michael O'Flaherty
Miss Pettitoes, Sailor…Elaine Petricoff
Mrs. Greenborough, Mrs. Jinks…Marian
    Primont
Aurelia Johnson, Madame
    Trentoni…Jeannine Taylor

Musical Numbers:

ACT I Love's Old Sweet Song…Fitch, Chorus
Strike Up the Band…The Band
Capt. Jinks of the Horse Marines…Charlie, Gussie, Capt. Jinks
Take Them Away They'll Drive Me Crazy…Capt. Jinks, Charlie, Gussie
If You've Only Got a Moustache…Charlie, Chorus
Dad's a Millionaire…Gussie, Chorus
Star Spangled Banner…Aurelia
Home Sweet Home…Aurelia, Chorus
A Mother's Smile…Capt. Jinks
Capt. Jinks of the Horse Marines (reprise)…Charlie, Gussie, Fitch, Peter, Chorus

ACT II Will You Love Me in December As You Do in May?…Capt. Jinks, Aurelia, Chorus
Champagne Charlie…Charlie, Gussie, Chorus
Shew Fly! Don't Bother Me…Piano Only
Last Rose of Summer…Aurelia
Those Tassels on Her Boots…Capt. Jinks, Chorus
Beautiful Dreamer…Capt. Jinks
Wilt Thou Be Gone Love?…Capt. Jinks, Aurelia
A Boy's Best Friend Is His Mother…Mrs. Jinks, Aurelia
Then You'll Remember Me…Capt. Jinks
La Traviata Waltzes…Dancers

ACT III Silver Threads Among the Gold…Chorus
That Gal Is a High Born Lady…Peter, Chorus
Whispering Hope…Capt. Jinks
Poor Kitty Popcorn…Aurelia, Chorus
Mermaid's Evening Song…Frau Hochspits, Mrs. Maggitt, Miss Pettitoes
Auld Lang Syne…Chorus
Wait 'Till the Sun Shines, Nellie…Chorus
Goodbye My Lady Love…Charlie, Gussie
Then You'll Remember Me (reprise)…Capt. Jinks
Capt. Jinks of the Horse Marines (reprise)…Capt. Jinks, Chorus
Wait 'Till the Sun Shines, Nellie…All

Licensing: Samuel French

Difficulties/Advantages: Even with doubling, a cast of fourteen stretches the definition of "little" a great deal. Moreover, unless it's a gay nineties sing-along you're after, this isn't very helpful. Its lugubrious book wouldn't work whether played sincerely, camped, or anywhere in between, although teeth-to-the-scenery performances of the caricatures might keep it afloat between songs. A much more useful compendium of the Victorian era would be the revue *Tintypes*.

Honky Tonk Highway

Book by Richard Berg
Music, Lyrics, and Additional Dialogue by Robert Lindsey Nassif

Another actors-play-their-own accompaniment show, and another excuse for a bunch of good ol' country-western songs.

Time and Place: 1970. Tucker's Roadhouse in Alton Falls, Tennessee.

Synopsis: On stage tonight: the Mountain Rangers reunion, one year after the death of their leader, Clint Colby. The reunion tells the story of Clint and the Rangers, who, not long ago, lived in a town so small the "new arrival moved here sixteen years ago." But Clint had ambitions and put together a band. The road was brutal, until one of their songs hit the radio. Then they were playin' big auditoriums instead of honky-tonks, and success, of course, busted them up. Clint never did have time for Jenine-Kate, who loved him from childhood, so she married Darrell, they went off to write their own songs, and she became a big star too. The others went back to their families. But Clint had a weak heart from childhood and died in his prime. This story is told by the band themselves, sometimes narrating and sometimes playing various parts. A blue cowboy hat stands for Clint, and when one of the men puts it on, he's Clint in an acted-out flashback.

Don't Tell Mama; June 3, 1994. Goodspeed Opera House; May 26, 1995.

Directed by Gabriel Barre.

Original Cast:

Matthew Bennett	Kevin Fox
Erin Hill	Rick Leon
David M. Lutken	Sean McCourt
Andy Taylor	Joyce Leigh Bowden
Jennifer L. Neuland	Steve Steiner
Ken Triwush	

Musical Numbers (everyone contributes to all the songs):

ACT I   I Found a Song
Chalhatchee
Far-off Lights
Come Out and Play
Follow Where the Music Goes
Perfect Strangers
Harmonica Perfect
I'll Be There
(Don't Want to) Follow (blues reprise)
Baby, I Love Your Biscuits (prerecorded)
Answer the Call

<table>
<tr><td></td><td>Heartbreak Hall of Fame</td></tr>
<tr><td></td><td>Answer the Call (reprise)</td></tr>
<tr><td>ACT II</td><td>Honky Tonk Highways</td></tr>
<tr><td></td><td>Mr. Money</td></tr>
<tr><td></td><td>Dr. Love (possibly prerecorded)</td></tr>
<tr><td></td><td>Daddy's Girl</td></tr>
<tr><td></td><td>Me, Myself and I</td></tr>
<tr><td></td><td>I'm So Happy, I Could Cry</td></tr>
<tr><td></td><td>Easier to Sing Than Say</td></tr>
<tr><td></td><td>Far-off Lights (reprise)</td></tr>
<tr><td></td><td>Music in This Mountain</td></tr>
<tr><td></td><td>Curtain Call</td></tr>
<tr><td></td><td>Baby, I Love Your Biscuits (prerecorded)</td></tr>
</table>

Licensing: Samuel French

Difficulties/Advantages: Since this particular country-western band tells their own story, you really have to have actors who are also country-western singers. The stage of the road-house shouldn't be a problem, and the costumes and props are pretty minor, just indications of various other characters the cast of four men and one woman sometimes play. The lyrics are solid and sentimental, and any time someone dies, you're bound to get a few tears, so performed well, this can be a helluva show.

I Can't Keep Running in Place

Book, Music, and Lyrics by Barbara Schottenfeld

A psychologist leads six women in an "assertiveness training workshop." More singing than in the real thing.

Time and Place: Contemporary. Six Wednesday night sessions, from late winter to early spring. A workshop space in the psychologist's Soho loft.

Synopsis: Beth has been married for twenty years to an oral surgeon who reads gum charts at dinner. Eileen's husband makes her feel guilty all the time. Sherry likes Mike but can't have an orgasm and can't ask for help from him. Alice is an actress so scared of success she has stopped working and gotten fat. Gwen can't even tell her husband she's at a group. Mandy is a Sarah Lawrence student there to observe for her psychology class but is more judgmental than observant. Michelle, the psychologist, has left her husband and two children to set up on her own and claims to love the independence, but we know the husband has a girlfriend, and her confidence is desperation. There's surprisingly little bonding, a lot of arguing, several sequences of role playing in which women play characters in the other's lives they couldn't possibly know, and some of the women get a little more assertive.

Westside Arts Theatre; May 14, 1981; 187 performances.

Directed by Susan Einhorn. Choreographed by Baayork Lee.

Original Cast:

Michelle...Marcia Rodd   Beth...Helen Gallagher
Eileen...Joy Franz   Alice...Evalyn Baron

Sherry...Bev Larson   Mandy...Mary Donnet
Gwen...Jennie Ventriss

Musical Numbers:

ACT I   I'm Glad I'm Here...Company
            Don't Say Yes If You Want to Say No...Michelle, Company
            I Can't Keep Running in Place...Eileen
            I'm on My Own...Michelle
            More of Me to Love...Gwen, Alice
            I Live Alone...Beth
            I Can Count on You...Alice, Company
ACT II   Penis Envy...Michelle, Company
            Get the Answer Now...Sherry, Company
            What If We...Michelle
            Almosts, Maybes and Perhapses...Beth
            Where Will I Be Next Wednesday Night?...Company

Licensing: Samuel French

Difficulties/Advantages: First production: 1980, but steeped in the argot of Women's Lib. The "Penis Envy" aria is about as clever as it gets. "If a man says what he means, he's direct. If a woman says what she means, she's curt." This variation on the classic gender complaint is about the level of originality here. Watching a Lara Croft film would be more inspiring of female assertiveness.

I Do! I Do!

Book and Lyrics by Tom Jones
Music by Harvey Schmidt
Based on "The Fourposter" by Jan de Hartog.

When producer David Merrick got Robert Preston and Mary Martin together for this classic two-hander play that *The Fantasticks'* composers were turning into a musical, he provided one of the most brilliant evenings in the theatre to ever delight audiences. Alone, they had lit up many musical stages. Together, they were brighter than the sun. Gower Champion, unable to turn two characters into a Busby Berkeley extravaganza, was remarkably restrained, and the show was both dazzling for the actors and heartfelt for the writing. This one should forever be in smaller theatres, for no two actors alive could fill the Broadway theatre as those two did.

Time and Place: The story covers 50 years of marriage, just before the turn of the century. A bedroom.

Synopsis: Young and in love, Michael and Agnes get married, fumble through their wedding night, raise two children, and bicker (he admits to an affair, she packs her bags, they get over it), all in act 1.

Act 2 finds them beginning to settle into old age by celebrating New Year's Eve at home, marrying off their daughter, going through male menopause and female menopausal depression, and heading into their retirement in happy acceptance of a well-lived life. In the end, they pack up and leave their four-poster bed to the next young couple. All this and a joyous and touching score takes place around the bed.

Photo: Judy Purple

I Do! I Do! at the Venice Little Theatre, Venice, FL.

46th Street Theatre; December 5, 1966; 4 previews, 560 performances.
Directed by Gower Champion.

Original Broadway Cast:

Agnes...Mary Martin   Michael...Robert Preston

Musical Numbers:

Aᴄᴛ I   All the Dearly Beloved...Both
             Together Forever...Both
             I Do! I Do!...Both
             Goodnight...Both
             I Love My Wife...He
             Something Has Happened...She
             My Cup Runneth Over...Both
             Love Isn't Everything...Both
             Nobody's Perfect...Both
             A Well Known Fact. . .He
             Flaming Agnes...She
             The Honeymoon Is Over...Both
Aᴄᴛ II   Where Are the Snows?...Both
             When the Kids Get Married...Both
             The Father of the Bride...He
             What Is a Woman?...She
             Someone Needs Me...She
             Roll Up the Ribbons...Both
             This House...Both

Licensing: Music Theatre International

Difficulties/Advantages: Either one of the two famous musical theatre performers who comprised the original cast would have been too big for off-Broadway. Together their magic could barely be contained on. Nevertheless, with only two characters and a simple set, this romantic and touching musical can be reproduced almost anywhere under almost any conditions, although the two roles are demanding. (In one number, he played the violin, she the saxophone, or do I remember that backwards?)

I Love My Wife

Book and Lyrics by Michael Stewart
Music by Cy Coleman

From a play by Luis Rego.

Actually a sex farce—the kind that runs for years in England, with intermittent songs by a four-piece band that keeps appearing around them in silly costumes—it was already a decade behind the times when it opened, eight years after the film *Bob and Carol and Ted and Alice* had already lampooned swinging and the sexual revolution. Nevertheless, it was very successful on Broadway, probably because it titillated the Long Island matinee ladies, and is included here because it only requires four actors, four actor/musicians, and a simple set or two.

Time and Place: The 1960s. Trenton, New Jersey.

Synopsis: Two men, convinced they ought to get in on the sexual revolution, attempt to stage an orgy with their wives, but end up with their own spouses, because, well, the title says it all.

Ethel Barrymore Theatre; April 7, 1977; 7 previews, 857 performances.

Directed by Gene Saks. Musical numbers staged by Onna White.

Original Cast:

Cleo.. Ilene Graff	Monica...Joanna Gleason
Wally...James Naughton	Alvin...Lenny Baker
Musicians:	
Stanley...Michael Mark	Quentin...Joe Saulter
Harvey...John Miller	Norman...Ken Bichel

Musical Numbers:

ACT I We're Still Friends...All
Monica...The Guys
By Threes...Wally, Harvey, Alvin
A Mover's Life...The Guys
Love Revolution...The Guys, Cleo
Someone Wonderful I Missed...Cleo, Monica
Sexually Free...Wally, Cleo, Alvin

ACT II Hey There, Good Times...Harvey, Stanley, Quentin, Norman
By the Way If You Are Free Tonight...Harvey, the Guys
Lovers on Christmas Eve...Monica, Wally
Scream...Harvey, Stanley, Quentin, Norman

Ev'rybody Today Is Turning On...Wally, Alvin
Married Couple Seeks Married Couple...Cleo, Monica, Wally, Alvin
I Love My Wife...The Guys
In Conclusion...Harvey

Licensing: Samuel French

Difficulties/Advantages: The four musicians sang in the original and even threw in a few lines of dialogue, but eliminating them from the stage altogether would probably be a simple matter, and they were wildly extraneous anyway. It was a directorial conceit that did nothing for the comedy except distract from it.

I'm Getting My Act Together and Taking It on the Road

Photo: Roger S. Belanger

I'm Getting My Act Together and Taking It on the Road at the Little Theatre of Fall River, MA.

Book and Lyrics by Gretchen Cryer
Music by Nancy Ford

The musical that asks "if it's at all possible for men and women to have decent constructive relationships with each other when our culture and our pasts so conspire against it. When we can hardly pick our way through the myths and distortions of what we are." In other words, a product of the Me Decade, in which sentences like that were common and many writers tried to develop ideas while losing sight of plot and character.

Time and Place: Now. Here.

Synopsis: Heather, a soap opera actress, is trying out a new cabaret act on her thirty-ninth birthday. Unfortunately, her manager doesn't think she should act her age and thinks she should sing nice songs, not the "ball-breaking hostility" she's recently expressed. Maybe this new feminism is a reaction to the roles she's always played, first as Daddy's little girl, then as a helpful housewife. Now divorced and pursued by a young man who plays guitar, she has decided to celebrate herself. Which may be why the author played the lead.

Anspacher Theatre; May 16, 1978; 1165 performances.

Directed by Word Baker.

Original Cast:

Joe...Joel Fabiani   Heather...Gretchen Cryer
Alice...Margot Rose   Cheryl...Betty Aberlin
Jake...Don Scardino

Musical Numbers:

Natural High...Heather, Alice, Cheryl, the Liberated Man's Band
Smile...Heather, Jake, Cheryl, Alice, the Band
In a Simple Way I Love You...Heather, the Band
Miss America...Heather, Alice, Cheryl
Strong Woman Number...Alice, Heather, Cheryl
Dear Tom...Heather
Old Friend...Heather
In a Simple Way I Love You (reprise)...Jake
Put in a Package and Sold...Heather, Alice, Cheryl
If Only Things Were Different...Jake
Feel the Love...Company
Lonely Lady...Heather (Music by Gretchen Cryer)
Happy Birthday...Heather, the Band
Natural High (reprise)...Company

Licensing: Samuel French

Difficulties/Advantages: A bit outdated—every girl singer sings "feminist" material now without a peep from her manager—and tailored for the original cast. But you can't argue with over 1,000 performances, and there's always a large audience for strong women in musical comedy.

Inside Out

Book by Doug Haverty
Music by Adryan Russ
Lyrics by Adryan Russ and Doug Haverty

It was inevitable that someone would dramatize/musicalize group therapy. (In fact, in 1974 a meeting of twenty-two Broadway dancers was almost precisely that; certainly it was therapeutic by all accounts. And the result was *A Chorus Line*.)

Time and Place: The not-too-distant past. A large metropolitan city in the United States, maybe New York.

Synopsis: Grace is the leader but, aside from organizing scenes in which the various members role-play each other and their families, doesn't seem to lead anyone anywhere. Sage interprets everything through astrology. Chlo is a single, gay mother of a teenaged boy; Molly would dearly love to be as thin as she was before children; and Liz is conflicted between her high-powered career and her house-husband and three children. Dena, who has just joined the group, is a singer who hasn't had a record in four years. The only progress anyone seems to make during the evening is that Dena, with the help of the others, puts together a new cabaret act, and record execs actually show up, leading to a final song that leaves us with the simple wisdom, "Just do it."

Players Theatre; November 26, 1985; 23 performances.

Directed by Henry Fonte. Choreographed by Gary Slavin.

Original Cast:

Dena...Ann Crumb	Grace...Harriett D. Foy
Molly...Kathleen Mahoney-Bennett	Liz...Jan Maxwell
Chlo...Cass Morgan	Sage...Julie Prosser

Musical Numbers:

ACT I   Inside Out...Company
Let It Go...Sage, Grace
Thin...Molly, Company
I Can See You Here...Grace
If You Really Loved Me...Company
Yo, Chlo...Dena, Chlo
If You Really Loved Me (reprise)...Chlo
Behind Dena's Back...Company
No One Inside...Dena
Inside Out (reprise)...Company
ACT II   Grace's Nightmare...Grace, Company
All I Do Is Sing...Dena
Never Enough...Chlo
I Don't Say Anything...Sage
The Passing of a Friend...Molly, Company
Things Look Different...Liz, Company
Do It at Home...Liz, Company
Reaching Up...Dena, Company

Licensing: Samuel French

Difficulties/Advantages: Six chairs and six roles for women who would have to bring a great deal to their character, because there's very little drama. Although as recent as the nineties, *Inside Out* seems mired in the sixties. Is the career/motherhood conflict really anything new? Are single moms this clueless today? Do we feel sorry for someone with only one hit record? I know we men are tough to live with, but get over it, ladies. You're just as difficult.

Just So

Conceived by Julianne Boyd
Book by Mark St. Germain
Lyrics by David Zippel
Music by Doug Katsaros

Based on Rudyard Kipling's *Just So Stories.*

A smart and clever children's musical that should help develop future theatregoers. When you've already done *You're a Good Man, Charlie Brown,* this should have them coming back.

Time and Place: The world's first day.

Synopsis: The Eldest Magician brings forth five animals and, for his big finish, Man. Man would like to know his story. Instead we learn how the Camel got his humps, how the Rhino got his skin, how the Leopard got his spots, how the Giraffe got his neck, and how the Elephant got his nose. A crocodile almost eats the Elephant, and other arguments ensue, indicating this world won't necessarily be in harmony. Finally the Eldest Magician gives Man a book. But all the pages are blank. He will have to write his own story.

Jack Lawrence Theatre; November 19, 1985; 6 previews, 30 performances.

Directed by Julianne Boyd. Choreographed by David Storey.

Original Cast:

Eldest Magician...Andre De Shields
Camel...Teresa Burrell
Elephant Child...Tina Johnson
Man...Jason Graae

Giraffe...Keith Curran
Rhino...Tom Robbins
Leopard...Tico Wells

Musical Numbers:

ACT I   Just So...Eldest Magician, Animals
The Whole World Revolves Around You...Eldest Magician, Animals, Man
Arm in Arm in Harmony...Man, Animals
Chill Out!...Djiin, Man
Camel's Blues...Camel
Eat, Eat, Eat...Rhino, Man, Animals
Itch, Itch, Itch...Rhino
Everything Under the Sun...Man
The Gospel According to the Leopard...Leopard, Man, Animals

ACT II   My First Mistake...Eldest Magician
Shadowy Forest of Garadufi Dance...Leopard, Animals
Giraffe's Reprise...Giraffe
The Answer Song...Kolokolo Bird, Elephant Child
I've Got to Know...Elephant Child
I Have Changed...Eldest Magician, Animals
Lullaby...Eldest Magician

Licensing: Samuel French

Difficulties/Advantages: An excellent children's musical that, if well performed, will not bore the parents who brought them. Lots of possibilities for the set—a barren desert that soon becomes populated with flowers, trees, and rolling hills. Costumes could be simple or elaborate (but stay short of too elaborate, as simplicity is a key here). You'll need a vibrant, flexible, talented Eldest Magician to drive the proceedings. Creationists will love it, but evolutionists shouldn't mind too much. Encourage literacy by selling the Kipling volume in the lobby.

The Last Five Years

Photo: Ed Krieger

The Last Five Years at the Laguna Playhouse, Laguna Beach, CA.

Music and Lyrics by Jason Robert Brown

Scenes from a relationship, mostly sung solo, in turn, by a young man and a young woman.

Time and Place: Contemporary. New York and Ohio.

Synopsis: The five years referred to are the years of the relationship and marriage of the actress Catherine and the writer Jamie. They meet, fall in love, marry. He becomes a very successful, fawned-over writer. He has an affair. She is a failure as an actress, having to play stock in Ohio too many summers, somewhat irked at the role of successful writer's wife she is consigned to. He leaves her. Here's the part that's not a cliché: we hear his journey in a series of songs in chronological order. This alternates with her story, done backwards, à la *Merrily We Roll Along*.

Minetta Lane Theatre; March 3–May 5, 2002.

Directed by Daisy Prince.

Original Cast:

Jamie Wellerstein…Norbert Leo Butz   Catherine Hiatt…Sheri Rene Scott

Musical Numbers:

>Still Hurting…Catherine
>Shiksa Goddess…Jamie
>See I'm Smiling…Catherine
>Moving Too Fast…Jamie
>I'm a Part of That…Catherine
>The Schmuel Song…Jamie
>A Summer in Ohio…Catherine
>The Next Ten Minutes…Jamie, Catherine
>A Miracle Would Happen…Jamie
>When You Come Home to Me…Catherine
>Climbing Uphill…Catherine
>If I Didn't Believe in You…Jamie
>I Can Do Better Than That…Catherine
>Nobody Needs to Know…Jamie
>Goodbye Until Tomorrow/I Could Never Rescue You…Catherine, Jamie

Licensing: Music Theatre International

Difficulties/Advantages: Neither of the two unique aspects of this brief musical—that all the songs are inner monologue while the two actors rarely interact with each other, and that Jamie's story is forward while Catherine's is backward—create any real dramatic effect; it's all in the power of the songs to create emotion. That carried the project—the writer is an award-winning theatre composer—but the idea that successful men have affairs and dump the first wife is neither original nor, here, mined for any depth or thoughtful ideas.

The Last Session

Book by Jim Brochu
Music and Lyrics by Steve Schalchlin
Additional Lyrics by John Bettis and Marie Cain

This musical's great strength is a witty and pithy confrontation between homosexuality and the church, the former represented by an out-of-the-closet singer/songwriter, the latter by an evangelical one. Ten songs are interspersed, because a recording session is the setting.

Time and Place: Tonight. A recording studio (a former fallout shelter under a house in Burbank, California).

Synopsis: Once a gospel/pop crossover star, Gideon gave up the fame because he didn't want to pretend to be straight all day. Now he's back in the studio to record a series of songs and letters to leave for his longtime companion, and then commit suicide because he has AIDS. Jim is the recording engineer and Vicki and Tryshia are back-up singers, but Vicki is also Gideon's first wife and Tryshia a good friend. Buddy is an ambitious young singer/songwriter who books himself into the session because Gideon is his hero. There's conflict aplenty, because Buddy turns out to be a Bible-quoting Christian who is appalled when he discovers Gideon's sexual orientation, and for most of the first act and well into the second, the crackling dialogue is an argument over what a good Christian is vis-à-vis sexual preference. Toward the end of the session, when the girls discover Gideon's plan for suicide, the arguments come faster. In the end, Gideon is talked out of it, and all sing a rousing chorus, because, "You can only lift the darkness when you care."

47th Street Theatre; October 17, 1997; 17 previews, 154 performances

Directed by Jim Brochu.

Original Cast:

Gideon...Bob Stillman   Jim...Dean Bradshaw
Tryshia...Grace Garland   Vicki...Amy Coleman
Buddy...Stephen Bienskie

Musical Numbers:

ACT I   Save Me a Seat...Gideon
The Preacher and the Nurse...Tryshia, Gideon, Vickie, Buddy
Somebody's Friend...Vicki, Tryshia, Gideon
The Group...Gideon, Tryshia, Vicki
Going It Alone...Buddy, Gideon
ACT II   At Least I Know What's Killing Me...Gideon
Friendly Fire...Buddy, Company
Connected...Gideon
The Singer and the Song...Tryshia, Company
When You Care...Gideon, Tryshia, Vicki, Buddy

Licensing: Samuel French

Difficulties/Advantages: You have to have four great singers, because that's their job; and four great actors, because the characters are sharply defined and wonderfully rich. The perennial problem with musical comedy is that those are the same four. The good news: no band is needed. The bad: your lead must play piano well. Easy set and costumes though.

The Last Sweet Days of Isaac

Book and Lyrics by Gretchen Cryer
Music by Nancy Ford

Two one-act musicals barely related by their themes of our isolated lives.

Time and Place: Could be today, could be the future. A city.

Synopsis: Act 1, "The Elevator," features a young man and a young woman trapped in an elevator, the young man attempting to convince the young woman to live life to the fullest every minute, as if each day were the last, which is a sincere if fumbling attempt to seduce her.

In act 2, "I Want to Walk to San Francisco," those two thirtysomethings are now nineteen-year-olds locked in separate prison cells, communicating by closed-circuit television. When a newscast on the monitor reports the young man's death, neither they nor the audience are sure if they are dead or alive. I didn't get it even after seeing it *and* rereading it, but my guess it that it's some sort of a statement about the solitary lives we lead, unconnected to each other but at the mercy of a totalitarian government—not uncommon protests at the time it was produced.

Eastside Playhouse; January 26, 1970; 485 performances.

Directed by Word Baker.

Original Cast:

        Isaac...Austin Pendelton   Ingrid...Fedricka Weber

Musical Numbers:

ACT I   "The Elevator"
            The Last Sweet Days of Isaac...Isaac
            A Transparent Crystal Moment...Isaac, Ingrid
            My Most Important Moments Go By...Ingrid
            The Last Sweet Days of Isaac (reprise)...Recorded
            Love, You Came to Me...Ingrid, Isaac
ACT II   "I Want to Walk to San Francisco"
            I Want To Walk to San Francisco...The Band
            Touching Your Hand Is Like Touching Your Mind...The Band
            Yes, I Know That I'm Alive...The Band
            Concert Section...The Band
                I Can't Live in Solitary
                Herein Lie the Seeds of Revolution
                Somebody Died Today

Licensing: Samuel French

Difficulties/Advantages: A band ("The Zeitgeist") performs the songs of the second act, but only the first act is worth doing. It has a wonderful score, and is a tour de force for two actors. There's a number of one-acts you could pair it with. "The Diary of Adam and Eve" from *The Apple Tree* would work well.

Little Mary Sunshine

Book, Music, and Lyrics by Rick Besoyan

A very broad spoof on the operettas of Rudolph Friml and Victor Herbert that enchanted millions in Europe and America in the early days of musical theatre and were carried on in the films of Jeanette MacDonald and Nelson Eddy.

Time and Place: Early in the 20th century. High in the Rocky Mountains.

Synopsis: We're in front of the Colorado Inn, where Little Mary Sunshine, raised by Chief Brown Bear of the Kadota Indian tribe (who found her lost in the forest), and her maid, Nancy, entertain many guests: forest rangers; young ladies of the Eastchester Finishing School; Ernestine Von Liebedich, a retired opera singer; and General Oscar Fairfax, a Washington diplomat. The rangers arrive to apprehend Yellow Feather, a renegade Indian (who, heaven forbid, didn't care to give up all the tribe's lands to the continent's latecomers), but spend more time courting the girls than seeking Yellow Feather. Booming baritone Captain "Big Jim" Warington has long been spooning for soprano Mary, and there are, happily, the same number of rangers as young ladies in the ensemble. The only yellow feather in the ointment is that the renegade Indian has sworn to have his way with Mary, not because of her trilling high notes but because she once turned him in when he was hiding in the inn.

    After a number of set pieces that may make it impossible for you to ever watch a Nelson Eddy/Jeanette MacDonald film again without laughing, Mary ends up lashed to a tree, but Big Jim saves her in time. A Washington diplomat arrives to grant the two remaining members of the tribe one-third of the state of Colorado—here the show unintentionally touches on some sensitive Indian Nation affairs entirely overlooked in the pre—politically correct fifties—and stays to tickle the young ladies, then settle down with the retired opera singer, who sings, and the mock-operetta is over.

Orpheum Theatre; November 18, 1959; 1,143 performances.

Book direction by Mr. Besoyan. Staged and choreographed by Ray Harrison.

Original Cast:

Chief Brown Bear...John Aniston
Cpl. "Billy" Jester...John McMartin
Capt. "Big Jim" Warington...William Graham
"Little Mary Sunshine" (Mary Potts)...Eileen Brennan
Mme. Ernestine Von Liebedich...Elizabeth Parrish
Nancy Twinkle...Elmarie Wendel
Fleet Foot...Robert Chambers

Yellow Feather...Ray James
Gen'l Oscar Fairfax, Ret....Mario Siletti
Young Ladies of the Eastchester Finishing School...Floria Mari, Jana Stuart, Elaine Labour, Rita Howell, Sally Bramlette, Leslie Daniel
Young Gentlemen of the United States Forest Rangers...Jerry Melo, Joe Warfield, Arthur Hunt, Ed Riley, Mark Destin, Ed Royce

Musical Numbers:

ACT I The Forest Rangers...Captain Jim, Forest Rangers
Little Mary Sunshine...Little Mary, Forest Rangers
Look for a Sky of Blue...Little Mary, Forest Rangers
You're the Fairest Flower...Captain Jim
In Izzenschnooken on the Lovely Essenzook Zee...Mme. Ernestine
Playing Croquet...Young Ladies
Swinging...Young Ladies
How Do You Do?...Forest Rangers
Tell a Handsome Stranger...Pete and Cora, Slim and Henrietta, Tex and Mabel
Once in a Blue Moon...Billy, Nancy
Colorado Love Call...Captain Jim, Little Mary
Every Little Nothing...Mme. Ernestine, Little Mary
What Has Happened?...Little Mary, Nancy, Mme. Ernestine, Young Ladies, Forest Rangers

ACT II Such a Merry Party...Nancy, Forest Rangers, Young Ladies
Say, Uncle!...General Oscar Fairfax, Young Ladies
Forest Rangers (Reprise)...Forest Rangers
Heap Big Injun...Billy
Naughty, Naughty Nancy...Little Mary, Young Ladies
Mata Hari...Nancy, Young Ladies
Do You Ever Dream of Vienna?...Ernestine, Oscar
Coo Coo...Little Mary
Colorado Love Call (reprise)...Captain Jim, Little Mary
Look for a Sky of Blue (reprise)...Company

Licensing: Samuel French

Difficulties/Advantages: This note in the acting edition of the musical would cover just about any of the many off-Broadway musical spoofs: "It is absolutely essential to the success of the musical that it should be played with the most warmhearted earnestness. There should be no exaggeration in costume, makeup or demeanor; and the characters, one and all, should appear to believe, throughout, in the perfect sincerity of their words and actions." Not so easy, considering lines like, "Dare I say that these infrequent meetings are the oasis in the vast desert of a poor Forest Ranger's lonely life," and "Yes, yes, a thousand times yes." Then there's the problem that few audiences today are old enough to have any idea of the operettas that *Sunshine* spoofs.

And yet...this seldom-produced, once-very-successful musical—like London's *The Boy Friend,* which had come to Broadway only five years earlier—is fun for all, performers and audiences. How that large cast all squeezed onto the stage of the Orpheum Theatre, I'll never know. With nine principals and twelve young men and women, small theatres are probably not its best venue any longer, but one could add any number to the chorus and stage a much larger production that looked more like the original Shubertinas (*Rose Marie* et al.), with long lines of chorus people. Cast opera students, be sure to have a sweeping, panoramic Colorado Rockies backdrop, and the laughs should roll in like a baritone's bluster. Otherwise, the costumes and sets are not difficult, and staging should be suitably wooden.

Little Shop of Horrors

Photo: Ed Matthews

Little Shop of Horrors at William Paterson University, Wayne, NJ.

Book and Lyrics by Howard Ashman
Music by Alan Menken

Based on the film by Roger Corman, screenplay by Charles Griffith.

This is the hilarious musical combining B- sci-fi movies and pop—with a subtle emphasis on fifties doo-wop—that launched the careers of composer Alan Menken and the late and greatly lamented writer/director Howard Ashman (a man whose understanding of the American musical form resurrected the fortunes of the Walt Disney company single-handedly when he structured the animated films *The Little Mermaid, Aladdin,* and *Beauty and the Beast* with theatre songs, thus setting the pattern that revived Disney's animation division, upon which all their financial success was based). The story of the man-eating plant that makes a fortune for a small florist and turns the meek Seymour into a man of accomplishment comes from a Roger Corman movie (Jack Nicholson played a small part), the low-budget attitude of which was delightfully transposed off-Broadway in the decrepit and familiar Orpheum Theatre. Its pastiche/rock score and funny story delighted audiences, particularly when tendrils from the ever-growing plant dropped down to devour them in the finale.

Time and Place: Today. Skid Row.

Synopsis: The little shop of horticulture (which also features three girls handily hanging around singing backup) features a few sad plants. There Mr. Mushnik and his two employees, Seymour and Audrey, are going out of business, until Seymour puts an exotic, unknown-species plant in the window, whereupon business booms dramatically. The plant, however, feeds only on human blood, and although Seymour is soon out of fresh fingers, the plant promises him untold success in life in exchange for more—a pretty straightforward, if Faustian, bargain. Though "no one deserves to die," there is always Audrey's boyfriend, a sadist (a dentist). Although he cannot find it within himself to shoot the guy, Seymour does find himself in a delicate philosophical situation: stuck in a special mask giving him nitrous oxide, the dentist needs Seymour's help to get it off. Seymour declines, watches him die laughing, and the curtain goes down on the plant happily enjoying the dentist's body parts.

In act 2, Seymour and Audrey have their love song, and the plant eats Mr. Mushnik when he threatens to expose Seymour with evidence that Seymour killed the dentist. By now the plant has started talking—and singing—with all the gusto of James Brown and encourages Seymour with grander and grander visions of success, which he is offered by a network executive, an editor, and a William Morris agent. When the plant tries to eat Audrey, however, Seymour has had enough and does battle. Unfortunately, he loses, at which point the plant prepares for world domination and turns on the audience. If the Faustian message isn't clear, the girls will sing you the warning: "Don't Feed the Plants!"

Orpheum Theatre; July 27, 1982; 2,209 performances.

Directed by Howard Ashman. Choreographed by Edie Cowan.

Original Off-Broadway Cast:

Chiffon…Marlene Danielle	Derelict…Matin P. Robinson
Crystal…Jennifer Leigh Warren	Orin, Bernstein, Snip, Luce, and
Ronnette…Sheila Kay Davis	Everyone Else…Franc Luz
Mushnik…Hy Anzell	Audrey II (manipulation) Martin P.
Audrey…Ellen Greene	Robinson…(voice) Ron Taylor
Seymour…Lee Wilkof	

Musical Numbers:

ACT I   Prologue (Little Shop of Horrors)…Chiffon, Crystal, Ronnette
Skid Row (Downtown)…Company
Da-Doo. . .Chiffon, Crystal, Ronnette
Grow for Me…Seymour
Don't It Go to Show Ya Never Know…Mushnik, Chiffon, Crystal, Ronnette, Seymour
Somewhere That's Green…Audrey
Closed for Renovations…Seymour, Audrey, Mushnik
Dentist!…Orin, Chiffon, Crystal, Ronnette

Mushnik and Son...Mushnik, Seymour
Feed Me (Git It)...Seymour, Audrey II
Now (It's Just the Gas)...Seymour, Orin
ACT II   Call Back in the Morning...Seymour, Audrey
Suddenly, Seymour...Seymour, Audrey
Suppertime...Audrey II
The Meek Shall Inherit...Company
Finale (Don't Feed the Plants)...Company

Licensing: Music Theatre International

Difficulties/Advantages: Don't let the film version of this off-Broadway musical deter you from appreciating the musical's wonderful theatricality, humor, and originality. Except for an ungainly scene stretched beyond necessity just for Steve Martin and Bill Murray to work together and an utterly wrong-for-the-story happy ending tacked on by Hollywood, the movie's fairly faithful but never found a cinematic way to capture the ebullience of the original, particularly in the musical numbers. Easy music to learn, delightful to perform, its three-member girl-group Greek chorus could be expanded if necessary. The costumes are pretty simple, the sets can be tacky, and the only important effect is the growing plant, which prop departments ought to have great fun with.

Lucky Nurse and Other Short Musical Plays

Words and Music by Michael John LaChiusa

This set of four very tiny, very metaphoric, sung-through near-operettas was produced at Playwrights Horizon on December 11, 1991. Directed by Kirsten Sanderson.

The various roles were all played by:

Chuck Cooper	Joe Grifasi
Mary Beth Peil	Alice Playten

Break

Time and Place: A construction site, high above a city.

Synopsis: Lunch break for two blue collar construction workers. One is pissed at the boss, the other amazed at the size of the lunch his wife packs. The blessed Virgin Mary appears but says its a mistake: she is supposed to be in Texas, has to get back to work. She does. They had a vision....But what does it mean?

Agnes

Time and Place: A city park.

Synopsis: A woman in a wheelchair has a confrontation with a thief. The woman dies. The thief leaves. It was what she wanted.

Eulogy for Mister Hamm

Time and Place: A hallway in a fleabag hotel.

Synopsis: A man, a woman, and a girl stand in the hallway, waiting to use the one bathroom. The man complains that the bathroom—and everything else about the hotel—is never repaired. He tells them that the superintendent died last night. The woman used a snow boot to destroy her room and would like to do the same to the bathroom. The girl dreams of going to San Francisco, where there's this guy who left her. When the door finally opens, it's the super, his death only a rumor. The bathroom is fixed.

Lucky Nurse

Time and Place: A city hospital nurses' lounge, a bar, a taxi, visitor's window of the hospital nursery.

Synopsis: A female nurse goes on duty, worried about having to put her dog to sleep. A male nurse goes off duty and to a bar, where he picks up a woman. She sleeps with him and leaves in the morning via cab, the cabbie lets her off in the park, and he appears in the hospital to drive the original nurse home. They observe a baby who has been found in a dumpster nearby.

Licensing: Dramatists Play Service

Difficulties/Advantages: Very interesting people, transcribed more by the music—nearly all really recitative—than their words and actions. Call it a song cycle of bizarre characters. Fourteen roles for good singers if you don't want to quadruple.

Lucky Stiff

Book and Lyrics by Lynn Ahrens
Music by Stephen Flaherty
Based on "The Man Who Broke the Bank at Monte Carlo" by Michael Butterworth.

That rare musical, a comic farce, a style you'll spot the moment one of the members is murdered and the rest of the performers step over his body to complete the opening number. The first full-length musical by the writers who later created *Once on This Island, My Favorite Year,* and *Ragtime.*

Time and Place: The Present. England, Atlantic City, and Monte Carlo.

Synopsis: English shoe salesman Harry dreams of a better life, which portends to arrive when he inherits six million dollars from an Uncle Anthony he has never met. All he has to do to claim it is take his uncle's dead body and a heart-shaped box on one last vacation to Monte Carlo. On the way, a young woman shadows him, and an Italian offers himself as a guide. Meanwhile in Atlantic City, Rita confesses to her brother Vinnie that she and her lover—he was Uncle Anthony—stole six million in diamonds from her husband, after which she accidentally shot her lover. Unfortunately for brother Vinnie, Rita has told her husband that Vinnie stole the money, now on its way to Monte Carlo. In Monte Carlo, Harry and dead Uncle Anthony (in a wheelchair, with dark glasses) stroll

Photo: Alan Zenreich

Lucky Stiff at the Conservatory of Theatre Arts, Leigh Gerdine College of Fine Arts, Webster University, St. Louis, MO.

around, but the Italian is still bothering him, and the young woman on the train turns out to be the representative from a dog orphanage that gets the money if Harry doesn't. All end up dancing in a nightclub, while Rita searches Harry's room, then pulls a gun on Harry when he returns.

Act 2. Harry manages to get away with Annabel, the dog lady, but loses the dead uncle. Still, a romance seems to be budding. The next morning, Harry and Annabel are found in bed, Uncle Anthony's corpse is returned by a maid, and Rita returns with the gun. A close look at the corpse, however, convinces Rita (she needs glasses only at convenient plot points) that the corpse is not her lover, Uncle Anthony, but a stranger, whereupon the Italian who has been following everyone reveals that he is Uncle Anthony. Brother Vinnie, meanwhile, has hooked up with the nightclub's chanteuse. (As if there weren't enough immorality going on, Vinnie is married.) They appear, demand the diamonds, get the box and leave for the good life. But they'll eventually discover that the corpse's heart is in the box. The diamonds are sewed into the corpse. Rita and her lover reconcile, take the corpse, and leave Harry and Annabel to the vacation in Monte Carlo that's all paid for.

Playwrights Horizon; April 26, 1988; 15 performances.

Directed by Thommie Walsh.

Album Cast:

Annabel Glick...Judy Blazer
Vinnie Di Ruzzi...Jason Graae
Dominique du Monaco...Debbie Shapiro
   Gravitte
Uncle Anthony, Luigi Gaudi...Paul Kandel
Harry Witherspoon...Evan Pappas
Solicitor, Monte Carlo Emcee,
   Boarder...Patrick Quinn

Landlady, Lady on Train, Airport
   Voice...Barbara Rosenblat
Boarder, Lady on Train, Screaming
   Woman...Mary Stout
Rita La Porta...Mary Testa
Boarder, Bellhop, Telegram
   Deliverer...Bruce Winant

Musical Numbers:

ACT I   Something Funny's Going On...Company
Mister Witherspoon's Friday Night...Harry, Landlady, Boarders, Uncle Anthony
Uncle's Last Request...Harry, Solicitor, Uncle Anthony
Good to Be Alive...Harry, Company
Rita's Confession...Rita, Vinnie
Lucky...Harry, Luigi
Dogs Versus You...Annabel, Harry
The Phone Call...Vinnie
Monte Carlo!...Monte Carlo Emcee
Speaking French...Dominique, Harry, Company
Times Like This...Annabel
Fancy Meeting You Here...Rita, Company

ACT II   Something Funny's Going On (reprise)...Company
Him, Them, It, Her...Harry, Company
Nice...Annabel, Harry
Welcome Back, Mr. Witherspoon (The Nightmare)...Company
Confession #2...Uncle Anthony, Harry, Annabel, Rita
Fancy Meeting You Here (reprise)...Rita, Uncle Anthony, Company
Finale: Good to Be Alive...Harry, Annabel, Company

Licensing: Music Theatre International

Difficulties/Advantages: As you can see, the cast is expandable. The plot is not: it's tight as a drum and wonderfully funny. Terrific roles, real musical comedy music, and great fun for all.

Man with a Load of Mischief

Book by Ben Tarver
Music by John Clifton
Lyrics by John Clifton and Ben Tarver
Adapted from the play *The Man with a Load of Mischief* by Ashley Duke.

Virginia Vestoff, soon to be Abigail Adams in *1776*, and Reid Shelton, much later to become Daddy Warbucks, were probably dazzling in this Fieldingesque musical, and needed to be, for the adaptation of the 1925 book creaks a little too much, although the tuneful, legitimate music and spirit of the thing could certainly carry the day.

Time and Place: Early in the 19th century. England, a wayside inn.

Synopsis: A lazy innkeeper and his henpecking wife host four mysterious strangers at their roadside inn when a lady's carriage becomes a runaway and a nobleman saves her. The evening turns on a variety of illicit relationships. The lady turns out to be the mistress of a prince, running away and returning to her former life as an actress. The nobleman is also running from the prince, due to debts incurred at gaming tables. He believes he might pay that debt by returning the mistress to the prince. When the lady doesn't succumb to his amorous advances, he takes the lady's maid into his confidence and his bedroom, and has his manservant attempt to seduce the lady in his place. This the man does, not so much for his master as himself, because he has long been an ardent admirer since her theatrical days. They fall in love.

Man with a Load of Mischief at Rep Stage, professional theatre in residence at Howard Community College, Columbia, MD.

Next morning it's clear that everyone had a bedmate. (Even the innkeeper boasts of his ability to satisfy his wife.) The impending arrival of the prince himself throws the nobleman's plans into disarray. The prince will assume the nobleman slept with the mistress and challenge him to a duel. The nobleman offers his man money to spirit away the mistress, and the two lovers happily run off together. Then the nobleman has to bribe the maid to admit she slept with him, so the prince will know he didn't sleep with the mistress. The maid, having demonstrated quite a nefarious mind of her own in the course of the play, doesn't immediately commit to helping him as the prince's horse's hoofbeats are heard offstage and the curtain falls.

Jan Hus Playhouse; November 6, 1966; 240 performances.

Directed by Tom Gruenewald. Choreographed by Noel Schwartz.

Original Cast:

An Innkeeper…Tom Moel His Wife…Leslie Nicol
A Nobleman…Raymond Thorne Charles, His Man…Reid Shelton
A Lady…Viginia Vestoff Louise, Her Maid…Alice Cannon

Musical Numbers:

Act I Overture
Wayside Inn…Innkeeper
The Rescue…Wife
Entrance Polonaise…Company
Goodbye, My Sweet…Lady
Romance!…Innkeeper, Wife, Lord, Maid
Lover Lost…Lady
Once You've Had a Little Taste…Maid
Hullabaloo Balay…Man
Once You've Had a Little Taste (reprise)…Maid, Wife, Innkeeper
Dinner Minuet…Company
You'd Be Amazed…Lord, Lady, Man
A Friend Like You…Lady, Lord
Wayside Inn (reprise)…Lord
Masquerade…Man

Man with a Load of Mischief…Lady
Masquerade (reprise)…Man
ACT II   Entr'acte
What Style!…Innkeeper
A Wonder…Lady
Make Way for My Lady…Man
Forget…Lord
Any Other Way…Wife, Innkeeper
Little Rage Doll…Maid
Romance! (reprise)…Lady
Man with a Load of Mischief (reprise)…Lady
Sextet…Company
Make Way for My Lady (reprise)…Man, Lady, Innkeeper, Wife

Licensing: Samuel French

Difficulties/Advantages: The main opportunity here is for a gorgeous set design and beautiful early nineteenth-century clothes. The plot is clunky and sometimes barely understandable, the dialogue salvageable by committed actors. The characters do offer singing actors a chance to display charisma, depth of passion, and extraordinary voices. The intrigues they plot and the romance they sing about all hinge on a Regency sense of social and sexual politics that have changed a good deal for both men and women, but as a period piece, it is quite educational.

Mayor

Book by Warren Leight
Music and Lyrics by Charles Strouse

Based on *Mayor* by Edward I. Koch.

Oddly enough, it was Big Apple Mayor Edward Koch himself who wanted a musical done based on his own memoirs. (It takes a lot of chutzpa to be the mayor of New York City.) He was always an easy mayor to satirize, as *Saturday Night Live* did so well so often, and the result is a mild spoof of a mayor's day, interspersed with some typical New Yorkers—yuppies, lovers, even tourists. It's a valentine to the city that combines just about every positive and negative aspect of a developed civilization. There's something of a story, but the cumulative effect is really that of a revue.

Directed by Jeffrey B. Moss. Choreographed by Barbara Siman.

Original Cast:

Douglas Bernstein	Marion J. Caffey
Keith Curran	Nancy Giles
Ken Jennings	Ilene Kristen
Kathryn McAteer	Lenny Wolpe as the Mayor

Musical Numbers:

ACT I   Mayor
You Can Be a New Yorker Too!
You're Not the Mayor
March of the Yuppies
Hootspa

	What You See Is What You Get
	Ballad
ACT II	I Want to Be the Mayor
	The Last "I Love New York" Song
	Good Times
	I'll Never Leave You (We Are One)
	How'm I Doin'?
	Finale
	My City

Licensing: Samuel French

Difficulties/Advantages: Outside of New York, this musical wouldn't make any sense. Even inside today, how many people remember the ebullient, bald-headed bachelor who presided over the city from 1977 to 1989? Maybe if Ed Koch gets his face on a postage stamp, you can revive it; otherwise, just insert your favorite songs into a Charles Strouse revue.

Me, Myself and I

Book and Lyrics by Alan Ayckbourn
Music by Paul Todd

Alan Ayckbourn—the Neil Simon of England—here writes a very interesting small musical, most definitely for adults. A woman seems to be having something of a nervous breakdown, questioning her life. If that sounds a cliché, in Ayckbourn's hands, it's both funny and piquant.

Time and Place: Lunchtime. A bar.

Synopsis: Mrs. Mary Yately of 14 Caldicott Gardens, Nettleford Estate, East Hopley, Near Nettleford, North Yorks, is being interviewed by Mr. Rodney Birch of the *Evening Paper* because she has won the Ideal Mum competition organized by the *Evening Echo*. He asks her the typical questions but gets quite confusing answers. No wonder, since Mary is most definitely a split personality, here represented by three actresses—Me, Myself, and I—(Id, Ego, and Libido?), two of which the reporter is unaware of. And if that isn't enough, she (they?) flirt and leave him a decent opening ("My husband isn't home Tuesdays and Thursdays").

Or perhaps not. Because in act 2, her husband shows up (looking astonishingly like the reporter), having heard from a neighbor that she has left the children and gone to a pub, whereupon he has had to leave his meeting and come to see what's wrong. You see, she hasn't at all been elected Ideal Mum and isn't being interviewed but perhaps has just gone off her rails a smidgen. At first attempting to coax her home, he finally—excellent husband—offers to spend more time with her, rather than go back to his meeting.

London premiere: The Orange Tree, Richmond; December 10, 1982.

London director: Kim Grant.

Original Cast (Scarborough):

Three women play Mary Yately as:

Me…Lavinia Bertram   Myself…Christine Kavanagh   I…Gillian Bevan
One man plays both:
Rodney Beech and Bill Yately…Michael Simpkins

Musical Numbers:

ACT I   Recit 1…Me, Myself, I, Man
          Somebody New…Me Myself, Man
          Song of My Childhood…Me, Myself, I, Man
          I Don't Want to Do It…Me, Myself, I
          My House…Me, Myself, I, Man
          Unlikely…Me, Myself, I
          Wife Swap Dance…Me, Myself, I
          Open for Love…Me, Myself, I
          Me, Myself and I…Me, Myself, I, Man
ACT II   Recit 2…Me, Myself, I
          No More…Me, Myself, I, Man
          Electric Woman…Me, Myself, I
          Closer…I, Man
          Teaching the Children…Myself
          Recit 3/Where…Me, Myself, I
          Have You Ever Thought?. . .Me, Man
          Another Bite…Me, Myself, I, Man
          Me, Myself and I (reprise)…Me, Myself, I, Man

Licensing: Samuel French

Difficulties/Advantages: This one seems to have metamorphosed through an unusually varied number of forms by the prolific writer, first as three separate "lunchtime shows," then as one play with musical prologue and epilogue, and finally as a full two-act musical with a variety of song forms. ("Some were successful, some weren't, usually because they were so complicated they'd have made even Sondheim scratch his head"—Ayckbourn.) The published form is quite interesting, with a sprinkling of laughs as well as pungent feelings—by a male playwright, no less—from a woman, if not quite on the verge of a nervous breakdown, then at least questioning her life's path. The ideas are certainly as relevant in American culture as English, but there's always the question for American theatres of whether to attempt English accents (and inevitably fail) or not, and risk sounding silly on lines such as "Jolly good." Since this is not a Nöel Coward comedy of manners, I'd suggest the latter, with the good enunciation of mid-Atlantic English. Aim for the truth of the characters, not their bearing or attitude.

Mirette

Book by Elizabeth Diggs
Music by Harvey Schmidt
Lyrics by Tom Jones

Based upon the picture book *Mirette on the High Wire* by Emily Arnold McCully.

Jones and Schmidt followed *The Fantasticks* with two great Broadway musicals—*I Do! I Do!* with only two characters is catalogued here—then spent a number of years in their own experimental workshop, resulting in several unique if uncommercial musicals. In the last several decades, they have pursued *Colette Collage* (also catalogued here), a musical version of *Our Town,* and this utterly charming story of a young girl who aspires to be a tightrope walker. None of these later three have made it to Broadway, partly because of poor productions (where oh where are the intelligent director/choreographers) and partly because of the profoundly conservative, spectacle-over-substance, fifteen-million-dollar state-of-the-commerce there.

Time and Place: 1899. A small hotel for actors in Paris.

Synopsis: Music Hall Artistes rent rooms from Madame Gateau, whose daughter, Mirette, ten years old, helps run the place. (Mirette's father, an actor, ran away to Brazil.) A mysterious man comes to rent a room and turns out to be the greatest of all high-wire walkers, the Great Bellini. He has retired but practices daily. Mirette sees him, tries out the practice wire when she is alone, and when he discovers her, begs to be taught. Not surprisingly, her mother is against the idea. Mother protests that Mirette is not Bellini, she must find her own life. But Bellini counters that perhaps Mirette isn't her mother either.

Before this issue is resolved, a few subplots emerge: Max, a great promoter of talent whom everyone knows, pays a visit. Gaby, a young dancer, gets a job at the music hall—some suspect due to her beauty more than her talent—and Tabac, a juggler and comic, loses his. When Mirette falls from the three-meter practice wire, her mother insists that Bellini cease the lessons, and Bellini does, telling Mirette he will no longer instruct her. In their argument, Bellini insults Mirette, and Mirette goes into a great depression. Bellini decides to leave. Mirette's mother insists he say goodbye to Mirette. When he does, he tells her why he is retired: because fear has overtaken him. She gives him courage, however, and he decides to make a great walk across the rooftops of Paris. A wire is stretched from the Eiffel Tower to the Palais du Chaillot. That night he attempts the walk but freezes. Mirette joins him, and together they cross. The Great Bellini is back...with his partner, Mirette.

The Goodspeed Opera House; July 1–Sept 18, 1998.

Directed by Andre Ernotte. Choreographed by Janet Watson.

Characters:

Madame Gateau	Mirette
Bellini	Tabac
Mme. Rouspenskaya	Clouk and Claire
Gaby	Camembert
Max	

Musical Numbers:

Aᴄᴛ I   Sitting on the Edge...Mirette
Madame Gateau's Colorful Hotel...Gateau, Mirette, Artistes
Maybe...Mirette, Rouspenskaya
Someone in the Mirror...Bellini
Irkutsk...Rouspenskaya
Practicing...Bellini, Artistes
Learning Who You Are...Bellini, Mirette
Juggling...Tabac, Orchestra
The Show Goes On...Camembert, Mirette, Artistes
Feet upon the Ground...Madame Gateau
Learning Who You Are (reprise)...Mirette
Clouk and Claire...Clouk, Claire, Orchestra
If You Choose to Walk upon the Wire...Bellini, Artistes
She Isn't You...Madame Gateau, Bellini

Act II   Entr'acte…Bellini, Mirette, Orchestra
The Great God Pan…Gaby, Artistes
The Great Bellini…Max, Mirette, Artistes
Sometimes You Just Need Someone…Mirette, Bellini
Madame Gateau's Desolate Hotel…Gateau, Bellini, Artistes
Finale…Company
    The Great Bellini
    Practicing
    Sometimes You Just Need Someone
    The Show Goes On

Licensing: Music Theatre International

Difficulties/Advantages: Either two of your actors, including the ten-year-old Mirette, can walk a high wire with reasonable assurance or you have to come up with a wonderfully theatrical way to suggest it. There's also the question of accents, which range throughout Europe, for this set-in-Paris musical. Sets and costumes should be beautiful, not necessarily realistic but stylish, because this is the rare small musical that isn't camp or comic, spoof or satire, but charming. All that said, it's well worth producing, and all ten roles should be rewarding to essay.

A New Brain

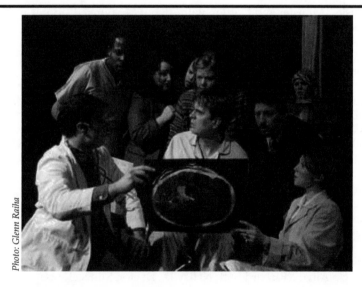

Photo: Glenn Raiha

A New Brain at the Capital Playhouse, Olympia, WA.

Book by William Finn and James Lapine
Music and Lyrics by William Finn

A sung-thru musical, filled with quartets and quintets and many "serious music" forms.

Time and Place: Contemporary. In the hero's life, much of which is in a hospital room.

Synopsis: Gordon, a gay songwriter slaving away on a children's television show and wishing he could write for Broadway, has a serious brain disorder (arterial venous malformation).

103

In one long act, he has an operation and lapses into a coma, but he comes out of it okay—unless you count the dream sequences in the coma. A female friend for someone to care about him, a homeless woman for commentary, a lover for passion, a mother for—well, he's gay, isn't he?—a doctor, a minister, several nurses, and his boss (the star of the TV show) for angst—all round out the cast of caricatures.

Mitzi E. Newhouse Theater at Lincoln Center; May 14, 1998; 40 previews, 78 performances.

Directed and choreographed by Graciela Daniele.

Original Cast:

Gordon Schwinn...Malcolm Gets
Mr. Bungee...Chip Zien
Mimi Schwinn, the Mother...Penny Fuller
Rhoda...Liz Larson
Roger Delli-Bovi...Norm Lewis, Christopher Innvar

Richard, the Nice Nurse...Michael Mandell
Lisa, a Homeless Lady...Mary Testa
Waitress, Nancy D., the Thin Nurse...Kristin Chenoweth
Dr. Jafar Berensteiner...John Jellison
The Minister...Keith Byron Kirk

Musical Numbers:

Frogs Have So Much Spring (The Spring Song)...Gordon
Calamari...Gordon, Rhoda, Waitress, Mr. Bungee
911 Emergency...Richard, Waitress, Doctor, Rhoda, Minister, Lisa
I Have So Many Sons...Gordon
Heart and Music...Minister and Gordon with All but Mr. Bungee Trouble in His Brain...Doctor, Mimi
Mother's Gonna Make Things Fine...Mimi, Gordon
Sailing...Roger, Gordon
Family History...Nancy D., Richard, Mimi
Gordo's Law of Genetics...Nancy D., Doctor, Minister, Rhoda, Richard, Lisa
And They're Off...Gordon with Nancy D., Doctor, Minister, Rhoda, Richard, Lisa
Just G. . .Gordon, Roger
Poor, Unsuccessful and Fat...Richard, Gordon, Mr. Bungee Sitting Becalmed in the Lee of Cuttyhunk...All but Mr. Bungee
Invitation to Sleep in My Arms...Gordon, Roger, Rhoda, Mimi
Change...Lisa
Yes...Gordon, Mr. Bungee with Nancy D., Doctor, Minister, Rhoda
In the Middle of the Room...Gordon, Mimi
Throw It Out...Mimi
Really Lousy Day in the Universe...Roger, Lisa
Brain Dead...Gordon, Roger
Whenever I Dream...Rhoda, Gordon
Eating Myself Up Alive...Richard with Nancy D., Doctor, Minister, Lisa
Music Still Plays On...Mimi
Don't Give In...Mr. Bungee with Gordon, Roger, Rhoda, Mimi
You Boys Are Gonna Get Me in Such Trouble/Sailing (reprise)...Richard, Gordon, Roger
Homeless Lady's Revenge...Lisa, Gordon, Roger
Time...Roger, Gordon
Time and Music...Minister, Gordon, All

Licensing: Samuel French

Difficulties/Advantages: Honestly, I am not prejudiced against gay-themed works. The *Boys in the Band* knocked me out, and *Jeffrey* had me rolling in the aisles (though I did like the film of *La Cage aux Folles* better than the musical). But these lyrics are less pithy than bitchy and whiny, when not inane ("Love is stupid and it bleeds" and "Life is a cause that you have to take up"), the music is in that never-never land between theatre and serious and would fall short in either category, and to say the characters are thin clichés is to give them too much substance. When Bock and Harnick were asked which came first, the music or the lyrics, Bock answered, "The book." That is the foundation of any good musical, no matter how it's delivered, and the modern manner of endless interior monologues in song and repetitive *geshries* will not replace one.

No Way to Treat a Lady

Book, Music, and Lyrics by Douglas J. Cohen

A tongue-in-cheek thriller with Oedipal overtones that could only have come from William Goldman, one of America's most versatile and humorous writers. Goldman's original novel was also a 1968 film defined by Rod Steiger's brilliant performance as the mad actor impersonating an Irish priest, a French waiter, an Italian delivery boy, and others to gain access to the women he murders. As a musical, it loses a lot, and it gains a tour de force performance only if a woman plays both mothers and all the victims.

Time and Place: Summer, 1970. New York City.

Synopsis: Kit and Morris have a similar problem: overbearing mothers. They're dealing with it in different ways. Morris is a cop with an inferiority complex, unable to commit to a woman. Kit is a serial killer, looking for press in the *New York Times* equal to that generated by his mother's glamorous acting career. We meet both men and both mothers pretty quickly in act 1. After that, Kit, the actor, kills a number of women (the best one is the hot Latin number who almost tangos him to death) and telephones Morris-the-detective complaining that he hasn't made the papers yet. Meanwhile Morris stumbles across a woman who is attracted to him. (Lucky guy. She's rich, cultured, good looking, and aggressively after him.) Of course, his obsession with catching the killer is standing in the way of his commitment, and she wishes he could choose but knows he can't.

By act 2, both Morris and the killer make the front page of the *Times* when Kit impersonates Morris to belay his latest victim. Then Kit ratchets up the game by making his play for Sarah, Morris's new girlfriend. Morris arrives in the nick of time, of course, but Kit manages to get the drop on them both. Instead, however, of using it as his chance to escape, he hallucinates his mother ("Bravo! You gave a performance at last!") and manipulates Morris into killing him. Happy ending: Morris moves out on his mother and marries Sarah.

York Theatre at St. Peter's; December 22, 1996; 42 performances.

World premiere directed by Jack Hofsiss. Choreographed by Chris Chadman.

Original Cast:

Christopher "Kit" Gill…Stephen Bogardus Morris Brummell…Peter Slutsker
Mother…June Gable Sarah Stone…Liz Callaway

Musical Numbers:

ACT I   I Need a Life…Morris, Kit, Flora
Only a Heartbeat Away…Kit, Mrs. Sullivan
So Far, So Good…Morris, Sarah
Safer in My Arms…Kit, Carmella
I've Been a Bad Boy/What Shall I Sing for You?…Kit, Morris, Alexandra
The First Move…Morris, Kit, Sarah
I Hear Humming…Flora, Morris
I Need a Life (reprise)…Sarah
Lunch with Sarah…Morris, Kit
So Far So Good (reprise)…Sarah
Front Page News Preview/You're Getting Warmer…Kit, Morris

ACT II   Front Page News…Kit, Morris, Sarah, Flora
So Much in Common…Sarah, Flora, Morris
Front Page News/What Shall I Sing for You? (reprise)…Kit
One More from the Top Preview…Kit
One of the Beautiful People…Sarah
Still…Sadie, Kit
I Have Noticed a Change/Morris's Life/Once More from the Top…Sarah, Kit, Flora, Morris
Front Page News/What Shall I Sing for You? (reprise)…Kit, Alexandra
So Far, So Good (reprise)…Morris, Sarah

Licensing: Samuel French

Difficulties/Advantages: Read the novel. See the movie. Then you'll probably want to do the show. Numerous workshops and productions since the premiere have led to a more or less definitive script from the author, but there's still a lot left for local directors to figure out. Kit's victims are usually all his mother (see Freud), and sometimes both mothers are played by the same actress. Harder to figure out is an economical set, since the play takes place in numerous apartments, sometimes more than one at once. Large theatres can, of course, use platforms and wagons and such, but that would overwhelm the four actors and be incompatible with the fundamental silliness of the production. Three of the four roles—both men and the mother/victims—are truly "tour de force," the musical's primary asset. And, oh yes, there's the murder-of-female-victims aspect, which may not be palatable to all organizations or schools. Still, this one has had a continuing life, so there's something attractive there.

Now Is the Time for All Good Men

Book and Lyrics by Gretchen Cryer
Music by Nancy Ford

A product of the then-current issue of the war in Vietnam, *Now Is the Time* may seem an idealistic and impressionistic drama today, but it's still a meaningful piece.

Time and Place: The 1960s. Bloomdale, Indiana, population 973.

Synopsis: Mike, who spent time in jail, begins teaching in a very small town that has very small ideas. Though the high school principal wants to be on Mike's side because Mike's father saved his life in World War II, he can't countenance such things as students taking notes in the margins of their books, making up limericks to the rhythm of a bouncing basketball, or arguing in class. It doesn't help that Mike begins dating Sarah, trying to open her mind to new ideas, when her husband only died nine months earlier and the principal has hopes for her himself. As act 1 closes, student Tommy gets his draft notice, although he's still a few days short of eighteen, and begins to voice the idea that he doesn't really want to go to war, something Mike has taught him that he may have to decide for himself, on his own.

Act 2 centers around an election for Bloomdale's "Man of the Century." The young people want to get behind Mike, but his nomination ignites a furor both in town and in Tommy's family, because Tommy's father, a veteran, is the competition. When Sarah's younger sister, jealous, spills the beans about Mike's prison term, he explains: in Vietnam he suddenly refused to kill and served time for it. Though the town thinks him a coward and hardly listens when he says his cowardice didn't come when he wouldn't kill but when he didn't openly declare himself a conscientious objector in the first place, Mike leaves town. But Sarah goes after him, leaving Albert—who had only wanted, and offered Sarah, "A Simple Life"—bereft.

Theatre De Lys; September 26, 1967; 22 previews, 111 performances.

Directed by Word Baker.

Original Cast:

Sarah Larkin...Sally Niven (a.k.a. Gretchen Cryer)
Eugenie Seldin...Judy Frank
Mike Butler...David Cryer
Tooney...Donna Curtis
Albert McKinley...David Sabin
Betty Brown...Margot Hanson

Esther Mason...Regina Lynn
Herbert Heller, the Coach...Art Wallace
Bill Miller...John Bennett Perry
Jasper Wilkins...Murray Olson
Ramona...Anne Kaye
Tommy...Steve Skiles

Musical Numbers:

ACT I   We Shall Meet in the Great Hereafter...Company
Keep 'Em Busy, Keep 'Em Quiet...Miller, Albert, Esther, Mike, Betty, Sarah, Jasper, Herbert
What's in the Air...Mike
Tea in the Rain...Sarah
What's a Guy Like You Doin' in a Place Like This?...Eugenie
Halloween Hayride...Betty, Tooney, Esther, Miller, Jasper, Tommy, Ramona
Katydid...Betty, Miller, Esther, Jasper, Tooney, Tommy, Ramona
See Everything New...Mike, Sarah
All Alone...Mike
He Could Show Me...Sarah
Washed Away...Tooney, Esther, Albert, Sarah, Herbert, Jasper, Miller, Tommy, Ramona, Betty
Stuck-Up.. Eugenie
My Holiday...Sarah, Mike
Down Through History...Tommy, Ramona
All Alone (reprise)...Tommy, Mike

ACT II   It Was Good Enough for Grandpa...Company
A Simple Life...Albert, Sarah
A Star on the Monument...Herbert, Miller, Jasper, Tommy
Rain Your Love on Me...Mike, Sarah
Stuck-Up (reprise)...Eugenie

There's Goin' to Be a Wedding…Herbert, Tooney, Tommy, Ramona, Betty, Miller, Esther, Jasper

All Alone Quintet (reprise)…Tommy, Ramona, Mike, Herbert, Tooney

Licensing: Samuel French

Difficulties/Advantages: Many projections and a turntable for the original production would seem to make this musical difficult for small theatres, but the projections are probably easy these days, with everyone a home-computer auteur, and the turntable is unnecessary. More difficult is the attack on mindless patriotism, never an easy subject. But "the show is conceived as a theatrical collage, a collection of scenes," and the scenes accumulate throughout the evening to make up a strong and meaningful—if now period—piece. If your college has a class on the sixties, this could be a great companion production.

Oil City Symphony

Book By Mike Craver, Mark Hardwick, Debra Monk, and Mary Murfitt
Music and Lyrics: Various Standards

"A celebration of suburban innocence and values." "The hokey pokey" with audience participation, and punch and cookies served by the cast at the end of the performance, will give you the idea of this satire on musical aesthetics that makes *Forever Plaid* seem positively hip-hop. Is the hokey pokey really that funny? Audiences thought so. Following an announcement that a yellow Honda Civic is parked in the principal's parking space, two men and two women—who between them play two pianos, accordion, synthesizer, vibraslap (is that an instrument?), violin, saxophone, flute, slide whistle, drums, and other percussion instruments—comprise the symphony for a small suburban town, and in the course of the evening play (or possibly murder would be a better word) many standard American songs, from the "Anvil Chorus" and a riotous polka to "In the Sweet Bye and Bye" and dueling pianos.

Time and Place: The present. An auditorium space.

Synopsis: A bit of detailed historical and technical information about the different instruments that the cast plays, and personal stories of how they came to know and love music, is about the only "book" material in this spoof on small towns, so arch and satiric that even small-town audiences should laugh.

Circle in the Square, Downtown; November 5, 1987; 626 performances.

Directed by Larry Forde.

Original Cast:

Mike Craver	Mark Hardwick
Debra Monk	Mary Murfitt

Musical Numbers:

Aст I   Count Your Blessings
Czardas
A Classic Selection: Anvil Chorus
A Popular Selection: In-a-Gadda-Da-Vida
Ohio Afternoon
Baby It's Cold Outside

ACT II

    The Hokey Pokey
    Beaver Ball at the Bug Club
    Beehive Polka
    A Patriotic Fantasy
    Dizzy Fingers
    Getting Acquainted
    Iris
    The End of the World
    Dear Miss Reeves
    Coaxing the Piano
    Bus Ride
    In the Sweet Bye and Bye
    My Ol' Kentucky Rock and Roll Home
    Exodus

Licensing: Music Theatre International

Difficulties/Advantages: The four performers—who could be expanded to, well, a symphony I suppose—have to play instruments, although not brilliantly, which makes this a real specialty musical.

Olympus on My Mind

Book and Lyrics by Barry Harman
Music by Grant Sturiale

Suggested by *Amphitryon* by Heinrich Von Kleist.

A funny little musical based on Greek myths. A burlesque sketch really, the kind the *Carol Burnett Show* did so well, here stretched to full length with songs and subplots.

Time and Place: The play is set in the ancient Greek city of Thebes, during the course of a 41-hour day.

Synopsis: Jupiter impersonates a mortal so he can spend the night with the lovely Alcmene. Unaccustomed to human emotions, he falls in love and is disappointed that she doesn't recognize his lovemaking as godlike. Meanwhile his son Mercury is required to impersonate Alcmene's maid's husband, but as the maid is a middle-aged shrew, Mercury avoids her by claiming to have lost his masculinity during the war. This frees her to pursue a life of debauchery with the chorus boys, at least until the real husband, Sosia, returns and walks right into his impersonator. Sosia is confused to see himself, but Amphitryon is furious that his wife spent the night with someone, although until Jupiter reveals himself, neither knows who it is. The act ends when the chorus reveals to the citizens that "Jupiter Slept Here!" although not before Delores, a voluptuous but entirely untalented chorus girl who is in the show because her husband, Murray the Furrier, is backing it, pushes her way downstage to exhibit herself in, and out of, Murray's furs.

    Naturally, in the second act, after several comic scenes based on mistaken identities, everything gets satisfactorily sorted out. Sosia beds his own wife only because she now thinks he's a god, Alcmene is grateful for the evening but still in love with her husband, and Jupiter returns to his heavenly seat as ruler of the universe much more wary of human emotions.

Olympus on My Mind at the Bristol Riverside Theatre, Bucks County, PA.

Actors Outlet, May 2, 1986; Lambs Theatre/Upstairs, July 15, 1986, 207 performances. Directed by Barry Harmon. Choreographed by Pamela Sousa.

Original Cast:

The Chorus
    Tom…Peter Kapetan
    Horace…Keith Bennett
Jupiter (a.k.a. Jove, Zeus)…Ron Raines
Charis…Peggy Hewett
Sosia…Lewis J. Stadlen

Dick…Andy Spangler
Delores…Faith Prince/Elizabeth Austin
Mercury…Jason Graae
Alcmene…Emily Zacharias
Amphitryon…George Spelvin

Musical Numbers:

ACT I   Welcome to Greece…Chorus
    Heaven on Earth…Jupiter, Alcmene, Chorus
    The Gods on Tap…Delores, Jupiter, Mercury, Chorus
    Surprise!…Sosia
    Love---What a Concept…Jupiter, Mercury
    Wait 'Til It Dawns…Mercury
    I Know My Wife…Amphitryon
    It Was Me…Sosia
    Back So Soon?…Amphitryon, Sosia, Chorus
    Wonderful…Alcmene
    At Liberty in Thebes…Charis, Chorus
    Jupiter Slept Here…Company

ACT II   Back to the Play…Chorus
    Something of Yourself (Don't Bring Her Flowers)…Mercury
    Generals' Pandemonium…Amphitryon, Jupiter, Sosia, Chorus

Heaven on Earth (reprise)...Sosia, Chorus
A Star Is Born...Delores, Company
Final Sequence...Amphitryon, Alcmene, Mercury, Jupiter, Charis, Sosia, Chorus
Heaven on Earth (finale)...Jupiter, Alcmene

Licensing: Samuel French

Difficulties/Advantages: The addition of the Delores of the chorus gag unfortunately turns the show into a burlesque of a spoof of a Greek myth, and ruins any chance it has to land in the category of *A Funny Thing Happened on the Way to the Forum,* one of the few successful farces in musical comedy—or even as one of the classic versions, numbering more than two dozen, of various playwrights' attempts to dramatize the Amphitryon legend. But for a small theatre with its tongue firmly in its cheek, this rare farce with songs could make for a funny and entertaining evening. In addition to the six principals, the script calls for a chorus of three men and a girl, the girl having some gags and one song, but the number of "generals" or "citizens of Thebes," not to mention high-kicking, tap-dancing backups to a couple of production numbers, could easily be extended or diminished for the size of the company or theatre. It does call for believable yet strenuous comic acting in the now-classic burlesque style, with which the mistaken identity sequences—in a neat comic concept, one actor plays both Jupiter and Amphitryon while two actors play Sosia and his imposter—should rise to utter hilarity. If you've already done *Forum* or don't have enough performers for it, this makes a great substitute.

Once on This Island

Book and Lyrics by Lynn Ahrens
Music by Stephen Flaherty

Based on the novel *My Love, My Love* by Rosa Guy.

Sung-thru (and not by Lloyd-Webber!) and without intermission, *Island* is a rousing musical that jumped its authors to the top of the Broadway heap. Many white Americans are unaware that blacks have a history of their own racism: the lighter the skin, the higher the class. This story is based on just that.

Time and Place: A stormy night. An island in the French Antilles.

Synopsis: The island is divided into the peasants (black) and the landowners (the "grands hommes," with pale brown skin). Among the peasants, a young girl is frightened by a storm, and to comfort her, the adults tell her an island legend, acting it out: A young girl named Ti Moune is orphaned, adopted, grows up, admires a glamorous stranger in an automobile, and prays to the gods that she will have a romantic adventure with him. The gods agree. Love, Death, Water, and Earth cause an automobile accident, and Ti Moune saves and nurses Daniel, pledging to the God of Death her own soul in exchange. When Daniel is returned to his home, Ti Moune follows. Daniel recovers, and he and Ti Moune fall in love, with a little help from the God of. He sings, however, "Some girls you marry, some you love." This is an unfortunate portent, as we now meet Daniel's fiancée, to whom he has been pledged since childhood. That's the way life is here. Ti Moune is distraught, but the gods pity her and turn her into a tree. And then one day, Daniel's son finds a peasant girl in its branches, and these two defy tradition and fall in love.

Booth Theatre; October 18, 1990; 19 previews, 469 performances.

Once on This Island at the Amas Musical Theatre, New York, NY.

Directed and choreographed by Graciela Daniele.

Original Cast:

Daniel…Jerry Dixon

Mama Euralie…Sheila Gibbs

Asaka, Mother of the Earth…Kecia Lewis-Evans

Little Ti Moune…Afi McClendon

Armand…Gerry McIntyre

Andrea…Nikki Rene

Tonton Julian…Ellis E. Williams

Erzülie, Goddess of Love…Andrea Frierson

Ti Moune…LaChanze

Agwe, God of Water…Milton Craig Nealy

Papa Ge, Demon of Death…Eric Riley

Musical Numbers:

We Dance. . .Storytellers

One Small Girl…Mama Euralie, Tonton Julian, Little Ti Moune, Storytellers

Waiting for Life…Ti Moune, Storytellers

And the Gods Heard Her Prayer…Asaka, Agwe, Papa Ge, Erzulie

Rain…Agwe, Storytellers

Pray…Ti Moune, Tonton Julian, Mama Euralie, Guard, Storytellers

Forever Yours…Ti Moune, Daniel, Papa Ge

Sad Tale of the Beauxhommes…Armand, Storytellers

Ti Moune…Mama Euralie, Tonton Julian, Ti Moune

Mama Will Provide…Asaka, Storytellers

Some Say…Storytellers

The Human Heart…Erzulie, Storytellers

Some Girls…Daniel

The Ball…Andrea, Daniel, Ti Moune, Storytellers

Forever Yours (reprise)…Papa Ge, Ti Moune, Storytellers

A Part of Us…Mama Euralie, Little Ti Moune, Tonton Julian, Storytellers

Why We Tell the Story…Storytellers

Licensing: Music Theatre International

Difficulties/Advantages: The authors have provided some dialogue substitutions so that actors of any race can, in the amateur market, perform this musical. Yet there's no getting around the fact that these characters are black, and good casting even requires some awareness of shading to distinguish the peasants from the landowners. Otherwise the basic premise would not make much sense.

Pageant

Book and Lyrics by Bill Russell and Frank Kelly
Music by Albert Evans
Conceived by Robert Longbottom

A satire on beauty pageants. The audience decides who wins. This is a great deal broader than the movie/Broadway musical *Smile,* the original beauty-contest spoof. And, oh yes, the female contestants are all played by men in drag.

Time and Place: This year. Your theatre, in your city.

Synopsis: Six contestants compete in evening gown, talent, swimwear, physical fitness, and beauty-crisis counseling, and each demonstrates his ability to be the spokesperson for the Glamouresse line of beauty products. One wins the "Miss Girlfriend" award, and when the scores of the five members of the audience chosen to be judges are tallied, a Miss Glamouresse is crowned by last year's winner. All emceed by a Bert Parks clone.

Blue Angel; May 2, 1991; 441 performances.

Conceived, directed and choreographed by Robert Longbottom. Co-choreographer: Tony Parise.

Original Cast:

Miss Bible Belt...Randl Ask
Miss Texas...Russell Garrett
Miss West Coast...John Salvatore
Frankie Cavalier...J. T. Cromwell
Miss Deep South...David Drake
Miss Industrial Northeast...Joe Joyce
Miss Great Plains...Dick Scanlan

Musical Numbers:

Natural Born Females...Contestants, Frankie
Something Extra.. Frankie
Miss Texas Talent...Miss Texas
Miss Deep South Talent...Miss Deep South
Miss West Coast Talent (dance)...Miss West Coast
Banking on Jesus...Miss Bible Belt Talent
It's Gotta Be Venus...Frankie, Contestants
Girl Power...Contestants
Something Extra (reprise)...Frankie
Goodbye...Frankie, Contestants
The Final Judgment...Tawney Jo
Miss Glamouresse...Frankie

Licensing: Samuel French

Difficulties/Advantages: Requires fairly elaborate costumes and hair—doubly difficult if your actor wears a size-fifteen high heel. Writer's notes: "Men in dresses may be funny by itself—for about five minutes. Then it's up to the characters." And: "The idea is to present male actors as female characters—not over-the-top drag queens." In fact, the gender-bending here is only an added joke. There's absolutely nothing that wouldn't be just as funny with the right actresses as contestants. On the other hand, the best actress in the world isn't going to get the laughs of a great drag queen.

Park

Book and Lyrics by Paul Cherry
Music by Lance Mulcahy

Time and Place: The present. Spring. A park.

Synopsis: Most of the first act is taken up with four strangers—a twenty-year-old boy, a twenty-eight-year-old girl, and a middle-aged man and woman—who meet in a public park and attempt to become friends. As soon as the young man says to the girl, "I came to the park to be born," you know you're in for some kind of allegory. The problem is, it's not clear what. Then, just as you think this is the most aimless musical you've ever seen, it turns out that the four are a family and have come to the park to work out a very dysfunctional relationship by playing a game of being strangers and telling each other secrets. The therapy doesn't work, and the first-act curtain descends on accusations and exits.

In act 2 they try again. What they say to each other—and the vague and simplistic lyrics they sing—is so nonsensical that their reconciliation at the final curtain is hardly comforting. Still, it's a relief that the musical is over.

John Golden Theatre; April 22, 1970; 5 performances, probably all previews, as they dared not open for critics.

Directed by John Stix. Musical staging by Lee Theodore.

Original Cast:

Young Man, Jamie…Don Scardino   Young Woman, Sara…Joan Hackett
Man, Austin…David Brooks   Woman, Elizabeth…Julie Wilson

Musical Numbers:

ACT I   All the Little Things in the World Are Waiting…Young Man
         Hello Is the Way Things Begin…Young Woman
         Bein' a Kid…Young Man, Young Woman
         Elizabeth…Man
         He Talks to Me…Woman, Man
         Tomorrow Will Be the Same…Quartet
         One Man…Woman
         Park…Young Man
ACT II   I Want It Just to Happen…Young Woman
         I Can See…Woman
         Compromise…Young Man
         Jamie…Young Man, Man
         Tomorrow Will Be the Same (reprise)…Ensemble
         I'd Marry You Again…Woman, Man
         Bein' a Kid (reprise)…Quartet
         Park (reprise)…Quartet

Licensing: Samuel French

Difficulties/Advantages: This four-character "Broadway" musical wouldn't work any better off than it did on. It was numbingly idiotic on stage, and read again thirty years later, even worse. When the American musical was healthy, lots of shows were mounted, which was a very good thing overall, but a few real turkeys slipped in among them. This one's exhibit A. Too bad, because it had a very talented cast, lost in a miasma of dialogue and lyrics about as pithy as Rod McKuen poetry.

Piano Bar

Story by Doris Willens and Rob Fremont
Music by Rob Fremont
Lyrics by Doris Willens

Time and Place: Happy Hour, on a rainy Tuesday in March of this year, or whatever year this is. Sweet Sue's Piano Bar, in the Murray Hill section of Manhattan. A neighborhood bar, but one that gets drop-in traffic, because it's near Grand Central Station. It has seen better days. Or nights.

Synopsis: This is a revue disguised as a musical. Two men and two women drop into a bar, where there is a piano player and a bartender. Encouraged by the piano player and fed a number of drinks by the bartender, the customers sing, mostly to us, about life's regrets. Eventually they pair off and, in that cynical New York way that Sondheim did much better in *Company*, underscore the notion that just about anything is better than loneliness. The whole thing is only mildly entertaining.

Westside Theatre; June 8, 1978; 133 performances.

Production staged and directed by Albert Takazauckas. Choreographed by Nora Peterson

Original Cast:

Bartender...Jim McMahon	Julie...Kelly Bishop
Prince...Joel Silberman	Walt...Richard Ryder
Ned...Steve Elmore	Debbie...Karen De Vito

Musical Numbers:

ACT I   Introduction...Prince
Sweet Sue's...Company
Today...Company
Pigeon-Hole Time...Ned
Congratulations...Debbie
Believe Me...Walt, Julie
Tango...Julie, Walt
Everywhere I Go...Debbie
Dinner at the Mirklines...Ned
Scenes from Some Marriages (The People Game)...Company
Personals...Prince
Nobody's Perfect...Company

ACT II   One Two Three...Company
Greenspons...Debbie
Moms and Dads...Company
Meanwhile, Back in Yonkers...Julie

Alas, Alack…Prince, Walt
New York Cliché…Debbie, Ned
It's Coming Back To Me…Julie, Walt
Tomorrow Night…Prince
Closing…Prince

Licensing: Samuel French

Difficulties/Advantages: If the fundamental clichés of society haven't changed since the post-war generation, the style has, which makes it hard to reproduce the kind of ideas represented here, even though they're still valid. If your theatre is lucky enough to have a singing pianist, pick out a famous composer, stage a revue set in a piano bar, and pass on this one.

Pump Boys and Dinettes

A Country Music Revue

Pump Boys and Dinettes at the Little Theatre of Fall River, MA.

Conceived and Written by John Foley, Mark Hardwick, Debra Monk, Cass Morgan, John Schimmel, and Jim Wann

Time and Place: The present. Highway 57—somewhere between Frog Level and Smyrna, North Carolina.

Synopsis: There's a gas station run by four good ol' boys, and a dinette across the street with a pair of sisters for waitresses. These six characters perform a bunch of good ol' country songs (which the original cast wrote), providing also their own accompaniment. There's no book, but the ambiance they create is terrific, if a long way from Dietz and Schwartz. Placed here instead of in the revue category simply because the "characters" are delicious.

Westside Arts Theatre, July 10, 1981; moved to Colonnades Theatre, October 1, 1981, 132 performances; then moved uptown to the Princess Theatre, February 4, 1982, for 573 more.

Although no director is listed, there's a thank you in the program to Word Baker for "fixing a few flats."

Original Cast:

Pump Boys…John Foley, Mark Hardwick, John Schimmel, Jim Wann
Dinettes.…Debra Monk, Cass Morgan

Musical Numbers:

ACT I   Highway 57…All
Taking It Slow…Pump Boys
Serve Yourself…L. M.
Menu Song…Dinettes
The Best Man…Prudie
Fisherman's Prayer…Pump Boys
Catfish…Pump Boys
Mamaw…Jim
Be Good or Be Gone…Rhetta
Drinkin' Shoes…All

ACT II   Pump Boys…Pump Boys
Mona…Jackson
The Night Dolly Parton Was Almost Mine…L. M.
Tips…Dinettes
Sisters…Dinettes
Vacation…All
No Holds Barred…All
Farmer Tan…L. M. and Dinettes
Highway 57 (reprise)…All
Closing Time…All
Greatest Hits (medley)…All

Licensing: Samuel French

Difficulties/Advantages: Several of the Red Clay Ramblers (see *Diamond Studs*) have metamorphosed into the Pump Boys and Dinettes, bringing their special brand of hillbilly rock 'n' roll with them. There's no reason your cast has to play their own instruments, and freed from guitars and all, there's probably much more opportunity for fun staging.

Radio Gals

Book, Music, and Lyrics by Mike Craver and Mark Hardwick

Arkansas women are running a pirate radio station, and the government itself isn't going to stop them.

Time and Place: The late 1920s, well before "The Crash." A warm spring day in the parlor of Hazel Hunt's home in Cedar Ridge, Arkansas.

Synopsis: Hazel Hunt retired from years of teaching music and was rewarded with a transmitter, whereupon she immediately set about producing a day-long radio show from her parlor. Having no idea that the airwaves are regulated, she "wavejumps," searching for a clear channel, often in the middle of a program. The story is a day of programming, replete with homegrown music. Unfortunately, the arrival of Mr. Abbott from the Department of Commerce throws a wrench into the proceedings. He discovers that Hazel and friends are breaking every possible rule. Also they are selling prohibition alcohol under the name of Horehound Compound. His final problem is that Gladys falls in love with him. When he takes off on his motorcycle to inform the government and close the station, Gladys follows. But so does Hazel, with her musket. (Not to fear, it couldn't fire a shot if the South rose again.)

They bring Abbott back and continue their day of broadcasting, even forcing Abbott to sing a song or two for their listeners. It turns out he has an excellent tenor. Before they can sign off for the day, Mr. Sarnoff of NBC calls to say that they have strayed onto his channel, he's heard their music, and he would like for them to participate in his trans-America broadcast. And he particularly likes Abbott's tenor. That's enough for Abbott to drop his briefcase and join the Radio Gals for a grand finale.

John Houseman Theatre; October 1, 1996; 17 previews, 39 performances.

Directed by Marcia Milgrom Dodge.

Original Cast:

Hazel Hunt…Carole Cook	Gladys Fritts…Rosemary Loar
Rennabelle…Klea Blackhurst	America…Emily Mikesell
Miss Mabel Swindle…Michael Rice	Miss Azilee Swindle…Mike Craver
O. B. Abbott…Matthew Bennett	

Musical Numbers:

ACT I   Sunrise Melody…Hazel and the Hazelnuts
Aviatrix Love Song…America and the Hazelnuts
If Stars Could Talk…Gladys, Rennabelle, America
When It's Sweetpea Time in Georgia…Miss Azilee
Dear Mr. Gershwin…Rennabelle
The Tranquil Boxwood…Gladys
There Are Fairies in My Mother's Flower Garden…Gladys
A Fireside, a Pipe and a Pet…O. B. Abbott
Edna Jones, the Elephant Girl…All
Paging the Ether/Play Gypsies Play…Hazel and the Hazelnuts

ACT II   Royal Radio…America and the Hazelnuts
Weather Song…The Hazelnuts
Buster He's a Hot Dog Now…Miss Mabel, Miss Azilee
Why Did You Make Me Love You?…O. B. Abbott
Old Gals Are the Best Pals After All…Hazel, Azilee, Mabel
A Gal's Got to Do What a Gal's Got to Do…Hazel
Whispering Pines…All
Wedding of the Flowers…All
Queenie Take Me Home with You…All

Licensing: Samuel French

Difficulties/Advantages: A rollicking rural farce and a collection of hillbilly songs combine to make this one so entertaining your audience won't notice how ludicrous it all is. But some of the women should play instruments, and only a breakneck pace and outstanding comediennes could keep your production afloat. Two of the older gals are customarily played by men.

Return to the Forbidden Planet

Photo: Nobby Clark

Return to the Forbidden Planet at the Queens Theatre, Hornchurch, UK.

A Play by Bob Carlton

A spoof on the classic sci-fi film *Forbidden Planet,* itself an update of Shakespeare's *The Tempest,* with rock 'n' roll songs from the fifties and sixties amid pseudo-Shakespearean dialogue ("There are more things in heaven and earth than are dreamt of in my laboratory," and "Out damned Blob, out I say!") A hit in England, less so in New York, possibly because spoofs and rock 'n' roll theatre were old hat by then. It's not *Rocky Horror,* with its original score, and like many off-Broadway spoofs, its plot is thin—the monsters from Prospero's id happen because he invented a mind-expanding drug—but if you love the golden oldies (see list below), it's a rollicking evening of classic rock, stitched together with some laughs. And unlike *Rocky Horror,* there's nothing untoward, so school kids could have a ball and get to wrap their articulation around Elizabethan iambic pentameter.

Time and Place: The 21st century, "a Friday, I think." The action all takes place on a 1950s B-movie spaceship.

Synopsis: A spaceship commanded by Captain Tempest crash-lands on D'Illyria, although not before the female Science Officer escapes on the ship's shuttlecraft. There, Prospero, formerly an evil scientist, insists that he is now reformed and comes aboard with his robot servant, Ariel. Fifteen years ago, he created a drug he called the X-Factor, which he claims will benefit mankind, but his wife, Gloria, stole the blueprints for the mind-expanding drug and banished him and their baby daughter to the planet. The daughter (Miranda) comes aboard, and Cookie, a crewman, falls in love with her, but she goes for the senior officer. Cookie sees them talking and overhears Miranda confessing her love.

He vows to avenge his unrequited love. Prospero drinks some of the X-Factor, and a strange feeling comes over him, while the crew worries about their situation. A huge monster approaches the ship. The Science Officer returns, escaping from the monster. It's Gloria! With Ariel's help, they fight off the monster's tentacles. Gloria schemes with Cookie—she wants the drug's formula, he wants Miranda. But Miranda dresses up like Marilyn Monroe to seduce the Captain. Cookie obtains the blueprint, which Ariel swallows. Prospero discovers that the monster is from his own id. Understanding that only his own death will dissolve the monster, he heads for the space lock and saves the ship and crew. Dillyria itself explodes, Gloria blesses the union of the Captain and Miranda, and we head back to Earth. Well, never mind. It's more about all the great songs and the clever take on half-Shakespearean, half-*Star Trek* dialogue.

The Bubble Theatre Company began the musical's odyssey in tents in 1983, and after a long gestation, it ended up on London's West End in September, 1989, for a three-and-a-half year run!

Directed by Bob Carlton. Choreographed by Rosy Sanders.

Original Cast:

Captain Tempest, a Starship Captain, Square Jawed, Boy's Own Paper Hero and Pipe Smoker...John Ashby

Doctor Prospero, a Mad Scientist, Marooned for 15 Years on the Planet D'Illyria...Colin Wakefield

Ariel, a Hip Robot...Nigel Nevinson

Cookie, the Ship's Cook, a Hopeless Romantic...Matthew Devitt

The Science Officer, a Woman with a Mysterious Past...Nicky Furre

Bosun Arras, All-Round Good Guy...Alan Barker

Navigation Officer, Prone to Panic During Intergalactic Emergencies...Kate Edgar

Miranda, Prospero's Daughter, Would-be Sorority Queen and Virgin...Anne Miles

Ensign Jock E. Schwartz, Friend to Cookie...Bill Dare

Newsreader, on Video Screen...Dr. Magnus Pyke

Musical Numbers:

ACT I
Wipeout...Instrumental
Great Balls of Fire...All
Don't Let Me Be Misunderstood...Prospero
Good Vibrations...Captain Tempest, Ariel
Ain't a Gonna Wash for a Week...Cookie
I'm Gonna Change the World...Captain Tempest, Prospero
Why Must I Be a Teenager in Love...Miranda
Young Girl...Captain Tempest
She's Not There...Cookie
All Shook Up...Prospero, Cookie, Miranda
Gloria...Crew

ACT II
5, 4, 3, 2, 1...Crew
Gloria (reprise)
Don't Let Me Be Misunderstood (reprise)...Science Officer
Who's Sorry Now?...Ariel
She's Not There...Instrumental
Tell Her...Science Officer, Cookie
War Paint...Ariel, Captain Tempest

Robot Man…Ariel
Shake, Rattle and Roll…Cookie
Go Now…Science Officer
The Young Ones…Captain Tempest, Miranda
We've Gotta Get Out of This Place…Ariel
Wipe Out and Telestar…Crew
Hey Mr. Spaceman…Miranda
Monster Mash…Prospero

Licensing: Margaret Ramsay Ltd., 14A Goodwin's Court, St. Martin's Lane, London WC2N 4LL

Difficulties/Advantages: The original director put the band—as the crew—on the flight deck and utilized hand-held microphones for all the dialogue as well as the songs, since the whole idea was a kind of intergalactic rock concert. Microphones with cords would probably look ridiculous today, and modern cordless amplification frees the hands for much better staging anyway. Video screens showed what happens outside the ship, but that isn't so difficult, or you could do without them easily. There's only one costume per actor, probably the tackier the better. There's more than a hint of *Star Trek* spoofing in this kind of thing, too, so I'd look to Kirk and Company for costuming. The ship can be accessorized just about any way you want, from tacky to high-tech. Above all, the songs must be presented well, since the baby boomers—and everyone since—are so familiar with the songs that you're competing with the originals. Finally, though I don't know how the original writer would feel about it, there's plenty of room for your own favorite songs.

The Roar of the Greasepaint, the Smell of the Crowd

Book, Music, and Lyrics by Anthony Newley and Leslie Bricusse

Imported from England because the first Newley/Bricusse musical, *Stop the World—I Want to Get Off*, had been a great success, this one didn't run as long or as far; yet it is every bit as good, take my word, and was still extremely original—coming to us in the "concept" or "allegorical" musical genre Newley and Bricusse had pioneered. The clever songs ("Put It in the Book"), the soaring melodies ("Who Can I Turn To?"), the powerful black anthem ("Feeling Good"), and more all add up to one of the most melodic scores ever written, and the themes, brilliantly interpreted by Newley as the humble Cocky and Cyril Ritchard as the self-satisfied, upper-class twit Sir, are as strong today as they ever were.

Time and Place: Now. On a game board.

Synopsis: Cocky and Sir arrive to once again play the game of life. Cocky, a have-not, always seems to lose, particularly because the rules are continually altered by Sir, a have, to suit himself. By the time the game is completed, Cocky and Sir admit they need each other, so they share the heavy load they arrived with and travel on.

Shubert Theatre; May 16, 1965; 231 performances.

Directed by Anthony Newley. Musical numbers staged by Gillian Lynne.

Original Cast:

Cocky...Anthony Newley
Sir...Cyril Ritchard
The Kid...Sally Smith
The Negro...Gilbert Price
The Girl...Joyce Jillson
The Bully...Murray Tannenbaum

The Urchins...Rawley Bates, Lori Browne, Lori Cesar, Jill Choder, Gloria Chu, Kay Cole, Marlene Dell, Boni Enten, Mitzi Feinn, Pamela Gruen, Linda Rae Hager, Cyndi Howard, Laura Michaels, Debbie Palmer, Heather Taylor

Musical Numbers:

ACT I   The Beautiful Land...The Urchins
          A Wonderful Day Like Today...Sir, Cocky, the Urchins
          It Isn't Enough...Cocky, the Urchins
          Things to Remember...Sir, the Kid, the Urchins
          Put It in the Book...The Kid, the Urchins
          With All Due Respect...Cocky
          This Dream...Cocky
          Where Would You Be Without Me?...Sir, Cocky
          Look at That Face...Sir, the Kid, the Urchins
          My First Love Song...Cocky, the Girl
          The Joker...Cocky
          Put 'em in the Box...The Urchins
          Who Can I Turn To?...Cocky

ACT II   That's What It Is to Be Young...The Urchins
          What a Man!...Cocky, Sir, the Kid, the Urchins
          Feeling Good...The Negro, the Urchins
          Nothing Can Stop Me Now!...Cocky, the Urchins
          Things to Remember (reprise)...Sir
          My Way...Cocky, Sir
          Who Can I Turn To?(reprise)...Sir
          The Beautiful Land (reprise) and Sweet Beginning...The Urchins
          Sweet Beginning...Cocky, Sir the Kid, the Urchins

Licensing: Tams-Witmark

Difficulties/Advantages: Only five principals and a group of "urchins," along with a single set, make this Broadway musical very presentable in all sorts of conditions; its haves vs. have-nots theme is as relevant as ever, perhaps more so, and the universality of the "game" and the timelessness of the musical score make it a show that needs to be revived more often— although, like all very theatrical pieces, it needs splendid performances and staging to entrance the audience. A great opportunity for a young cast. Though Cocky and Sir are large, difficult roles, the urchins are usually a chorus of young girls.

The Rocky Horror Show

Book, Music, and Lyrics by Richard O'Brien

By now no one in the civilized world isn't familiar with the phenomenal cult success of the film version of this English Fringe rock musical that camps on science-fiction B-

The Rocky Horror Show at the Santa Rosa Junior College Summer Repertory Theatre, Santa Rosa, CA.

movies and the Frankenstein story. Originally a hit in England, then Los Angeles, then just about everywhere—except New York (where it was mistakenly put into a Broadway theatre).

Time and Place: The 1950s, although only Brad and Janet are from that odd civilization. A spooky mansion.

Synopsis: Following a friend's wedding, Brad and Janet become engaged. Then, on a trip through a dark and stormy night to visit their old tutor Dr. Scott, their car blows a tire, and they stumble into a castle and meet some odd types doing "The Time Warp" dance, and a Sweet Transvestite from Transsexual Transylvania, who soon has them in their underwear. Invited to Frank's laboratory, they witness the creation of Rocky, a blond hunk made to order for a Sweet Transvestite. Later, Frank sleeps with, and satisfies, both Brad and Janet (a neat trick, so to speak). Janet, heretofore a virgin, likes it, enough to sing and hook up with Rocky. When Frank finds out that Rocky has been cheating on him—and Dr. Scott arrives representing the government—he transforms everyone into a chorus line for a garter-and-stockings number that exploits the general theme of the show: "Don't dream it, be it." But his servants, Riff-Raff and Magenta, get the upper hand with a ray gun, dematerialize Frank and Rocky, and return happily to their native planet.

Well, the plot doesn't really matter anyway. It was the outrageous performance by Tim Curry, and the rock 'n' roll songs—particularly Eddie the delivery boy's delivery of "Hot Patootie"—that carried *Rocky Horror* into cinematic myth. Many small musicals have tried and failed to capture the same style of camp. None have come even close.

The Royal Court Theatre Upstairs, London, June 16, 1973; Roxy Theater, Hollywood, March 24, 1974 (9-month run); Belasco Theater in Manhattan (converted to a cabaret), March 10, 1975, 4 previews, 45 performances.

All productions directed by Jim Sharman.

Original Roxy Cast:

The Belasco Popcorn Girl (Trixie)...Jamie Donnelly
Janet...Abigale Haness
Brad...Bill Miller
Riff-Raff...Ritz O'Brien
Magenta...Jamie Donnelly
Rocky...Kim Milford
Doctor Scott...Meat Loaf

Narrator...William Newman
Columbia...Boni Enten
Frank...Tim Curry
Eddie...Meat Loaf

Musical Numbers:

Science Fiction Double Feature...Magenta
Damn It Janet...Brad, Janet
Over at the Frankenstein Place...Brad, Janet, Company
Sweet Transvestite...Frank
The Time Warp...Riff-Raff, Company
The Sword of Damocles...Rocky, Company
I Can Make You a Man...Frank, Company
Hot Patootie...Eddie
Touch-A Touch-A Touch Me...Janet, Company
Once in a While...Brad
Eddie's Teddy...Dr. Scott, Company
Planet Schmanet and Wise Up Janet Weiss.....Frank
Floorshow/Rose Tint My World...All
I'm Going Home...All
Super Heroes...Brad, Janet, Company
Science Fiction Double Feature (reprise)...Magenta

Licensing: Samuel French

Difficulties/Advantages: Not for the Bridgewater Ladies Cultural Assembly, but more fun for the actors than a cast party with spiked punch. The doubling brings this cast down to nine, with four "phantoms"—back-up singers—which are not absolutely necessary, but can, on the other hand, be increased to just about as many as can learn the Time Warp steps. The euphonious and exuberant score is easy to learn and an absolute joy to sing, but produce this at your own risk—expect the younger half of the audience to be dressed more exotically than your cast and to sing along, the older half to walk out.

Romance/Romance

Two One-Act Musicals

Book and Lyrics by Barry Harman
Music by Keith Herrmann

ACT I: "The Little Comedy"

Based on the short story by Arthur Schnitzler.

Time and Place: The turn of the century. In and around the city of Vienna.

Synopsis: A wealthy, handsome rake, tired of the usual "arrangements" and having just given up his latest mistress, disguises himself as a poor poet to seek an adventure. A woman "with a history," having given up her latest lover, disguises herself as a poor millinery

124

Romance/Romance, "Summer Share," Bristol Valley Theater, Naples, NY.

girl and ventures into the street. Naturally, they meet and fall in love. Three weeks into their idyllic life, both decide to appear as themselves and tell the truth. There is a near immediate understanding when they appear in their finest clothes, and much laughter. But negotiations commence. Is love gone?

ACT II: "Summer Share"

Based on *Pain de Ménage* by Jules Renard.

Time and Place: Today. The living room of a contemporary beach house in the Hamptons.

Synopsis: Two couples share a summer rental. One's husband and the other's wife have long been best friends, but tonight they gradually move toward having an affair. With the others asleep, they slip out of the house with every intention to do so but return almost immediately, too guilty to consummate. When the curtain falls, reality has, for the second time tonight, intruded on romance.

Helen Hayes Theater; April 20, 1988; 307 performances.

Directed by Barry Harman. Choreographed by Pamela Sousa.

Original Cast:

ACT I	"The Little Comedy"		
	Alfred Von Wilmers…Scott Bakula	Josefine Weninger…Alison Fraser	
	"Him"…Robert Hoshour	"Her"…Deborah Graham	
ACT II	"Summer Share"		
	Lenny…Robert Hoshour	Barb…Deborah Graham	
	Sam…Scott Bakula	Monica…Alison Fraser	

Musical Numbers:

ACT I   "The Little Comedy"
The Little Comedy…Alfred, Josefine

Goodbye, Emil…Josefine
It's Not Too Late…Alfred, Josefine
Great News…Alfred, Josefine
Oh, What a Performance!…Alfred, Josefine
I'll Always Remember the Song…Alfred, Josefine
Happy, Happy, Happy…Alfred
Women of Vienna.. Alfred
Yes, It's Love…Josefine
A Rustic Country Inn…Alfred, Josefine
The Night It Had to End…Josefine
The Little Comedy (finale)…Alfred, Josefine

Aᴄᴛ II   "Summer Share"
Summer Share…All
Think of the Odds…Barb, Lenny
It's Not Too Late (reprise)…Sam, Monica
Plans A and B…Monica, Lenny
Let's Not Talk About It…Sam, Barb
So Glad I Married Her…All
Small Craft Warnings…Barb, Lenny
How Did I End Up Here…Monica
Words He Doesn't Say…Sam
My Love for You…Lenny, Barb
Moonlight Passing Through a Window…Sam
Now…Monica
Romantic Notions…Sam, Barb, Lenny, Monica

Licensing: Samuel French

Difficulties/Advantages: These two one-acts go well together, and you can utilize four actors or eight. Strong books, if inconsequential, and a decent but forgettable score.

Ruthless!

Book and Lyrics by Joel Paley
Music by Marvin Laird

What Ever Happened to Baby Jane? Gypsy, All About Eve, The Women, The Bad Seed, Sweeney Todd, Valley of the Dolls, Mildred Pierce, and Shirley Temple—all these and more are alluded to in this high-camp send-up of show business, in which a child would— and literally does, several times—kill for stardom, beginning with the lead in her school play, "Pippi Goes to Tahiti—The Musical." Tawdry, brash, and a pizzicato note short of wildly over-the-top are some of the descriptions critics lavished on this uneven tale of three generations of women in a family for whom the lure of celebrity causes larceny, mezzo-soprano belting, and sudden explosions of tap-dancing. The Teacher, the Competition, and the Star add to the shenanigans of several women, one ballsy child, and a female agent played by a man in drag, in a successful off-Broadway musical spoof of show business in general and forties movie clichés in particular. In other words, a gay male point of view on backstage Broadway and Hollywood.

Players Theatre; May 13, 1992; 40 previews, 302 performances.

Directed by Joel Paley.

Ruthless! at the Mounds Theatre, St. Paul, MN.

Photo: Chad Allen

Original Cast:

Sylvia St. Croix…Joel Vig
Tina Denmark…Laura Bundy
Louise Lerman/Eve…Joanna Baum

Judy Denmark…Donna English
Myrna Thorn…Susan Mansur
Lita Encore…Denise Lor

Musical Numbers:

ACT I   Prologue…Sylvia
Tina's Mother…Judy
Born to Entertain…Tina
Talent…Sylvia
To Play This Part…Tina
Teaching Third Grade…Miss Thorn
Where Tina Gets It From…Judy, Sylvia
The Pippi Song…Louise
Kisses and Hugs…Tina, Judy
I Hate Musicals…Lita
Angel Mom…Judy, Tina

ACT II   Entr'acte/Montage…Judy, Tina
A Penthouse Apartment…Eve
It Will Never Be That Way Again…Ginger
I Want the Girl…Sylvia
Parents and Children…Ginger, Tina
Ruthless!…Ginger, Sylvia, Tina
Talent (reprise)…Tina

Ruthless! (reprise)...Company
Unkie's Muncle...Ruth Del Marco

Licensing: Samuel French

Difficulties/Advantages: Brash performers are the requirement here, those larger-than-life folks who leave tooth marks on the scenery. Eight women—although the principal role of the Agent was played in drag in New York—and a little girl who would just kill to be a star. Your audience won't have to get all the references to enjoy the very broad humor, but it helps.

Sally Blane, World's Greatest Girl Detective

Book by Helen Sneed and Peter Webb
Music and Lyrics by David Levy and Leslie Eberhard

Having no idea where or when this musical played, but knowing that Leslie Eberhard was a talented writer, I'm simply going to quote the catalogue from Dramatists Play Service, and you can investigate further if you like.

Synopsis: "Sally Blane, a pretty and indomitable seventeen-year-old, has solved mysteries all over the globe and has helped thousands of people in distress. Early in this, her latest adventure, she discovers that her father, Lane Blane, is being held hostage by a coffee cartel in Latin America. With her omnipresent chaperone, Fricka Norse, and her plump chum, Amaryllis White, Sally sets forth to save her Dad. Her boyfriend, Scotty Schuykill, wants her to stay home with him and do normal things like go to school. Sally can't resist another mystery, though, and takes off for foreign soil.

"Aboard the SS Privilege, bound for Latin America, Sally is stalked by the menacing (though bumbling) Blister Owen. She also meets up with Consuelo and Lupe Wordsworth, two helpless waifs who are returning to the land of their birth to hunt for their inheritance, the Wordsworth Fortune. Sally vows to help them. Once in Latin America, she is introduced to Connie and Lulu's sinister aunt, Tia Esmerelda, who seems to know more about the whereabouts of Sally's father than she should.

"Aided only by her flashlight and a magnifying glass, Sally is run down by a sinister sedan, beaten up by a thug, rendered unconscious by a drug-soaked handkerchief, kidnapped, hit on the head, poisoned by a mysterious devil doll, lured through the hazardous tropical rain forest, and pushed down an old stone well by her own father. And that's only act 1!

"In act 2 she finds time to become fluent in Spanish, learn the tango, discover the missing fortune, save her father's life, and subvert a massive plot to take over the entire Southern Hemisphere. Just before the curtain, Sally is reconciled with Scotty and promises to go back to school. A mysterious gun shot rings out, and Sally charges off on her next case."

Cast: 3 men, 7 women

Licensing: Dramatists Play Service

Salvation

Book, Music, and Lyrics by Peter Link and C. C. Courtney

There was a time when the idea of rock music as theatre music was aborning and almost any tune with a solid rhythm could excite an audience in a small off-Broadway theatre. This musical capitalized on that.

Synopsis: A history of the Christian Church told in a revival meeting of disgruntled children of the twentieth century.

Jan Hus Playhouse; September 24, 1969; 239 performances.

Directed by Paul Aaron. Dance movement by Kathryn Posin.

Original Cast:

Ranee…Yolanda Bavan
Monday…C. C. Courtney
Boo…Boni Enten
Betty Lou…Marta Heflin

Farley…Peter Link
Mark…Joe Morton
Dierdre…Annie Rachel
LeRoy.. Chapman Roberts

Musical Numbers:

Salvation
In Between
1001
Honest Confession Is Good for the Soul
Ballin'
Let the Moment Slip By
Gina
Stockhausen Potpourri
If You Let Me Make Love to You, Then Why Can't I Touch You?
There Ain't No Flies on Jesus
Deadalus
Deuteronomy XVII Verse 2
For Ever
Footloose Youth and Fancy Free
Schwartz
Let's Get Lost in Now
Back to Genesis
Tomorrow Is the First Day of the Rest of Your Life

Licensing: Music Theatre International

Difficulties/Advantages: Replacements during the run included Barry Bostwick and Bette Midler, which just goes to show you how desperate performers are to get that big break. This wasn't it for either of them, but if you caught them in the show, consider yourself lucky.

Shelter

Book and Lyrics by Gretchen Cryer
Music by Nancy Ford

After a great start with *Now Is the Time for All Good Men* and the funny and tuneful first act of *The Last Sweet Days of Isaac,* both off-Broadway, Cryer and Ford lost their position as the leading lights of the next generation of musical comedy writers with this one.

Time and Place: The present. A television studio set.

Synopsis: Maud is filming a commercial for cooking oil and coming apart at the same time, because her husband left her that morning. They wrap the commercial, but Michael, the writer, asks her to stay. Seems he lives there, in the television studio, on the house set, along with a computer that interacts with him. There is a subtle seduction going on, but beyond that, most of the first act contains dialogue such as, "Words alter the way we experience things," until they presumably go to bed.

The next morning, the cleaning lady enters, and it becomes clear that she sleeps with Michael too. Then his wife, Gloria, appears. Wednesday—that's the name of the cleaning lady, because she comes on Wednesdays, although she came a day early this week—is fired. Maud leaves. Gloria leaves. Michael is quite satisfied with himself. Or something like that.

John Golden Theatre; February 6, 1973; 16 previews, 31 performances.

Directed by Austin Pendleton. Musical staging by Sammy Bayes.

Original Cast:

Maud...Marcia Rodd	Michael...Terry Kiser
Wednesday November...Susan Browning	Gloria...Joanna Merlin
Television Crew...Charles Collins, Britt Swanson	Arthur...Tony Wells
Voice of the Director...Philip Kraus	

Musical Numbers:

ACT I   Changing...Maud
Welcome to a New World...Arthur, Michael
Woke Up Today...Maud
It's Hard to Care...Michael, Arthur, Maud
Mary Margaret's House in the Country...Maud
Woman on the Run...Arthur
Don't Tell Me It's Forever...Arthur, Maud, Michael

ACT II   Sunrise...Arthur
I Bring Him Seashells...Wednesday
She's My Girl...Michael, Maud
He's a Fool...Maud
Something Good Together...Maud, Michael, Arthur, Wednesday
He's a Fool...Wednesday, Maud
Going Home with My Children...Maud, Arthur
Sleep, My Baby, Sleep...Michael

Licensing: Samuel French

Difficulties/Advantages: Nonsensical dialogue was probably the chief cause for this one being one of the biggest flops Broadway ever saw. Utterly silly even then, its sixties meaning-of-life prose and lyrics sound nearly comical today. There are three good parts for women, though, and it's the rare musical that makes a man out to be about as absurd as television sitcoms usually do.

Show Me Where the Good Times Are

Book by Lee Thuna
Music by Kenneth Jacobson
Lyrics by Rhoda Roberts
Suggested by Molière's *The Imaginary Invalid.*

An adaptation of the great Molière play, cleverly reset among America's Jewish immigrants early in the twentieth century on Henry Street. This one should have been a big Broadway musical à la *Hello, Dolly!* but didn't have the cash and so fell between Broadway and off-Broadway. Historical footnote: it was the first production to open the brand-new Edison Theatre, a 500-seat gem in the middle of the Broadway theatre district.

Time and Place: Spring 1913. New York City, the bedroom of Aaron's house on Henry Street and various places on the Lower East Side.

Synopsis: The hypochondriac who spends most of his time in bed is, in this version, the patriarch of a Jewish immigrant family, plotting to marry his daughter to a doctor so he can have full-time medical care. Unfortunately for his scheme, she is in love with an impoverished actor, and they elope. At the same time, his wife, after five years married to a patient, has lost her patience, and his sister has had enough of his bullying too. He fakes his own funeral, discovers his daughter's true feelings for him—and his wife's lack thereof—and finally finds himself feeling better (quite a shock for a hypochondriac). The sister marries the manager of the troop, who gives the young actor a small part (in spite of his stutter). The actor marries the daughter and all go on tour, leaving the invalid alone…until his wife returns to find him healthy, and they are reconciled. In other words, all the usual plot machinations Molière is famous for, in a kind of Yiddish theatre version.

Edison Theatre; March 5, 1970; 29 performances.

Directed by Morton Da Costa. Choreographed by Bob Herget.

Original Cast:

Aaron…Arnold Soboloff	Rachel…Gloria LeRoy
Annette…Neva Small	Bella…Cathryn Damon
Maurice…John Bennett Perry	Kolinsky…Christopher Hewett
Rothstein…Edward Earle	Dr. Perlman…Mitchell Jason
Thomas Perlman…Michael Berkson	Madame Schwartz…Renee Orin

Men and Women of the Lower East Side: Austin Colyer, Kevin Daly, Denny Martin Flinn, Lydia Gonzalez, Maria Hero, Peggy Hewett, Sara Louise, Donna Monroe, James E. Rogers, Peter Sansone.

Musical Numbers:

ACT I   How Do I Feel?…Aaron with Rachel, Annette, Bella
         He's Wonderful…Annette, Rachel
         Look Up…Annette, Rachel, Bella
         Show Me Where the Good Times Are…Bella, Company
         You're My Happiness…Aaron, Bella
         Cafe Royale Rag…Orchestra
         Staying Alive…Kolinsky, Rachel, Company
         Open Up Your Pores…Bella, Kolinsky, Rachel, Company
         One Big Happy Family…Aaron, Maurice, Bella, Annette,
         Rachel, Thomas, Kolinsky, Perlman
ACT II   Follow Your Heart…Bella, Ladies
         Look Who's Throwing a Party…Aaron, Guests
         When Tomorrow Comes…Maurice
         One Big Happy Family (reprise)…Aaron, Perlman
         Let Us Put Them to the Test…Aaron, Rachel, Kolinsky
         I'm Not Getting Any Younger…Bella and Her Fellas
         Who'd Believe?…Aaron

Licensing: Samuel French

Difficulties/Advantages: Except for the rousing title tune, I don't recall the score at all. This is strange, because I was in the show from first to last. I do recall that the idea was a splendid one. Why more Molière musicals haven't been attempted I don't know. He's a natural. The production was woefully inadequate, either because it should have been a big *Hello, Dolly!* type musical, or a chorusless, more intimate one (but that would have done me out of a job). It fell between the two, underbudgeted, underimagined, and understaged. The cast was wildly talented individually, although Arnold Soboloff, a wonderful character actor, wasn't up to carrying a musical—so few modern men are— and Chris Hewett didn't have as much of an opportunity to display his splendid comedic charisma (so much in evidence in the film *The Producers*, the 1970 Lincoln Center revival of *Trelawney of the Wells,* and his Captain Hook) as he should have. Neva Small earned the role of Chava in the film *Fiddler on the Roof*, then grew up. Gloria LeRoy, an eccentric dancer from burlesque, grew old. Triple threat Cathryn Damon never really got out of Gwen Verdon's shadow, and Michael Berkson, after truly lighting up our stage and that of *Walking Happy,* went back home to civilian life. Eddie Earle waited for more material that never came, but dazzled me with his principal credit: understudy and replacement for Anthony Newley in the original Broadway *Stop the World.* Broadway is about as tough a profession as you could ever imagine. But they, and all the show's troupers, were wonderful, dazzling people, and "in those years we lived our best, and what has come after, and what there is to come, can never carry us to those heights again."

Smoke on the Mountain

A Gospel Comedy Musical
Written by Connie Ray
Conceived by Alan Bailey

A good excuse for a gospel sing.

Time and Place: A Saturday night in June 1938 ("The United States is in the last years of the Great Depression. Organized religion is at its peak"). The sanctuary of the Mount Pleasant Baptist Church in Mount Pleasant, North Carolina, just west of Hickory near the Blue Ridge Mountains.

Synopsis: The Sanders family has been booked this Saturday night by Pastor Oglethorpe, whose car broke down in front of their grocerette and filling station. They return—after a five-year hiatus—to the gospel circuit with a visit to his church, and stir the audience with their witness, sermons, stories, and songs...until the two twins do some dancing, which so upsets two old ladies in the congregation—on whom the Pastor is obviously counting for much financial support—that they leave and faint. The consternation ends act 1.

A few more sequences occur, in which we meet the black sheep of the family (reformed) and Mother (with an odd sermon of her own). The slight romantic attraction between the Pastor and Sister June is a loose plot end never raveled. Not much story means no climax, but it's a tight-knit, solid excuse for gospel singing, and there's nothing more uplifting than that.

Tried out at the McCarter Theatre; then opened off-Broadway at the Lamb's Theatre on May 13, 1990, 11 previews, 452 performances.

Directed by Alan Bailey.

Original Off-Broadway Cast:

Mervin Oglethorpe, Pastor of Mount Pleasant Baptist Church...Kevin Chamberlin
The Sanders Family

Burl, Father...Reathel Bean	Vera, Mother...Linda Kerns
Stanley, Uncle...Dan Manning	Dennis...Robert Olsen
and Denise, Twins...Jane Potter	June, Sister...Connie Ray

Miss Maude and Miss Myrtle, two spinsters, are in the "congregation" (the audience), but it's unlikely two audience members will react with all the indignation of two very conservative Baptist society ladies over some of the goings-on with the humor two actors could inject, so you might want to cast them yourself.

Musical Numbers:

ACT I
The Church in the Wildwood...The Sanders Family
Wonderful Time Up There...Stanley, the Sanders Family
Build on the Rock...The Sanders Family
Meet Mother in the Skies...Stanley, Burl
No Tears in Heaven...Vera, Dennis, the Sanders Family
Christian Cowboy...Dennis, Denise
The Filling Station...Burl, Stanley, the Sanders Family
I'll Never Die, I'll Just Change My Address...Denise
Jesus Is Mine...Pastor Oglethorpe, Burl, Stanley, Dennis
The Blood Medley: Nothing but the Blood, Are You Washed in the Blood?..., There Is Power in the Blood, There Is a Fountain Filled with Blood...The Sanders Family
I'll Live a Million Years...The Sanders Family

ACT II
I Wouldn't Take Nothing for My Journey Now...Vera
Everyone Home but Me...Stanley
I Wouldn't Take Nothing for My Journey Now...The Sanders Family
Angel Band...Denise, the Sanders Family
Bringing in the Sheaves...Pastor Oglethorpe, the Sanders Family
Whispering Hope...Burl, Vera, the Sanders Family

Inching Along…The Sanders Family
I'm Using My Bible for a Road Map…Dennis, the Sanders Family
I'll Walk Every Step of the Way…Burl
I'm Taking a Flight…Vera, Dennis, Denise
Life's Railway to Heaven…The Sanders Family
Smoke on the Mountain…The Sanders Family
I'll Fly Away…The Sanders Family
When the Roll Is Called Up Yonder…The Sanders Family

Licensing: Samuel French

Difficulties/Advantages: The playwright warns that these are real people, not caricatures, but unless your theatre is deep in the Bible Belt, you're going to have to act these parts, however authentically: a family of hillbilly gospel singers. The biggest hurdle: the Sanders family plays their own instruments—piano, guitar, string bass, and percussion. Banjo, fiddle, autoharp, ukulele, and harmonica can be used as available. The set is simple: a poor rural church, with several pews, a pulpit, a couple of chairs, a piano, and two upstage doors. The costumes should be cheap and simple; there's little room for creativity. These people are very poor Southerners, and it's 1938. Unless you've got a handful of true gospel singers with a hankerin' to act, don't attempt this. But if you do, you could raise the roof, with some solid laughter in between the vocals.

And with a success like that, you just knew they'd be back. So if you try *Smoke* and it goes well for you, the next holiday season you can produce the…

Sanders Family Christmas

A Play with Gospel Music
Written by Connie Ray
Conceived by Alan Bailey

Time and Place: 1941. Mount Pleasant Baptist Church in Mount Pleasant, North Carolina.

Synopsis: Pastor Oglethorpe has invited the Sanders Family Gospel Group: Burl; his brother Stanley, who spent a year and a half in jail before becoming a singing star on the radio; his wife Vera (at the piano); his nineteen-year-old twins Dennis and Denise; and June (who can't sing, but signs), in her mid-twenties, to sing and witness at his church. There's a bit about them all being late, due to the snowstorm, and lots of news about the neighborhood (Wilbur Passmore is swollen to twice his size), but basically each family member tells a story (bears witness) and there's a heap of rousing Christmas music. During intermission they go outside to light the tree and manage to put out the fire in the manger scene.

The second act is more of the same, with one exception: Pastor Oglethorpe asks June to marry him. She says yes, and a "Bells" medley closes out the festivities.

Musical Numbers:

ACT I   Good Christian Men, Rejoice…The Sanders Family
Christmas Time's A-Comin'…The Sanders Family
Angels We Have Heard on High…The Sanders Family
A Country Kind of Christmas…The Sanders Family
Cactus Christmas Tree…Dennis, Denise
Merry Christmas Down Home…The Sanders Family

I Wonder as I Wander...Denise
Christmas in the Mountains...Burl, Stanley, Mervyn, Dennis, Vera
Onward Christian Soldiers. . .The Sanders Family
I'm on the Battlefield...The Sanders Family
Keep on the Firing Line...All
Hold Fast to the Right...Vera and Family
Joy to the World...The Sanders Family

ACT II Did You Ever Go A-Sailing...Stanley, Burl, Dennis, Denise
Longing for That Hallelujah Day...The Sanders Family
I've Been Changed...Mervyn, All
Noche de Paz...All
Grandpa's Done Gone Crazy...All
Bring a Torch, Jeanette Isabella...Mervyn, Vera, Denise
Nose to Nose...All
Away in a Manger...The Sanders Family
Bell Medley: Caroling, Caroling; Jingle Bells; Christmas Bells; With Bells On...The Sanders Family
Beautiful Star of Bethlehem...All
Oh Come All Ye Faithful...All
Hark the Herald Angels Sing...All
Go Tell It on the Mountain...All
We Wish You a Merry Christmas...All

Licensing: Samuel French

Difficulties/Advantages: Most difficult requirement: the members of the Sanders Family have to accompany themselves, playing piano, guitar, and string bass, as well as banjo, fiddle, autoharp, ukulele, harmonica, and various percussion instruments as available. According to the script: "The setting should evoke a small Baptist church whose minister is paid so little that he has to take a part-time job at the local pickle plant. The costumes should likewise be appealing but plain." Couldn't be easier than that. Your audience is the "congregation" and should have a spiritually good time. Also: "These characters are not Southern caricatures or religious buffoons, but real people." (The distinction escapes me, but then I've never much appreciated the Southern accent.)

Something's Afoot!

A Murder Mystery Musical

Book, Music, and Lyrics by James McDonald, David Vos, and Robert Gerlach
Additional Music by Ed Linderman

Included here because a cast of ten and a single set make it reasonable for small theatres to produce, *Something's Afoot* actually played Broadway, which was probably a mistake. It's a lightweight musical spoof of English drawing-room whodunit murder mysteries, particularly the classic "And then there were..." plot from Agatha Christie's *Ten Little Indians.* With a splendid cast of English character actors, which it didn't get on Broadway, and a brilliantly rigged set (the Broadway production was an underfinanced regional import), it ought to be quite entertaining. It isn't much of a mystery—anyone with a slight background in Christie will figure it all out by the third song—but it is well written and offers a wonderful opportunity for the kind of committed carica-

Something's Afoot! at the Oregon Cabaret Theatre, Ashland, OR.

tures we haven't seen since the days of Sydney Greenstreet, Peter Lorre, and Margaret Rutherford.

Time and Place: Late spring, 1935. The entrance hall to Rancour's Retreat, the country estate of Lord Dudley Rancour, located on an island in the middle of a lake, somewhere in the English lake district.

Synopsis: No sooner than six guests have arrived, the butler announces that the lake has risen, making the road impassable. He also announces that their host is dead. Then, to make sure suspicion doesn't fall on the butler, he is killed by an exploding staircase, leaving the guests, the maid, and the caretaker to care for themselves. They soon discover that their host has been shot. A young man caught in the storm on the lake takes refuge in the house, and while at first assumed to be the murderer, is not, although he is present when the only telephone whose line isn't cut rings. When the doctor answers it, he is gassed. Several guests turn out to have motives, and everyone sings that they are "Suspicious!" of everyone else. The storm cuts out all the lights, the grand-dame touches a light switch and is electrocuted. Four down and seven to go as the first-act curtain falls.

The nephew, no sooner than he finds a will that cuts him out, is fatally clubbed to death by a trick sconce. Then the colonel dies from a poisoned dart. Miss Tweed solves it all, but is killed before she can announce the identity of the murderer. This leaves the ingénue and the juvenile. They come across a recording explaining that the ingénue is in fact Lord Rancour's adopted daughter and that he, just before committing suicide, booby-trapped the house so there would be no one to contest her inheritance. Unfortunately, she and her young man drink a toast from a poisoned bottle of wine, and then there were none.

Lyceum Theatre; May 27, 1976; 61 performances.

Directed by Tony Tanner.

Original Broadway Cast:

Lettie…Neva Small
Clive…Sel Vitella
Dr. Grayburn…Jack Schmidt
Lady Grace Manley-Prowe…Liz Sheridan
Miss Tweed…Tessie O'Shea

Flint…Marc Jordan
Hope Langdon…Barbara Heuman
Nigel Rancour…Gary Beach
Col. Gillweather…Gary Gage
Geoffrey…Willard Beckham

Musical Numbers (the authors request that the program not list who sings what, presumably because you could then read your program and tell who dies next and who doesn't):

A Marvelous Weekend
Something's Afoot
Carry On
I Don't Know Why I Trust You (But I Do)
The Man with the Ginger Moustache
Suspicious
The Legal Heir
You Fell out of the Sky
Dinghy
I Owe It All
New Day

Licensing: Samuel French

Difficulties/Advantages: Great for community theatre, if you're looking for a musical spoof on English drawing-room mysteries in the Agatha Christie mode. Several hurdles: a (deadly) working set, ten veddy British accents (two Cockney and the rest upper-class). One would love to see a good English Rep. theatre perform this musical.

Song and Dance

Music by Andrew Lloyd Webber
Lyrics by Don Black and Richard Maltby Jr.

From England, where Lloyd Webber wrote a set of variations on Paganini's A Minor Caprice for his brother, a cellist, that proved irresistible as a dance piece. A year later, the prolific Webber wrote a series of songs for a television musical (entitled "Tell Me on a Sunday") about an English woman in New York going through the ups and, often, downs of a series of love affairs. An enterprising producer stuck the two together for a full evening of live West End theatre, where it was very successful. Unfortunately, in America, a number of changes were made that caused the leading character to, in the words of one critic, go from "a deeply ordinary and real heroine," to a "campy kook." An attempt to link the two pieces also muddied the originally pristine waters.

Palace Theatre in London, March 26, 1982, 781 performances (a second season at the Shaftesbury produced another 149 performances); Royale Theatre on Broadway, September 18, 1985, 15 previews, 475 performances.

Directed by Don Black. Choreographed by Peter Martins.

Original Broadway Cast:

Emma…Bernadette Peters
Joe…Christopher d'Amboise

Man from the Streets…Gregg Burge
Woman in Gold…Mary Ellen Stuart

The Women…Charlotte d'Amboise, Denise Faye, Cynthia Onrubia, Mary Ellen Stuart

The Men…Gregg Burge, Gen Horiuchi, Gregory Mitchell, Scott Wise

Customer…Gen Horiuchi

Two Singles…Cynthia Onrubia, Denise Faye

Woman in Grey Flannel…Cynthia Onrubia

Musical Numbers (the leading lady sings all songs in Act I; Act II is all dance):

Take That Look off Your Face
Let Me Finish
It's Not the End of the World
First Letter Home
Sheldom Bloom
Capped Teeth and Caesar Salad
You Made Me Think You Were in Love
Second Letter Home
Unexpected Song
The Last Man in My Life
Come Back with the Same Look in Your Eyes
Lets Talk About You
Tell Me on a Sunday
I Love New York
Married Man
I'm Very You, You're Very Me
Third Letter Home
Nothing Like You've Ever Known

Licensing: Rodgers and Hammerstein Theatre Library

Difficulties/Advantages: If at all possible, go back to the original London version, which will give you either a strong one-act musical to go with some of the others catalogued here or a second act for which your local choreographer can lavish his or her unconfined attention. You'll need a diva to pull off act 1 and a dancer or dancers for act 2, and you'd have to be a serious Lloyd Webber fan to want to do it, but there's loads of room for creativity, possibly this project's only advantage.

Song of Singapore

Book by Allan Katz and Erik Frandsen, Michael Garin, Robert Hipkens, and Paula Lockheart

Music and Lyrics by Erik Fandsen, Michael Garin, Robert Hipkens, and Paula Lockheart

Primarily an excuse for a lot of original swing numbers, the plot—carried out by the actual band members in the original production—is raced through like a Gene Krupa number in this big-band spoof that touches on everything from *Maltese Falcon* and *Casablanca* to various South Sea mellers, with the ambiance of *Seven Sinners* starring Marlene Dietrich.

Time and Place: Early December 1941. Freddy's Son of Singapore Cafe, a nightclub on the Singapore waterfront.

Synopsis: In a smokey dive, a band entertains, a corrupt policeman installs a Shanghai Lil—type to run the place, and a Hindu staggers in with a fish wrapped in newspaper, then dies. Inside the fish are the infamous stolen jewels of Jun Kin Po, which girl-singer Rose of Rangoon promptly runs off with. Fortunately it's intermission, so the blind piano player and other poor musicians can go after her. If that's not a strong enough first-act curtain, we are reminded that the Japanese are about to invade.

Rose returns in act 2, having no idea where she put the jewels in the fish, since her running joke is that she has amnesia. She cooked the fish, but not to worry, she suddenly remembers she is Amelia Earhart. A second Hindu arrives and delivers a jeweled fish. Before the band can take it and fly out of Singapore, even before they can play another forties tune, the local policeman returns. No real gun play, but Chah Li gets the drop on him and runs off with the jewels. The band packs up, says goodbye to Singapore, and Rose/Earhart flies them to Pearl Harbor…on December 6.

Song of Singapore Theatre; May 23, 1991; 459 performances.

Directed by A. J. Antoon. Additional musical staging by Lynne Taylor-Corbett.

Original Cast:

Spike Spauldeen…Erik Frandsen	Freedy S. Lyme…Michael Garin
Hans van der Last…Robert Hipkens	Rose…Donna Murphy
Chah Li…Cathy Foy	Inspector Marvin Kurland et al…Francis Kane
Kenya Ratamacue…Oliver Jackson Jr.	Taqsim Arco…Earl May
Zoot DeFumee…Jon Gordon	T-Bone Kahanamoku…Art Baron

Musical Numbers:

Act I Song of Singapore.. Band
Inexpensive Tango…Spike
I Miss My Home in Haarlem…Hans
You Gotta Do What You Gotta Do…Rose
The Rose of Rangoon…Spike
Necrology…Band
Sunrise…Rose
Never Pay Musicians What They're Worth…Freddy
Harbour of Love…Kurland
I Can't Remember…Rose
I Want to Get offa This Island/Harbour of Love…Band/Kurland

Act II Foolish Geese…Chah Li
Serve It Up…Rose
Fly Away Rose…Hans, Freddy, Spike
I Remember…Rose, Band
Shake, Shake, Shake…Freddy, Band
We're Rich…Band
Sunrise/Song of Singapore…Band

Licensing: Samuel French

Difficulties/Advantages: Another in that incredibly popular genre for off-Broadway musicals, the spoof. The gimmick here is that the band comprises the show's characters, and the whole thing takes place in a nightclub in Singapore in the early 1940s. However, it doesn't matter which characters play which instruments, or even if any of them do, so the casting is entirely up to a local production, and the orchestrations can vary according to availability and ability. It also fits in that wonderful category of environmental theatre, wherein the audience can be part of the set—see also *Diamond Studs* (a Western saloon) and *Smoke on the Mountain* (a church)—this one a Singapore nightclub.

Splendora

Book by Peter Webb
Music by Stephen Hoffman
Lyrics by Mark Campbell
Based on the novel by Edward Swift.

Time and Place: Now. A small town in East Texas.

Synopsis: The town is represented by Sue Ella, Maga Dell, and Zeda Earl (among others who appear more Southern than Texan at times). It dramatizes the plight of Timothy John, a boy who, after being raised as a girl by his grandmother, ran away, and has now returned as "Jessica" at curtain's rise. The simple plot finds Jessica doing the town a lot of good in her position as librarian of the bookmobile and restorer of county-courthouse architecture (something allegorical there but it slipped by me), until the assistant pastor falls in love with her, whereupon she has to admit to being a he. The theatrical gimmick, original if nothing else, is that both he and she are on stage throughout the show, with she interacting throughout act 1 and he stepping up in act 2, the alter ego only visible to the audience (which is certainly confused at first but warms to the idea). When he finds "himself," he thanks his Jessica-self but sends her away, then disappears (as does his suitor, wielding a Bible and mumbling scriptures). If all this sounds rather fanciful, it is, but it worked for most critics and was well received for its Sondheimesque score.

American Place Theater, November 9, 1995; 14 performances.

Directed by Jack Hofsiss. Musical staging by Robert La Fosse.

Original Cast:

Sue Ella Lightfoot…Evalyn Baron	Maga Dell Spivy…K. T. Sullivan
Jessica Gatewood…Nancy Johnston	Timothy John Coldridge…Michael Moore
Brother Leggett…Ken Krugman	Zeda Earl Goodrich…Laura Kenyon
Agnes Pullens…Kathy Robinson	Lucille Monroe…Susan Rush

Musical Numbers:

Act I
In Our Hearts…Maga Dell, Zeda Earl, A. P., Lucille, Sue Ella
How Like Heaven…Jessica, Timothy John
Don't Get Me Started…Sue Ella
Pretty Boy…Lucille, Zeda Earl, A. P.
Home/Say Goodnight…Timothy John, Jessica
Gossip 1: "Poor Sad Thing. . ."…Lucille, Zeda Earl, A. P.
With Her…Timothy John
Gossip 2: "Up at Dawn. . ."…Lucille, Zeda Earl, A. P.
In Small and Simple Ways…Brother Leggett
Gossip 3: "Warms My Soul. . ."…Lucille, Zeda Earl, A. P., Maga Dell
Dear Heart…Jessica, Brother Leggett
How Little I Know…Jessica
Had He Kissed Me Tonight…Jessica
If He Knew…Timothy John

	Good Hearts, Rejoice…Maga Dell, Zeda Earl, A. P., Lucille

Good Hearts, Rejoice…Maga Dell, Zeda Earl, A. P., Lucille
What Is, Ain't…Sue Ella
Promise Me One Thing…Jessica, Brother Leggett, Timothy John

ACT II
Love Crawls In…Timothy John, Jessica
I Got Faith in You…Sue Ella, Timothy John
All The Time in the World…Timothy John, Jessica, Brother Leggett
A Man Named Dewey…Maga Dell
I Am Beauty…A. P.
Don't Get Me Started (reprise)…Sue Ella
Miss Crepe Myrtle…Zeda Earl, A. P., Lucille, Maga Dell
Grateful…Timothy John
Finale: My Name Is Timothy John…Timothy John, Zeda Earl, A. P., Lucille, Maga Dell
In Our Hearts (reprise)…Maga Dell, Zeda Earl, A. P., Lucille, Sue Ella

Licensing: Dramatists Play Service

Difficulties/Advantages: This gender-bender musical has six rich roles for women and two for men, with a wide variety of songs and plenty of design opportunities where creativity would count more than spectacle. The transsexual nature of the plot isn't for every community, but it's done with taste and humor.

Spokesong

Or, The Common Wheel

By Stewart Parker
Music by Jimmy Kennedy
Lyrics by Stewart Parker

Really, a play with music.

Time and Place: The early 1970s, with flashbacks to the 80 years preceding. Belfast, Northern Ireland.

Synopsis: The Protestants and the Catholics are at war, as are the IRA and the British, and the town's a rubble of hatred and bombings. In the midst of this, a man who has grown up in a bicycle shop and now runs it (a losing proposition) falls in love with a woman. To say that Boy Loses Girl, then Boy Gets Girl, understates this powerful play. Boy almost loses girl to his brother, a younger man who returns home after five years in London and is going to sell the shop, which he owns. Fed up with Belfast, the woman almost goes back to London with him. At the last, however—and after she blackmails her own father over his leadership of the local extortionist/terrorists and figures out that the brother is working for them—she moves into the shop to help carry on the bicycle business. All in all, it's the sometimes funny, sometimes sad struggle of the peacefully inclined to live among so much inherited hatred, with the bicycle vs. the automobile (as if the bombings weren't enough, there's a freeway coming through the shop soon), a neat metaphor for the effects of progress.

First presented in 1975 at the Dublin Theatre Festival; American premiere at Long Wharf Theatre, New Haven, Connecticut, February 2, 1978; Broadway premiere: Circle in the Square Theater, March 15, 1979.

Directed by Ken Frankel.

Original American Cast:

The Trick Cyclist...Joseph Maher	Frank...John Lithgow
Daisy...Virginia Vestoff	Francis...Jose Summer
Kitty...Maria Tucci	Julian...John Horton

Musical Numbers:

Act I Daisy Bell
Beautiful Daisy Bell
The Parlour Song
Cocktail Song
Cowboy Song
Act II Music Hall Song
Spokesong
Army Song
Spinning Song
Army Song (reprise)
The Anthem
Daisy Bell

Licensing: Samuel French

Difficulties/Advantages: Irish accents? Learning to ride a unicycle? Singing? That's nothing for thespians. But this isn't really a musical, and the numbers are more commentary than drama. In fact, if no one can sing, you could perform the play without them. It wouldn't be as theatrical, but it would be every bit as powerful.

Starblast

Book and Lyrics by Barry Harman
Music by Grant Sturiale

A children's musical, strictly for elementary and middle school audiences, although these days I'd say that middle schoolers are more into Chris Rock movies. Nevertheless, Barry Harman (author of the little musicals *Romance/Romance* and *Olympus on My Mind*) and composer Grant Sturiale have concocted a swift hour of fun for the little ones, with strong messages of self-confidence, all relating to the computer games they're all playing.

Time and Place: The future. Another planet.

Synopsis: When P-T-III, an intergalactic space traveler, lands on a distant planet, its inhabitants give him only one hour to clear off or fight them. A broken spaceship keeps him grounded, so he wanders around the planet, seeking help. In a reverse on Dorothy's three friends in Oz, three aliens he comes across give him plenty of advice, but each disappears when he asks for help. Time's up, and he battles them with a giant joy stick—and wins, only to discover that there are more and more levels. How many? As many as it takes for them to vanquish him. Fortunately, Peter wakes up from his dream about now, just in time for our audience to learn a lesson in his final song: "I Can Dream."

Lehman College, The Bronx; December, 1983.

Directed by Barry Harman. Choreographed by Michael Lichtefeld.

Musical Numbers:

> Overture
> Use Your Imagination…The Players
> Where in the Universe Am I?…P-T-III and Figments of His Imagination
> Keep Yourself Together…Elwood, P-T-III
> Elwood's Exit…Elwood
> Reach for the Stars…Allura, P-T-III
> Be Logical/Go with the Flow…Beep/Blip
> You're Not Alone…Vitalis and Space Greasers
> Call on Your Friends…Vitalis, P-T-III, Greasers
> Where in the Universe Am I? (reprise)…P-T-III
> Hallelujahs…Gospelettes
> Look to Your Inner Space…Mother Space, Gospelettes
> Starblasters—Level One…Starblasters
> Starblasters—Level Two…Starblasters
> Starblasters—Level Three…Starblasters
> I Can Dream…P-T-III
> Use Your Imagination…Full Company
> Sing Me a Holiday Song…Full Company (optional for holiday version)

Licensing: Samuel French

Difficulties/Advantages: Three men and two women can do it all, usually in a minivan and station-wagon tour of elementary schools, but if you want to get all the kids involved, as many as several dozen can be employed in various roles, as well as a chorus of "Starblasters, Gospelettes, Greasers and Figments."

Starmites

Book by Stuart Ross and Barry Keating
Music and Lyrics by Barry Keating

Another attempt to bring pulp fiction—in this case science-fiction comic books—to the musical stage, with tongue firmly in cheek. Nine years of workshops, regional theatre productions, and backer's auditions finally brought the show to Broadway, but it was probably best in its original incarnation at the tiny Ark Theatre and should have learned its lesson from *Little Shop of Horrors,* which, in spite of its huge success, never ventured uptown but chose to remain off-Broadway, where camp belongs. While not in a class with *The Rocky Horror Show* (even when mimicking "Time Warp" with its own second-act dance, "The Cruelty Stomp")—particularly because the lyrics are too often mundane—this space-rock musical boasts at least a bit of feminism, as the leading role is a teenage girl with no self-esteem who becomes a superhero. The trouble with camp, however, is that it is too often confused with gay, and the wonderful role of Diva, the kind of amazon women who in comic book illustrations could schwing the imagination of any teenage boy, was played on Broadway as a butch lesbian.

Time and Place: Now. Earth and Innerspace (a parallel universe).

Synopsis: Eleanor is a young teen misfit who is into comic books. Literally. She becomes Milady, the Earth Girl who can save the Starmites from the villainous Shak Graa, provided she can obtain the Cruelty from Diva. (That's some sort of space-age musical instrument—in varying productions an electric guitar and French horn.) Diva wants to marry her daughter off to Space Punk, who really loves Milady but agrees because otherwise Diva's Banshees will destroy the Starmites, his cohorts and backup doo-wop singers. Space Punk has his principals, however, so Diva uses her Chamber of Psychosorcery to place her daughter's spirit in Milady's body (giving the female lead a third role). Before the marriage can take place, Trinkulus, until now a lowly, lisping minstrel, reveals himself to be the real Shak Graa and takes Bizarbara, thinking she's Milady, to his sacrificial pit. When it is revealed that the wrong sacrifice will destroy his power, the heroic Eleanor/Bizarbara throws herself in, while the Eleanor/Milady (quick costume changes here) battles Shak and wins. But Orgala—some sort of force we haven't heard much from—informs Diva that Milady is her real daughter, and they are reunited, as are Eleanor and her mother (also played by the Diva actress) in a world in which comic books reign supremo.

Criterion Center Stage Right; April 27, 1989; 60 performances.

Directed and staged by Larry Carpenter. Choreographed by Michele Asaf.

Original Cast:

On Earth:
    Eleanor...Liz Larsen
    Mother...Sharon McNight
Innerspace:
    Shak Graa...Ariel Grabber
    Spacepunk...Brian Lane Green
    Trinkulus...Gabriel Barre
Starmites:
    Ack Ack Ackeman...Bennett Cale
    Herbie Harrison...Victor Trent Cook
    Dazzle Razzledorf...Christopher Zelno
Diva...Sharon McNight
Bizarbara...Liz Lasen
Banshees:
    Shotzi.. Mary Kate Law
    Canibelle...Gwen Stewart
    Balbraka...Freida Williams
    Maligna...Janet Aldrich
Droids...John-Michael Flate, Ric Ryder

Musical Numbers:

PROLOGUE Prelude/Prologue...Shak Graa, Eleanor, Punk, Starmites
            Superhero Girl...Eleanor
ACT I   Starmites...Starmites, Punk
            Trink's Narration...Trinkulus, Starmites
            Afraid of the Dark...Starmites, Punk, Eleanor, Trink
            Little Hero...Eleanor, Starmites
            Attack of the Banshees...Banshees
            The Cruelty...Trinkulus
            Hard to Be Diva...Diva, Banshees
            Love Duet...Punk, Eleanor

Love Duet (reprise)…Eleanor
The Dance of Spousal Arousal…Balbraka, Bizarbara, Banshees
Finaletto…Company

ACT II   Bizarbara's Wedding…Bizarbara, Banshees
Milady…Punk, Starmites
Beauty Within…Diva, Bizarbara
The Cruelty Stomp…Trink, Company
Reach Right Down…Starmites, Diva, Banshees, Eleanor
Immolation.. Punk, Eleanor, Shak Graa, Starmites
Starmites/Diva (reprise)…Diva, Banshees, Starmites
Epilogue
Finale…Company

Licensing: Samuel French

Difficulties/Advantages: Could have been a hoot and a holler for Trekkies and Wookies, but finally it's a poor man's *Rocky Horror Show.*

Stop the World—I Want to Get Off

Book, Music, and Lyrics by Anthony Newley and Leslie Bricusse

A concept/allegorical musical from England, before *Company* but after *Allegro.* If a little familiar now, it was au courant and astonishing at the time, set in a circus arena, all the characters as clowns, Littlechap in whiteface, a chorus of young girls (with one woman playing four), and an oboe standing in for Littlechap's father-in-law. Subtitled a "new style" musical, it was indeed a successful version of the very concept that Rodgers and Hammerstein had unsuccessfully attempted with *Allegro,* an allegorical story of Everyman from birth to death. With spectacle becoming the most valuable commodity in Broadway entertainments these days, we're not going to see many more one-set musicals, but one can see here—and in *A Chorus Line,* possibly the last of the one-set musicals—just how entertaining book, music, and lyrics alone can be.

Time and Place: It doesn't really matter.

Synopsis: Anthony Newley, already a child star in English films, played Littlechap—who marries the boss's daughter, is "lumbered" with kids, and generally acts like a heel as he rises to the top of business, becomes a member of Parliament, then regrets much of his life ("I was only ever in love with one person in my life—and that was me!") in one of the most recorded songs of all time, "What Kind of Fool Am I?"

Shubert Theater; October 3, 1962; 555 performances.

Original Cast:

Littlechap…Anthony Newley   Evie, Anya, Ilse, Ginny…Anna Quayle
Jane…Jennifer Baker   Susan…Susan Baker

Musical Numbers:

ACT I   The A.B.C. Song…Chorus
I Wanna Be Rich…Littlechap, Chorus
Typically English…Evie, Littlechap
A Special Announcement…Chorus

Lumbered…Littlechap
Glorious Russian…Anya
Meilinki Meilchick. . .Littlechap, Anya, Chorus
Gonna Build a Mountain…Littlechap, Chorus
Typische Deutsche…Ilse, Chorus
Family Fugue…Littlechap, Evie, Susan, Jane
Nag! Nag! Nag!…Littlechap, Evie, Susan, Jane, Chorus

ACT II All American…Ginnie
Once in a Lifetime…Littlechap, Girl
Mumbo Jumbo…Littlechap, Chorus
Welcome to Sunvale…Chorus
Someone Nice Like You…Littlechap, Evie
What Kind of Fool Am I?…Littlechap

Licensing: Tams-Witmark

Difficulties/Advantages: Requires an astonishingly talented leading man and a very versatile leading lady—unless you use four different actresses for the women in his life—but the chorus can be great fun, and the theatrical nature offers endlessly creative staging possibilities that could enhance (or destroy, as when Sammy Davis Jr. starred in the worst revival of a musical ever) this gem of a musical. Traditionally it's been set in a kind of circus arena, but there's an enormous opportunity for creativity, so long as you don't overshadow the story or performances.

They're Playing Our Song

Book by Neil Simon
Music by Marvin Hamlisch
Lyrics by Carole Bayer Sager

Though not officially an off-Broadway musical—it opened and ran successfully on Broadway—this is an ideal "little" musical, for it can (and should) be done with only two characters. In fact, it really ought to be considered a play with music, first because the first act has only six tunes and the second only three; second because there's not much plot-driving to the score, the songs mostly inner-monologue love songs, although the title tune is one of musical theatre's most joyous. *Song* is Hamlisch's first musical after *A Chorus Line*, and smarting from some stupid critics' misunderstanding that that score didn't boast enough hummable melodies (it boasted something much better, a powerful dramatic skein), here he took the opportunity to write popular hits, and most of them are. Original performances by Broadway musical newcomers child-of-the-fifties comedian Robert Klein and daughter-of-TV-royalty Lucie Arnaz were spontaneous and ingratiating, if firmly in the category of nonsinging actors. Neil Simon's multi-laughs book and the charming pop songs of Hamlisch and Sager carried this two-character musical into the hearts of New Yorkers, even if they didn't coexist with each other all that easily. (There's also a chorus of three boys and three girls, about which more below, but they had nothing to contribute as they stumbled through inane staging, popping up from behind couches and refrigerators and rearranging the furniture.) *Song* is actually the true love story of its composer and lyricist as told by Neil Simon (whose three other Broadway librettos—*Little Me*, *Sweet Charity*, and *Promises, Promises*—make up a quartet of the funniest musical books ever written, neck and neck with *A Funny Thing Happened on the Way to the Forum* by Larry Gelbart and *How to*

Succeed in Business Without Really Trying by Abe Burrows, Willie Gilbert, and Jack Weinstock). If love stories were all as zippy and witty as Simon's, the divorce rate would be lower.

Time and Place: Today. In and around New York.

Synopsis: Vernon is an Oscar- and Grammy-winning composer, and Sonia is a starving lyricist with one hit behind her. Introduced by their agent to write some songs, they become attracted to each other. (It's too cosmopolitan to be called "love," although there's plenty of that in the song lyrics, but "romance" will do.) They head for a weekend bungalow in Quogue, she fighting off an attachment to an ex-boyfriend, all nervous energy and quirky clothes, he all arrogance covering a lack of self-confidence. After mild frustrations and Neil Simon jokes, they consummate the relationship. (Sorry, that's during intermission.)

Act 2 begins back in the city. She moves in. Flash-forward past days and nights of songwriting, and things aren't going so well. We never quite know why, but they break up in the middle of making a demo. He goes to California, gets hit by a car. She wistfully visits him in the hospital, he wistfully visits her back in New York, and they decide to try again. Hugs and curtain.

Imperial Theatre; February 11, 1979; 1,082 performances.

Directed by Robert Moore. Musical numbers staged by Patricia Birch.

Original Cast:

Vernon Gersch...Robert Klein	Sonia Walsk...Lucie Arnaz

Voices of Vernon Gersch...Wayne Mattson, Andy Roth, Greg Zadikov
Voices of Sonia Walsk...Helen Catillo, Celia Celnik Matthau, Debbie Shapiro

Musical Numbers:

ACT I
Fallin'...Vernon
Workin' It Out...Vernon, Sonia
If He/She Really Knew Me.. Sonia, Vernon
They're Playing Our Song...Vernon, Sonia
If She/He Really Knew Me (reprise)...Vernon, Sonia
Right...Sonia, Vernon
Just for Tonight...Sonia

ACT II
When You're in My Arms...Vernon, Sonia
I Still Believe in Love...Sonia
Fill in the Words...Vernon

Licensing: Samuel French

Difficulties/Advantages: The first thing future productions should do is dump that insipid chorus. That leaves two good roles with the juicy, flowing dialogue of Neil Simon, a comedy style that is never dated, as long as it's not played for laughs. A few simple sets make it ideal for a small theatre. If the actors can sing pop music well, all the better. If they can't, well, neither could the Broadway stars.

The Thing About Men

A Musical Comedy Affair

Book and Lyrics by Joe DiPietro
Music by Jimmy Roberts

Based on the screenplay *Men* by Doris Dörrie.

A sharply funny farce that took the foreign film market by storm when the original film arrived decades ago, and is every bit as entertaining now as an off-Broadway musical, with a good helping of that most difficult of song forms: comic.

Time and Place: Contemporary. New York.

Synopsis: Tom is a man among men: suit and tie, four-bedroom suburban house, commute to advertising office, Porsche, wife and two kids, veteran of fifteen-year marriage and several affairs. Now his wife Lucy is having an affair, and the double standard appalls him. He moves out. He secretly follows her to spot her lover, whose roommate has just vacated the premises. Tom moves in with Sebastian, the starving artist his wife is having an affair with. Of course he doesn't tell Sebastian he's the husband. (Priest: "So let me get this straight—you're an adulterer who's moved in with his unfaithful wife's nonmonogamous lover.") Finale act 1: Lucy is coming for brunch, to see, for the first time, her lover's bohemian slum-loft, and to meet his roommate!

When Lucy arrives, Tom has gotten into a gorilla suit, complete with mask, so his identity is not discovered. (Don't ask. It works.) He decides to get Sebastian to fall in love with someone besides his wife and introduces him to Cindi, a model. They kiss, but Sebastian doesn't feel the excitement. This tells him that he really loves Lucy, and he proposes. Tom admits to himself that the better man won and decides that if Sebastian is going to marry his soon-to-be-ex wife, he should have a steady job, and coaches Sebastian to stop painting from his own style and do advertising. Tom arranges an interview, and Sebastian gets a job. The affair, however—under the pressure of Sebastian's rising star as a Competent Male—cools off. Finally the three of them run into each other and all is revealed. Everyone has grown, and Tom and Lucy will try again.

Promenade Theatre; August 27, 2003–February 15, 2004.

Directed by Mark Clements. Musical staging by Rob Ashford.

Original Cast:

Tom…Mark Kudisch
Lucy…Leah Hocking
Sebastian…Ron Bohmer
One "Man" played multiple roles: Darryl, Tom's Assistant; Manuel, a Taxi Driver; a Grunge Teenager; a Bartender; a Priest; Bernard, a Maitre D'; Lance, a Waiter; Another Bartender; a Sushi Deliveryman; a Stylist; and others…Daniel Reichard
One "Woman" played multiple roles: Jessica (Tom's colleague with whom he's having an affair); a Mother; Okasana (Sebastian's roommate); a Bar Fly; Edith, Sebastian's Neighbor; Janice, a Gym Employee; Cindy, a Model; Juke Box Singer; a Sushi Deliverywoman; a Stylist; Vivian, a Secretary…Jennifer Simard

Musical Numbers:

ACT I   Oh, What a Man...Man, Woman, Lucy, Tom
               No Competition for Me...Manuel and Tom, Sebastian
               Opportunity Knocking.. Tom
               Free, Easy Guy...Sebastian
               Take Me into You...Sebastian, Lucy
               Because...Lucy
               No Competition (reprise)...Tom
               The Confession...Priest
               The Greatest Friend/Downtown Bohemian Slum...Sebastian, Tom, Lucy

ACT II   Restaurant Sequence...Maitre' D, Sebastian, Cindy, Waiter
               Take Me into You (reprise)...Lucy
               Highway of Your Heart...Woman
               The Better Man Won...Tom
               The Road to Lucy...Tom, Sebastian
               Make Me a Promise/New Beautiful Man...Young Lucy, Tom, Sebastian, Woman Stylist, Man Stylist
               What Men Will Do for Love...Tom
               Time to Go Home...Tom
               Because (reprise)/Back at the Office...Tom, Lucy

FINALE ACT II...Company

Licensing: Rodgers and Hammerstein Theatre Library

Difficulties/Advantages: Requires strong singers/actors to pull this off, but worth it. A man and a woman play a number of juicy roles, so you can cast more than the minimum five if you like. Several places—their house, his loft, a bar, the street, a restaurant—are evoked, but you can't slow down for set changes. It's very cinematic, so come up with a unit concept.

Three Guys Naked from the Waist Down

Book and Lyrics by Jerry Colker
Music by Michael Rupert

The three original actors managed a break-neck pace of kamikaze comedy about as funny as the Monkees. And frankly, stories of stand-up comics who want to be the next Seinfeld and then complain about success don't play to much sympathy among people who would gladly sell out but don't get an offer. Still, a projection-filled production runs smoothly, and the roles are plums for comic actors.

Time and Place: Today. In show business.

Synopsis: Three stand-up comics team up, get a shot on Carson, succeed, sign with the William Morris office, get a TV series (*Hello, Fellas,* a.k.a. *Killer Cops in Drag*) that makes them famous, go on a world tour (in drag), and make a feature film that bombs. Given all that success, naturally they feel that they've sold out, and they self-destruct. One commits suicide, a second returns to his roots as a comedy club emcee, and the third gets his own TV show.

Minetta Lane Theatre; February 5, 1985; 20 previews, 160 performances.

Directed by Andrew Cardiff. Choreographed by Don Bondi.

Original Cast:

Ted Klausterman...Scott Bakula   Kenny Brewster...John Kassir
Phil Kunin...Jerry Colker

Musical Numbers:

ACT I   Promise of Greatness...Ted
         Angry Guy/Lovely Day...Phil
         Don't Wanna Be No Superstar I...Ted, Phil
         Operator...Kenny
         Screaming Clocks (The Dummies Song)...Ted, Phil, Kenny, Mr. Dirtball, Spike, Steve
         Don't Wanna Be No Superstar II...Ted, Phil, Kenny
         The History of Stand-Up Comedy...Ted, Phil, Kenny
         Dreams of Heaven...Kenny
         Don't Wanna Be No Superstar III...Ted, Phil, Kenny
ACT II   The American Dream...Ted, Phil, Kenny
         What a Ride I...Ted Phil, Kenny
         "Hello, Fellas" Theme...Ted, Phil, Kenny
         "Hello Fellas" TV Special World Tour...Ted, Phil, Kenny
         What a Ride II...Ted, Phil, Kenny
         What a Ride III...Ted, Phil, Kenny
         "Three Guys Naked from the Waist Down" Theme...Ted, Phil, Kenny
         I Don't Believe in Heroes Anymore...Ted

Licensing: Samuel French

Difficulties/Advantages: The film *Airplane* reestablished from vaudeville the idea that comedy, when delivered in huge quantities at a breakneck pace, need only score on one out of three jokes, and you've got 'em. A local version of this show can work. On the other hand, does anyone really want to see another I-sold-out-and-now-success-is-a-bitch story?

The Threepenny Opera

Book and Lyrics by Bertolt Brecht
Music by Kurt Weill
English Adaptation of Book and Lyrics by Marc Blitzstein
Based on John Gay's *The Beggar's Opera.*

Stuart Little, in his book on the history of off-Broadway, writes: "Not before or since has Brecht succeeded in New York on any large scale. Broadway theatres such as the Martin Beck and the Lunt-Fontane, where a *Mother Courage* and an *Arturo Ui* later played, seemed inappropriately commodious and elegant, as if a Gothic cathedral were sheltering a congregation of revivalists. Brecht in New York has been more successful in miniature." The Theater de Lys, then, was an ideal venue in which to introduce this seminal musical, which was revived in 1954 off-Broadway after a Broadway production in 1933 that failed. Though forced to close due to a prior booking of the de Lys, thereafter, Brooks Atkinson appended a line at the end of all his reviews of other Theatre de Lys shows: "Bring back *The Threepenny Opera.*" The producers finally did, on September 20, 1955, and it had the longest run of any musical in the history of the

The Threepenny Opera at the Williamstown Theatre Festival, Berkshires, MA.

American theatre to that time.

The first and most famous of the Bertolt Brecht/Kurt Weill musicals, staged in 1928 in Berlin during the heyday of the Weimar Republic cultural explosion (and in the shadow of the rising Nazi tide), premiered in Berlin in 1928 at the Theater am Schiffbauerdamm. *Threepenny Opera* is influenced both by Brecht's growing interest in Karl Marx's communism and Piscatur's "epic" theatre style. Weill meanwhile—they had met only a year earlier when Weill had given a Brecht play a good review, and together become interested in opera—was known as a coming young modern composer: jazzy, dissonant, and contrapuntal. Their first collaboration was the "songspiel" known as *The Little Mahagonny*, performed during a boxing match in Baden-Baden during 1927.

In March of 1928, a young actor named Ernst-Josef Aufricht leased the Theater am Schiffbauerdamm and cast around for plays. Approaching Brecht, he committed to a new translation of John Gay's 1728 *The Beggar's Opera*, the first integration of songs (mostly existing popular folk ballads of the early eighteenth century) and dialogue to establish the form one day to be known as musical comedy. Brecht began a German translation but brought Weill in to write modern melodies. In a process not unlike today's workshop approach to musicals, Brecht began with a number of the original songs but gradually replaced them all, inserting his own lyrics and some additional scenes that do not appear in *The Beggar's Opera*. Brecht wrote the finale and the "Ballad of Mack the Knife" during rehearsals.

Following Murphy's Law (Murphy being a stage manager) that anything that can go wrong, will, the lead, Carola Neher, dropped out, and her replacement had to learn the role in four days. Helene Weigel contracted appendicitis and her part—that of a brothel Madame—had to be cut. The actress playing Mrs. Peachum, Rosa Valetti, had moral objections to the "Song of Sexual Obsession" and forced that to be cut as well. The actress playing Lucy had her solo eliminated when she couldn't handle it, Lotte Lenya's billing was left out of the program, and the first performance was forty-five minutes too long. Nevertheless, opening night turned out to be the greatest theatrical triumph of the period.

Probably what makes the musical so successful with wide audiences is that it was written during a period in which Brecht was only beginning to study Marxist ideas, and it isn't as polemical or didactic as his later writing. Its success was due more to the fact that it practically created a new theatrical genre, spoofing Wagnerian opera on the one hand and utilizing the integration of songs in a play on the other, that hadn't yet been seen. Weill's wonderful, if dissonant, melodies ensured dazzled audiences. Only secondary was the attack on society's morals and thus its appeal to an audience beyond the elite upper class. Subsequent English translations were very effective, because Brecht and Weill had set the play not in Germany but in:

Time and Place: 1837, at the beginning of Queen Victoria's reign. Soho, England.

Synopsis: There, Peachum controls the city's beggars, Macheath is the Don of London's gang of criminals, and Tiger Brown is a corrupt police officer. As for the women, Peachum's daughter Polly elopes with Macheath, Tiger's daughter Lucy is pregnant by him, and Low-Dive Jenny and Suky Tawdry are whores with whom Macheath cavorts weekly. The whores are bribed by Peachum to turn Macheath in (well, if it was your daughter, wouldn't you?), and he goes to jail. Polly takes over Mac's business. He soon escapes, however, but Tiger Brown ends up in a moral dilemma: arresting him again, Brown will lose a good chunk of his bribes, but if he doesn't, Peachum promises to get all his beggars to disrupt the coronation of the Queen, which is scheduled to take place the next day. Though Polly and Lucy commiserate that they have both been stood up and don't know where Mac is, Mrs. Peachum discovers that he is shacked up with Suky Tawdry and insists that he be arrested again. He is, and his hanging is scheduled for six a.m. the next morning, nearly simultaneous with the coronation. At that time, the cast assembles around Mac's jail cell for a finale, Mac's men unable to raise the money for a bribe. About to die, Mac's last speech is Brecht's (still relevant) theme that all the small-time crooks are being put out of business by the larger, equally crooked corporations. This, however, being a musical comedy—and Brecht's theatrical style allowing for plenty of address to the audience—Peachum announces that we will in fact have a happy ending. In a deus ex machina, a special order arrives from the Queen, pardoning Macheath and awarding him a knighthood.

World premiere: Berlin, 1928; Broadway: April 4, 1933, 12 performances; off-Broadway: Theatre de Lys, March 10, 1954, 2,705 performances.

Off-Broadway production directed by Carmen Capalbo.

Off-Broadway Cast:

Streetsinger…Jerry Orbach	Jenny…Christiane Felsmann
Mr. J. J. Peachum…Emile Renan	Filch…William Duell
Macheath…Gerald Price	Polly Peachum…Cynthia Price
Readymoney Matt…Stan Schneider	Crookfinger Jake…Maurice Shrog
Bob the Saw…Joseph Mascolo	Walt Dreary…Noam Pitlik
Reverend Kimball…Carroll Saint	Tiger Brown…Alfred Spindelman
Betty…Mary Harmon	Molly…Marion Sele
Dolly…Nona Chandler	Coaxer…Betinna Barrett

Smith...Rome Smith   Lucy Brown...Ann Mitchell
1st Constable...Len Ross   2nd Constable...Noam Pitlik
Messenger...William Duell

Musical Numbers (titles tend to change from translation to translation; these are from the Manheim/Willett version):

Prologue: Ballad of Mack the Knife...Streetsinger

ACT I
Morning Anthem...Peachum
The "No They Can't" Song...Peachum, Mrs. Peachum
Wedding Song...Macheath's Men
Pirate Jenny...Polly
Army Song...Macheath's Men
Love Song...Macheath, Polly
Barbara Song...Polly
First Threepenny Finale—The World Is Mean...Polly, Peachum, Mrs. Peachum

ACT II
The Ballad of Sexual Obsession...Mrs. Peachum
Polly's Song...Polly Peachum
Ballad of Immoral Earnings...Macheath
Ballad of Good Living...Macheath
Jealousy Duet...Lucy, Polly
Second Threepenny Finale—How to Survive...Macheath, Jenny

ACT III
Ballad of Sexual Obsession (reprise)...Mrs. Peachum
Song of the Insufficiency of Human Endeavor...Peachum
Solomon Song...Jenny
Call from the Grave...Macheath
Ballad of Forgiveness...Macheath
Third Threepenny Finale...Mounted Messenger, Company

Licensing: Requires permission from Bertha Case, 42 West 53rd Street, New York, New York 10019. Also, check the translation you wish to use. The Rodgers and Hammerstein Theatre Library reps the well-known Marc Blitzstein translation. Eric Bentley is a respected Brecht scholar, and the Manheim/Willett translation, commissioned by Joe Papp, restores some of the nastier bits that were cleaned up for the sensibilities of American audiences in the 1930s.

Difficulties/Advantages: The Catch-22 of *Threepenny Opera* is that while Stuart Little's assessment is quite accurate, and the show is at its most effective in an intimate setting, its cast of eleven large and several small roles, a chorus, and jazz-band orchestrations make it hard to produce in anything less than at least a medium-size theatre. Thus, while Broadway revivals have all suffered the fate of the original, small theatres have avoided producing it. Probably the original Theatre de Lys production, operating under contemporary union salaries, would lose money today even while selling out. Only colleges seem to be able to bridge the gap.

The material appeals to them as well. The old adage "Honor among thieves" is well-disproved here, and the thieves are clearly not the only class of society to which Brecht is referring. Lots of pro-proletariat, agit-prop productions flourish where young directors are happy to skewer the establishment. And that's a good thing, because Weill's score is one of the great treasures of the musical theatre and shouldn't be lost. The broad satire lends itself to almost any imaginative setting, from the past to the future, and any design elements, from symbolic to realistic. Too often, however, productions follow the design style of the Broadway musical *Cabaret*—girls in torn stockings and garter belts spreading their legs to sing—fixing their concept on the sex and sleaze of Berlin in the twenties, when, although *Cabaret* takes place there and then, Brecht and Weill, *writing* then, in fact set their piece in a time and place cultures apart: England's Victorian docks and dives.

Touch

A Country Rock Musical

Book by Kenn Long in Collaboration with Amy Saltz
Lyrics by Kenn Long
Music by Kenn Long and Jim Crozier

The Plowright Players, a sixties commune using a barn as a theatre (someone's Dad's?), developed this piece and brought it to the big city. Their storyline: a number of young people come to the big, neon-lit city out of restlessness, but there find the usual difficulties of earning a living and retreat to the country, where—in act 2—they form a commune. This attracts the attention of the locals, who have no sympathy for this organic farming, hippie tribe, and conflict results. One of them is beaten up and their garden is destroyed. Peace and love prevail, however, as the group decides not to retaliate but to spread their message of a new beginning for all mankind.

Village Arena Theatre; November 8, 1970; 422 performances.

Directed by Amy Saltz.

Original Cast:

Awol...Norman Jacob
Wyan...Kenn Long
Roland...Gerard S. Doff
Patti...Susan Rosenblum
Alex...Dwight Jayne

Guiness...Barbara Ellis
Melissa...Phylis Gibbs
Mark...Peter J. Mitchell
Susan April...Ava Rosenblum

Musical Numbers:

ACT I   Declaration
Windchild (Music and lyrics by Gary Graham)
Cities of Light
Sitting in the Park
I Don't Care
Goodbyes
Come to the Road
Reaching, Touching

ACT II   Quiet Country
Guiness Woman
Susan's Song
Maxine!
Tripping
Garden Song
Watching
The Hasseltown Memorial Squaredance
Confrontation Song
Alphagenesis

154

Licensing: Unknown

Difficulties/Advantages: In the sixties, a number of touchy-feely musicals attempted to bring the message of tune in/turn on/drop out into dramatic form. It worked with *Hair* and *Your Own Thing.* This one would be long forgotten, except that a cast album was left behind.

Trixie True, Teen Detective

Book, Music, and Lyrics by Kelly Hamilton

An attempt to spoof the teen detective fiction of the 1940s—let's call it the off-Broadway side of *City of Lights.*

Time and Place: The mid-1940s. The New York offices of Snood Publishing and the mythical town of Cherry Hill, New Jersey.

Synopsis: Trixie is a Nancy Drew type, as typed by a hard-drinking writer stuck in the offices of Snood Publishing. He'd rather be authoring the great American novel. His story: In Cherry Hill, New Jersey, the versatile True captures criminals, bakes a cake, and is preparing a tap routine for tonight's broadcast. Miss Olga, however, who is teaching her the terpsichore, is a spy, and the taps are going to sound out the secret formula from the Cherry Hill Weapons Plant. Trixie would catch on, of course, except that by the end of act 1, the writer, not getting along with his hard-driving, snood-wearing publisher, has decided to make this the case that Trixie can't solve and put her in a situation that is going to make this the last case she ever works on, and thus the last Trixie True book he has to write.

Bound and gagged in a submarine and headed for the bottom with explosive tap shoes (really), Trixie True would indeed fail her last case if back at the Snood publishing company, writer Joe Sneed didn't suddenly unlock the long dark tresses under the snood and the hidden romantic side of Miss Snood—now Rita from Argentina to him—and when she offers him the chance to take over the company, he hurriedly types up a final chapter in which Trixie, using her tap shoes of course, is saved by her fiancé Dick, who happens to be passing by with the Coast Guard, and all is well.

Theatre de Lys; December 7, 1980; 94 performances.

Directed by Bill Gile. Musical staging by Arthur Faria.

Cast

Joe…Gene Lindsey	Al…Jay Lowman
Miss Snood…Marilyn Sokol	Trixie True…Kathy Andrini
Dick Dickerson…Keith Rice	LaVerne…Alison Bevan
Bobby…Keith Caldwell	Madame Olga…Marilyn Sokol
Wilehelm…Jay Lowman	

Musical Numbers:

ACT I   Trixie's on the Case!…Joe, Al, Miss Snood, Trixie, Crooks
This Is Indeed My Lucky Day…Trixie
Most Popular and Most Likely to Succeed…Dick, Bobby, Maxine, LaVerne
Mr. and Mrs. Dick Dickerson…Dick, Trixie
Juvenile Fiction…Miss Snood
A Katzenjammer Kinda Song…Olga, Wilhelm
You Haven't Got Time for Love…Dick, Trixie

Licensing: Samuel French

Difficulties/Advantages: Although the cartoon sets would be fun to build—they were originally stylized to suggest the pulp fiction of the 1940s—there's nothing much here. The story-within-the-story is silly and shallow enough, but the story—of the alcoholic writer who tries to bury Trixie for good, then leaps at the chance to spend the rest of his life publishing her—is just plain inane.

Two by Two

The Biblical Musical

Book by Peter Stone
Music by Richard Rodgers
Lyrics by Martin Charnin

Based on the play *The Flowering Peach* by Clifford Odets.

When Danny Kaye starred, he mugged, ad-libbed, and chewed the scenery while the rest of the cast fumed. Richard Rodgers called his show "one-by-one vaudeville." But Kaye was a comic genius, warmly welcomed back to the theatre by audiences that hadn't seen him there since *Lady in the Dark.* When he tore a ligament in his leg, he even performed the show in a wheelchair. It is axiomatic that authors and directors cast stars (Zero Mostel, Danny Kaye, Robert Morse, Jerry Lewis, Pearl Bailey) for their outstanding—and improvisational—comedic talent, then complain loudly when they depart from the book with antics that delight—and bring in—audiences. They don't return their royalties, however, and *Two by Two* ran almost a year.

Time and Place: Before, during, and after the flood. In and around Noah's home, on the ark, and atop Mt. Ararat.

Synopsis: Noah is told to build an ark. (God is represented by thunder and lightning, which makes the casting much easier.) His family isn't so hot on the idea. Indeed, he has to knock his youngest son unconscious to get him aboard. A buxom young woman from town comes aboard, because every species (you knew this) has to be in pairs.
　　　　It rains all during intermission.
　　　　It only takes forty days and forty nights for the middle son to lust after the buxom lass and the youngest son to confess his love for his older brother's wife. The exchange is made. So much for the subplot. A rainbow is both God's promise that he will never again destroy the world and a touching finale.

Imperial Theatre; November 10, 1970; 8 previews, 343 performances.

Directed and choreographed by Joe Layton.

Original Cast:

Noah...Danny Kaye   Noah's Wife, Esther...Joan Copeland
Shem...Harry Goz   Leah...Marilyn Coope
Ham...Michael Karm   Rachel...Tricia O'Neil
Japheth...Walter Willison   Goldie...Madeline Kahn

Musical Numbers:

ACT I   Why Me?...Noah
Put Him Away...Shem, Ham, Leah
The Gitka's Song...The Gitka
Something, Somewhere...Japheth, Family
You Have Got to Have a Rudder on the Ark...Noah, Shem, Ham, Japheth
Something Doesn't Happen...Rachel, Esther
An Old Man...Esther
Ninety Again!. . .Noah
Two by Two. . Noah, Family
I Do Not Know a Day I Did Not Love You...Japheth
Something, Somewhere (reprise)...Noah

ACT II   When It Dries...Noah, Family
Two by Two (reprise)...Noah, Esther
You. . .Noah
The Golden Ram ...Goldie
Poppa Knows Best...Noah, Japheth
I Do Not Know a Day I Did Not Love You (reprise)...Rachel, Japheth
As Far as I'm Concerned...Shem, Leah
Hey, Girlie...Noah
The Covenant...Noah

Licensing: Rodgers and Hammerstein Theatre Library

Difficulties/Advantages: With only eight characters and two sets, this Broadway musical has a lot to offer as a "little musical," with a charming, if not particularly powerful, score.

Martin Charnin, the sole surviving author, is attempting to return the script to the original ensemble piece the authors envisioned—prior to Danny Kaye—but which version is available from the R & H organization, you'll have to ask.

Weird Romance

Two One-Act Musicals of Speculative Fiction

Music by Alan Menken
Lyrics by David Spencer

Act I: "The Girl Who Was Plugged In"

Book by Alan Brennert and David Spencer

Based on the story by James Tiptree Jr.

Synopsis: In the first of these two *Twilight Zone* musicals, a bag lady's mind is placed in the body of a beautiful blonde by a corporation that has manufactured a star in order to control her, because the new law against advertising means that you can sell products only with celebrity endorsements. The CEO's son is assigned to take care of the girl, and he falls in love without knowing what the "mind" really looks like. In short, it's a sci-fi twist on the old romantic story of inner beauty versus the package.

ACT II: "Her Pilgrim Soul"

Book by Alan Brennert

Based on his original story.

Synopsis: A scientist working on holograms finds himself with one of a fetus that takes on a life of its own, grows into a young woman, and engages in a relationship with the scientist, whose own home life is a bit stalled over his absorption in his work and his unwillingness to have children yet. The heroine can't leave the lab, so the scientist doesn't either, and eventually he learns the story of her life with the man she loved. That man turns out to be him in a former life, and her holographic life turns out to be the completion of the real thing, which was foreshortened when she died of a miscarriage. The point of her brief "visit," then, is to convince the scientist to move on in his own life, and he does, rekindling his relationship with his wife.

WPA Theatre; May 12, 1992; 50 performances.

Directed by Barry Harmon. Choreographed by John Carrata.

Original Cast:

Daniel, Fan, Technician,
   Reporter...Danny Burstein
P. Burke, Nola...Ellen Greene
Isham, Kevin...Jonathan Hadary
Delphi, Fan, Susan...Marguerite
   MacIntyre
Carol, Fan, Voice Coach, Technician,
   Voice...Jessica Molasky

Shannara, Rebecca, Makeup Specialist,
   Technician...Valarie Pettiford
Zanth, Movement Coach, Technician,
   George Lester...Eric Riley
Paul, Johnny Beaumont...Sal Vivano
Joe, Chuck, John Ruskin...William
   Youmans

Musical Numbers:

ACT I   "The Girl Who Was Plugged In"
     Weird Romance...Shannara, Zanth
     Stop and See Me...P. Burke
     That's Where We Come In...Isham, P. Burke, Technicians
     Feeling No Pain...Delphi, Joe
     Pop! Flash!...Handlers, Delphi, Isham, Joe, Reporter(s)
     Amazing Penetration...Isham, Female Assistants
     Eyes That Never Lie...Paul
     No One Can Do...Joe, P. Burke
     Worth It...Delphi, P. Burke
     Eyes That Never Lie (reprise)...Paul
     Final GTX Sequence:
        Weird Romance Motif...Zanth, Shannara
        Stop and See Me...Delphi, P. Burke
     Weird Romance (Act I Finale)...Zanth, Shannara

ACT II   "Her Pilgrim Soul"
     Opening Sequence:
        Weird Romance Motif...Disembodied Female Voice

I Can Show You a Thing or Two...Johnny Beaumont
Happy in Your Work...Daniel
My Orderly World...Kevin
My Orderly World (fragment)...Carol
Need to Know...Daniel
You Remember...Kevin, Nola, Daniel
You Remember (Part 2)...Kevin, Nola
Another Woman...Carol, Kevin
Pressing Onward, Moving Forward...Nola, Susan, Chuck, Kevin, Lester, Daniel
I Can Show You a Thing or Two...Johnny Beaumont
A Man...Rebecca, Carol
Pressing Onward, Moving Forward (reprise)...Ruskin
Someone Else Is Waiting...Nola, Kevin
I Can Show You a Thing or Two (Act II Finale)...Johnny Beaumont

Licensing: Samuel French

Difficulties/Advantages: Nine actors with lots of doubling, or lots of actors. Principals can play parallel parts in both acts, or the principals in the first can be ensemble in the second, and vice versa. In other words, there are few or many roles, depending on the resources of your theatre. The score is filled with (read "too many").

The suspension of disbelief that the musical form requires coupled with the leap of faith necessary for fantasy and science fiction adds up to a combo that no show has yet successfully delivered, *Via Galactica (Road to the Stars)*, the futuristic Galt McDermot musical that followed that composer's wildly successful *Hair*, being only the most vivid example. (It closed instantly.) These two one-acts come a bit closer, but when romance is weird, it's difficult to write the soaring songs that true passion can instigate.

What About Luv? (a.k.a. Love)

Book by Jeffrey Sweet
Music by Howard Marren
Lyrics by Susan Birkenhead

Based on the play *Luv* by Murray Schisgal.

From the very successful original play comes an unsuccessful musical version, partly because of the songs and partly because the kind of humor Schisgal utilized seems a little lame today.

Time and Place: The 1960s. New York.

Synopsis: Harry is about to jump from a bridge when old college chum Milt comes along, and they reminisce. Milt has married Ellen and is living in the suburbs and playing golf, while Harry is down and nearly out, having lost the will to live. Milt convinces Harry that love is the answer. It is for Milt, anyway, although it's not for his wife but for his mistress that he pines. In fact, Milt is meeting Ellen here at the bridge and plans to throw her into the river. When she arrives, Milt introduces Harry to Ellen and leaves the two of them together, hoping that love will blossom enough to grant him a divorce. After exchanging sad childhood stories, Ellen explains her problem: she's smart as a

What About Luv? at the Hofferber Repertory Theatre, North Bend, OR.

quiz-show winner. But that hasn't helped her marriage, and she pulls out a knife, although unsure whether she should kill husband Milt or herself. Looking out over the abyss, Ellen and Harry fall in love with each other, a reasonable solution.

But not for two unreasonable Murray Schisgal characters. There follows a classic comedy scene from the 1960s play in which, to prove their love, they begin abusing each other. First a step on the toe, then a kick in the shins, a tearing off of clothes. When he throws her mink coat off the bridge, she asks him to jump. (It doesn't read as funny as it is. See the film version featuring Jack Lemmon, Peter Falk, and Elaine May, three funnier film comics you couldn't ask for.) Milt returns in time to stop them, and when Harry and Ellen run off with each other, he realizes he can join his girlfriend.

Act 2. It's a year later, and Milt runs into Ellen. He admits that his second wife has run out on him and that he has fallen back in love with Ellen. But it's too late. Ellen and Harry have married. But Harry is driving Ellen crazy, and she too wants to return to Milt.

The best way to do this, they decide, is to push Harry off the bridge. Since he was going to jump last year anyway, it's not such a crime. Harry arrives in time for this plot, but a series of events, inexplicable on paper, leads to both Harry and Milt falling off the bridge several times. No matter, as they always reappear, if soaking wet. In the end, Milt and Ellen reconcile and promise to name their baby after Harry, who isn't quite back where he started (a suicide), because now he believes in love.

Audrey Wood Theatre; April 15, 1984; 17 previews, 27 performances.

Original Cast:

Harry...Nathan Lane		Milt...Stephen Vinovich
	Ellen...Judy Kaye	

Musical Numbers:

> Reunion
> Poly Arts U.
> Paradise
> Carnival Ride
> The Chart
> Harry Meets Ellen
> Election Statistics
> I Believe in Marriage
> Somebody
> The Test
> Yes, Yes, I Love You
> How Beautiful the Night Is
> What a Life
> Lady
> If Harry Weren't Here
> My Brown Paper Hat
> Do I Love Him
> What About Love?

Licensing: Music Theatre International

Difficulties/Advantages: The characters this farcical situation relies on are a bit mired in the 1960s, the comic side of John Updike's unhappy suburbanites. If you must give this feather-weight piece a try, do the play. The music adds very little. It's hard enough to be funny, harder still to drive a play to greater and greater heights of hilarity, necessary for a farce. Why have to start over every five minutes following a song?

Whispers on the Wind

> Book and Lyrics by John B. Kuntz
> Music by Lor Crane

With dialogue such as:
> Time!
> The end of darkness,
> Just before you were.
> Wrapped
> In the pencil-pure,
> Untouched parchment of tomorrow

and lyrics such as:
> Midwestern summer, blackberry green and honeysuckle slow. . .

Whispers is not so much a musical as a song cycle, in this case one that limns the life of a boy who grows up in the Midwest, drops out of college to go to New York, gets a temporary job, and falls in love. Five actors—two baritones and a tenor, a soprano, and an alto are their only specific characteristics—speak the poetry and sing the songs that comment upon a life so ordinary and typical as to be uninteresting, thus one of off-Broadway's most notorious flops, notorious because it played the legendary Theatre de Lys and because it featured David Cryer, Nancy Dussault, and Mary Louise Wilson, three of the brightest lights of that generation's musical theatre. Even they couldn't make of the words anything theatrical, partly because of the form but mostly because even as poetry, the writing was banal.

Theatre de Lys; June 3, 1970; 13 previews, 9 performances.

Directed by Burt Brinckerhoff.

Original Cast:

Narrator...David Cryer

First Man...Patrick Fox

Second Woman...Mary Louise Wilson

First Woman...Nancy Dussault

Second Man...R. G. Brown

Musical Numbers:

ACT I   Whispers on the Wind
         Welcome, Little One
         Midwestern Summer
         Why and Because
         Children's Games
         Miss Cadwallader
         Upstairs-Downstairs
         Strawberries
ACT II   Is There a City?
         Carmen Vincenzo
         Neighbors
         Apples and Raisins
         Things Are Going Nicely
         It Won't Be Long
         Prove I'm Really Here
         Finale
         Also written for the show, and on the record:
         The Children's Sake
         Down the Fields
         In the Mind's Eye
         Then in the Middle
         The Very First Girl

Licensing: Samuel French

Difficulties/Advantages: *Whispers* can't be counted out as a possibility. Nevertheless, expect to enjoy working on it, but don't expect the audience to enjoy sitting through it.

Yankee Ingenuity

Book and Lyrics by Richard Bimonte

Music by Jim Wise

Based on *Fashion* by Anna Cora Mowatt.

One of two musical versions of the first American comedy written by a woman, a play that satirized the desire of many Americans at the time (1845) to imitate the manners of European society, and to join families with names like Astor and Vanderbilt in the upper crust.

Time and Place: 1845. Broadway, just off Union Square, New York City, the Tiffany drawing room and one bedroom.

Synopsis: Mrs. Tiffany aspires to high society. Mr. Tiffany thinks he was better off as a peddler, particularly when his clerk, Snobson, blackmails him for having forged a client's name to steal some money. What Snobson wants is Seraphina Tiffany's hand in marriage, but he'll have to get in line behind a poet, a yachtsman, and a French count. The count wins, but he's a fraud, after her money, exposed by the French maid he was once in cahoots with and the orphan Gertrude, who turns out to be the true granddaughter of Adam Trueman, Mrs. Tiffany's brother. Colonel Howard loves Gertrude for who she seems to be and not for her money, which works out just as Grandpa Trueman planned. So when the count turns out to be penniless and can't get his hands on Seraphina's jewels, thanks to a clever butler, everything works out all right. And if you followed all that, you're a better man than I am, Gunga Din.

Meadow Brook Theatre, Rochester Michigan; April 22, 1976.

Directed by Terence Kilburn. Choreographed by Don Price.

Original Cast:

Zeke…Phillip Piro	Elizabeth Tiffany…Marianne Muellerleile
Gertrude…Michele Mullen	Seraphina…Terri McRay
Snobson…Robert Grossman	Antony Tiffany…Max Showalter
Millinette…Cheryl Giannini	T. Tenneyson Twinkle…James Winfield
Augustus Fogg…Thomas C. Spackman	Colonel Howard…Stephen Berger
Count Jolimaitre…Terrence Baker	Adam Trueman…James D. O'Reilly

Musical Numbers:

ACT I   The Upper Crust of Broadway…Mrs. Tiffany
The American Way…Millinette, Zeke
Old New York…Mr. Tiffany
How I Wonder…Seraphina, Gertrude
The Way You Use Your Fan…Mrs. Tiffany, Seraphina
A Love That Was Meant to Be…Gertrude, Colonel Howard
Yankee Ingenuity…Zeke, Trueman, Mr. Tiffany
Keep Up Appearances…Company

ACT II   The Guess-Who Gavotte…Mrs. Tiffany, Company
Save the Last Waltz for Me…Seraphina, Count, Company
Yankee Ingenuity (reprise)…Zeke, Gertrude
Ya Never Know…Snobson
Free…Gertrude
Times Gone By…Mr. and Mrs. Tiffany
Ya Never Know (reprise)…Snobson
Finale: Upper Crust and Yankee Ingenuity…Company

Licensing: Samuel French

Difficulties/Advantages: Lines such as "Life in a democracy would be ideal, if it weren't so hard to find good servants" and "Education makes a woman nervous and discontented" hint that the original play may have been pretty funny. In fact, both this version and *Fashion* make it pretty clear that the original play might best be performed without musical adaptations.

You're a Good Man, Charlie Brown

Book, Music, and Lyrics by Clark Gesner
Based on the comic strip *Peanuts* by Charles M. Schulz.

On Tuesday, March 7, 1967, at tiny Theatre 80 St. Marks in New York's Greenwich Village, Charles Schultz's classic cartoon figures were realized on stage for the first time. They did so, according to Walter Kerr in the *New York Times* the next morning, "Without losing a drop of the ink that made their lifelines so human," demonstrating that, simple as those few lines were, Schulz had in fact created not just cartoons, but rich, multilayered characters.

Peanuts' now-classic stage incarnation began with an album of songs by Clark Gesner, inspired by the Peanuts gang and released by MGM records in 1966. Gesner had been writing songs for Captain Kangaroo and for the Jules Monk revues at Plaza Nine. Barbara Minkus, Lucy on the record, played it for acquaintance Arthur Whitelaw, who had been hoping to produce a musical version of his favorite comic strip ever since he was a wide-eyed sixteen-year-old in love with Broadway musicals. Although Whitelaw had to convince a reluctant Gesner that the album should be a show, when he called Schulz, he discovered that the cartoonist himself had long thought his characters would work on the musical stage. Whitelaw hired director Joseph Hardy, and they began to look for a cast.

Not an easy task. What actors could possibly impersonate the Peanuts gang, much less the famous canine? One can only imagine how frustrating auditions must have been, seeing all those typical actors from Broadway musicals of the 1960s and trying to envision them as Charlie and company. And yet, as often happens in New York theatre, little by little a unique set of actors appeared. The creators eventually found a film major from N.Y.U. (Bob Balaban, as Linus); a blonde in a polka-dot tie (Karen Johnson, as Peppermint Patty); a refugee from TV commercials and children's theatre (Reva Rose, as Lucy); a short, sturdy Yalie who could play a dog better than Lassie (Bill Hinnant, as Snoopy); his younger brother, acting in repertory in Rhode Island (Skip Hinnant, as Schroeder); and a drummer/poet/songwriter from Iowa who was heading into pop music (Gary Burghoff, as Charlie Brown, an actor eventually to immortalize Radar O'Reilly on the long-running television series M*A*S*H). This group of enthusiastic if inexperienced actors were then given…no script, for the director Joseph Hardy, musical director Joseph Raposo, songwriter Clark Gesner, and their cast had only stacks of wonderful Schulz cartoons, a nearly new 200-seat theatre in the East Village, and a deadline a month away. In years to come, this sort of thing would be called either foolhardy or a "workshop." In February of 1967 it must have been great, chaotic fun. Gesner combined several strips into longer scenes. Director Hardy gave each of the actors a huge book of strips and told them to pick the ones they liked best about their characters.

In fact the little musical never did come up with a "book." No surprise, as the bookwriter listed, "John Gordon," doesn't exist but is a pseudonym for all those present who labored to organize Schulz's whimsical incidents and universal wisdom. The musical, like the lives of Charlie Brown and his friends, is loosely structured. Whether Charlie is hoping that the little red-headed girl will notice him, or Snoopy is pondering the ways of the world, we move from baseball game to piano practice, from homework to lunch, from kite flying to recess, in a delightfully random and unhurried way. The theatrical framework, however, is Hardy's strong concept of "A Day in the Life," for the show moves from morning to evening.

You're a Good Man, Charlie Brown
at the Plymouth Playhouse, Minneapolis, MN.

When the Peanuts gang finally took to the stage, the actors were well suited to their parts. None could sing or dance. Lucy in particular had a singing voice like fingernails on a blackboard. Quite unlike the slick, booming voices of uptown Broadway, the "little" cast—six undersized, eager actors—didn't contradict the classic prototypes but, in their simplicity, encompassed them.

Sitting there in the East Village—surrounded by the sixties loss-of-innocence counterculture, hippies, flower power, and rock 'n' roll—the little musical from the heart of Americana quickly established itself as a smash hit. There followed the virtual invention of a new business plan for hit shows, the "sit-down" company, placing local versions in cities all across the United States and eventually worldwide, from Japan to Copenhagen. Since then, generation after generation has delighted in the stage incarnation of Schulz's characters, with its pithy, straight-to-the-heart truisms and exuberant songs.

Theatre 80 St. Marks; March 7, 1967; 1,597 performances.

Directed by Joseph Hardy. Choreographed by Patricia Birch.

Original Off-Broadway Cast:

Linus…Bob Balaban   Charlie Brown…Gary Burghoff
Patty…Karen Johnson   Schroeder…Skip Hinnant
Snoopy…Bill Hinnant   Lucy…Reva Rose

Musical Numbers:

ACT I   You're a Good Man, Charlie Brown…Company
         Schroeder (Moonlight Sonata)…Lucy, Schroeder
         Snoopy…Snoopy
         My Blanket and Me…Linus
         Kite…Charlie Brown
         Dr. Lucy…Lucy, Charlie
         Book Report…Charlie, Lucy, Linus, Schroeder

165

Act II   The Red Baron...Snoopy
T-E-A-M (The Baseball Game)...Company
Queen Lucy...Lucy, Linus
Peanuts Potpourri...Snoopy, Linus, Schroeder
Little Known Facts...Lucy, Linus, Charlie
Suppertime...Snoopy, Charlie
Happiness...Company

Licensing: Tams-Witmark

Difficulties/Advantages: Although orchestrations are available, the score is ideally presented with only piano, drums, and bass (listen to the marvelous Vince Guaraldi trio that scores the TV specials) and can be done effectively with piano only.

    "Almost immediately after we opened, I began thinking about a sequel," said Arthur Whitelaw, the original show's producer. And who doesn't dream of repeating a success? In this case, the treasure trove of strips barely allowed the original to scratch the surface, so, nine years later, this time starring the dog, came...

Snoopy!!!

Book by Warren Lockhart, Arthur Whitelaw, and Michael L. Grace
Music by Larry Grossman
Lyrics by Hal Hackaday

Directed by Arthur Whitelaw. Choreographed by Marc Breaux.

Original Cast:

Snoopy...Don Potter
Peppermint Patty...Pamela Myers
Lucy...Carla Manning
Woodstock...Alfred Mazza

Charlie Brown...James Gleason
Sally...Roxann Pyle
Linus...Jimmy Dodge

Musical Numbers:

Act I   The World According to Snoopy
Edgar Allan Poe
I Know Now
The Vigil
Clouds
Where Did That Little Dog Go?
Daisy Hill

Act II   Friend
The Great Writer (It Was a Dark and Stormy Night)
Poor Sweet Baby
Don't Be Anything Less
The Big Bow-Wow
Just One Person

Licensing: Tams-Witmark

Difficulties/Advantages: What a wonderful opportunity for a small theatre to do both shows in rep with the same cast, a four-hour marathon of one of the great creations of American pop culture. A great show, too, for young people to perform, and since the original, we have *Annie* to prove that there's plenty of young talent out there. Wouldn't it be great to see kids playing the kids of Peanuts?

In 1999 a revival of the original—with two new songs not by Clark Gesner, orchestrations for a five-piece chamber ensemble, and the character of Peppermint Patty replaced by Sally Brown—was produced on Broadway. According to the licensing organization, "A new perspective has been added by emphasizing the insatiable insouciance of the characters that was held in check in the original." It was? With a multi-ethnic cast in an uptown theatre (the Ambassador), the revival was ill-advised and poorly done, and flopped miserably. Not that Charlie Brown can't be done in a larger theatre setting, but "Broadway" is far too grand for this great Little Show That Could. If you license this one, don't fall for the "revised" version.

Your Own Thing

Book by Donald Driver
Music and Lyrics by Hal Hester and Danny Apolinar
Suggested by William Shakespeare's *Twelfth Night.*

The first off-Broadway musical to win the New York Drama Critics Circle Award and the Outer Critics Circle Award for best musical, it was a big hit when it opened at the little Orpheum theatre at the height of the sixties, then mounted successful companies throughout the country. Its score is tuneful in a bubble-gum pop style, its story a clever redaction of Shakespeare's *Twelfth Night, or What You Will* (itself taken from *Appalonius and Silla* by an unknown Greek author). Among the first to connect the hairstyles and dress of the sixties with the Elizabethan era, Puerto Rican songwriters Hal Hester and Danny Apolinar chose the public-domain, pants-part Shakespeare comedy for their second assault on Broadway (having already written a musical based on another property, the rights to which were denied). Together with a friend who owned the Orpheum theatre, they raised the $30,000 necessary to mount the show, then engaged Donald Driver to write the book and direct. Driver, dropping all of Shakespeare's subplots and concentrating on the principal romantic quadrangle, filled in the humor with comments by the great and near-great, from Queen Elizabeth and Buddha to W. C. Fields and John Wayne, all with the clever and then original use of slides and recordings. Its success was based on its charm, ingratiating performances, and most of all, style. The production featured twelve slide projectors, two movie projectors, and two tape recorders—one of the earliest "multimedia" productions, a technique soon to be successfully appropriated by just about all the performing arts. No Broadway musical so captured the sixties as *Hair*, and no off-Broadway musical so captured them as this one, with its song "Do Your Own Thing" leading the way.

Theatrical trivia department: Clive Barnes, then the critic for the *New York Times*, the most powerful review a show could garner, couldn't attend the scheduled opening night, a Friday, but agreed to stay in town for the weekend if they would postpone their opening to Saturday. Taking a chance, they did, and he gave the show an excellent review ("a cheerful, joyful and blissfully irreverent musical…as modern as today"). It's still as modern as then.

Time and Place: The imaginary kingdom of Illyria (which looks suspiciously like New York in the sixties).

Synopsis: At sea, a shipwreck separates brother/sister singing duo Sebastian and Viola when Sebastian is talked into going back to the sinking ship for their arrangements. On land, music manager Orson has lost a member of his quartet Apocalypse to the draft, and risks losing thirty weeks of bookings, beginning at Olivia's discotheque, she who refuses to accept Orson's declarations of love. Viola dresses as a boy, auditions, gets the job as the missing Apocalypse, and carries a letter to Olivia for Orson. While she's gone, Sebastian shows up for the same job, but Orson can't tell the siblings apart. He sends a series of letters to woo Olivia, not realizing—as Olivia doesn't either—that there are two messengers, not one. In the event, Olivia falls for Sebastian and Viola for Orson. There follow comic complications rising to Mack Sennett pitch, until Sebastian and Viola appear onstage together and all is resolved for the "Now Generation."

Orpheum theatre; January 13, 1968; 933 performances.

The entire production was staged by Donald Driver (it has long been rumored that Michael Bennett, a friend of Driver and Leland Palmer, helped out with the staging, and the slickness of some of the musical numbers supports this).

Original Cast:

Danny...Danny Apolinar
Michael...Michael Valenti
Olivia...Marion Mercer
Sebastian...Rusty Thacker
Nurse...Imogene Bliss

John...John Kuhner
Orson...Tom Ligon
Viola...Leland Palmer
Purser/Stage Manager...Igors Gavon

Musical Numbers:

No One's Perfect, Dear...Sebastian, Viola
The Flowers...Viola
I'm Me! (I'm Not Afraid)...Apocalypse
Baby! Baby!...Apocalypse, Viola
Come Away, Death...Sebastian
I'm on My Way to the Top...Sebastian
She Never Told Her Love...Viola
Be Gentle...Viola, Orson
What Do I Know?...Viola
Baby! Baby! (reprise)...Apocalypse, Sebastian, Viola
The Now Generation...Apocalypse, Viola
The Middle Years...Sebastian
The Middle Years (reprise)...Olivia
When You're Young and in Love...Orson
Hunca Munca...Apocalypse, Company
Don't Leave Me...Olivia, Sebastian, Orson
Do Your Own Thing...Company

Licensing: Tams-Witmark

Difficulties/Advantages: The orchestra—an electric organ, an electric guitar, an electric fender base, and percussion—shouldn't be too difficult to arrange these days. Very dependent on the empathy it gained with lyrics such as "Our generation is now!" this musical might now be subtitled "Our generation was then." And with lines such as "What's his bag?" and "Just the right square can be awfully groovy" alternating with beautiful paragraphs from the original Shakespeare, this would have to be done tongue firmly in cheek as a period piece. The jokes would garner more groans than laughs these days, but with the right insouciance and breakneck rhythm, it could be as entertaining as it was then, with a cultural history lesson thrown in for those who never heard of the sixties.

Zombie Prom

Book and Lyrics by John Dempsey
Music by Dana P. Rowe

Based on a story by John Dempsey and Hugh Murphy.

Rebel with a good cause: he's a zombie.

Time and Place: The nuclear fifties. The hallways and classrooms of Enrico Fermi High School, the newsroom of *Exposé* magazine, a television studio, and Toffee's bedroom.

Synopsis: Toffee's parents forbid her to see the orphan Jonny—who spells his name without the H in spite of the principal's insistence—so he commits suicide by jumping into the local nuclear plant's waste-treatment silo. This is no cause to cancel the prom, but Toffee, without a boyfriend, won't be going—that is, until Jonny returns as a Zombie. But Principal Strict has a rule: no zombies. He can't return to school, and he can't go to the prom. And if that's not bad enough, Toffee is reluctant to take him back. (The green goo all over him is putting her off.) When Eddie, a reporter, shows up to get the story, he runs into Miss Strict. It's been a long time, but clearly something happened between them years ago.

By the end of intermission, a full-scale rebellion develops. Let the undead back into high school! Miss Strict suspends the baseball team and the pep squad in retaliation, and if there's any more trouble, she'll cancel the prom! Eddie puts Jonny on TV, where he manages, through his stage fright, to say (sing) that he'll never be through with love. Toffee, seeing him, wonders, "What's a girl to do when her dead boyfriend asks her to the prom?" Miss Strict reminds everyone that no zombie is to appear at the prom, but Eddie reminds Miss Strict that they had a torrid affair during their own high school days. Well, Jonny and Toffee do appear at the prom and are crowned King and Queen. Miss Strict is about to close down the dance, when Eddie appears and insists she tell the whole story: She too was in love in high school with the local bad boy. *They* weren't allowed to go to *their* prom, so she snuck out of the house and drove around with him, parked, and yes, lost her virginity. Trouble was, she got pregnant and had to sneak out of town to give birth and have the child adopted. So she's now going to see that the same thing doesn't happen to Toffee. Only Eddie has a surprise, besides the one that he was the bad boy. He has discovered that Jonny is their son! She relents, they're a family again, and the kids enjoy their zombie prom.

Variety Arts Theatre; March 26, 1996; 28 performances.

Directed by Philip Wm. McKinley. Choreographed by Tony Stevens.

Original Cast:

Miss Delilah Strict…Karen Murphy	Toffee.. Jessica-Snow Wilson
Candy…Rebecca Rich	Coco…Cathy Trien
Ginger…Natalie Toro	Jonny Warner…Richard Roland
Joey…Marc Lovci	Josh…Jeff Skowron
Jake…Stephen Bienskie	Eddie Flagrante…Richard Muenz

Musical Numbers:

ACT I   Enrico Fermi High...Toffee, Jonny, Coco, Candy, Ginger, Josh, Jake, Joey, Miss Strict
Ain't No Goin' Back...Toffee, Jonny, Kids
Jonny Don't Go...Toffee, Girls
Good as It Gets...Toffee, Kids
The C Word...Toffee, Jonny, Kids
Rules, Regulations and Respect...Miss Strict, Kids
Ain't No Goin' Back (reprise)...Jonny, Toffee, Kids
Blast from the Past...Jonny, Kids
That's the Beat for Me...Eddie, Secretaries, Copy Boys
The Voice in the Ocean...Jonny, Toffee
It's Alive...Jonny, Miss Strict, Kids
Where Do We Go from Here?...Jonny, Toffee, Kids
Case Closed Trio. . Eddie, Miss Strict, Jonny

ACT II   Then Came Jonny...Miss Strict, Jonny, Toffee, Kids
Come Join Us...Ramona Merengue, Motorwise Gasoline Guys, Eddie
How Can I Say Good-Bye?...Jonny, Motorwise Guys
Easy to Say...Toffee, Girls
At the Dance...Eddie, Miss Strict
Exposé...Eddie, Miss Strict
Isn't It?...Kids
How Do You Stand on Dreams?...Toffee, Jonny
Forbidden Love...Toffee, Jonny, Kids
The Lid's Been Blown...Eddie, Miss Strict, Kids
Zombie Prom...Company

Licensing: Samuel French

Difficulties/Advantages: If your audience has seen *Grease* too many times, this is for you. Moreover, the strong contemporary music will delight your teenage performers, and the story has resonance for everyone, from boomers to kids. The original ten actors doubled, so there's a dozen more small parts. If in the next few years every high school in America hasn't produced *Zombie Prom,* their curriculum is deficient.

Part Two: The Themed Revues

One great thing about revues is their versatility. In many schools and community theatres, cast size is determined by the number of performers who sign up. The distribution of material can be based more or less on the distribution of talent among your performers.

Another is that they usually allow for a great deal of creativity from production to production. If you're producing Dames at Sea, *you pretty much have to provide the deck of a battleship, one way or another. But these shows generally feature sketches and songs, the latter often presentational, on a unit set. The design elements are pretty much up to you. Sets and costumes can vary as much as the designer's creativity allows.*

And although the licensing companies will scream when I say this, revue material is generally flexible. Moving songs and sketches here and there to suit your talent and your staging won't cause a problem. Whether your program is an hour, ninety minutes, or a full-fledged evening often depends on your audience's patience.

Whatever decade you're interested in, whatever theme you like, here are a number of small musical revues that will suit your budget and, hopefully, your audience.

The All Night Strut

A Musical Celebration of the 1930s and 40s.
Conceived by Fran Charnas

A collection of mostly well-known songs from the two decades, performed one after the other, with no story or even characters.

Theatre Four; October 4, 1979; 6 performances.

Directed and choreographed by Fran Charnas.

Original Cast:

Andrea Danford   Jess Richards
                           Jana Robbins

Musical Numbers:

ACT I Chattanooga Choo-Choo
Minnie the Moocher
Brother, Can You Spare a Dime
In the Mood
Gimme a Pigfoot and a Bottle of Beer
A Nightingale Sang in Berkeley Square
Fascinating Rhythm
Java Jive
World War II Medley: GI Jive, Shoo Shoo Baby, White Cliffs of Dover, Rosie the
Riveter, You're a Lucky Fellow Mr. Smith, Praise the Lord and Pass the
Ammunition, Comin' in on a Wing and a Prayer, I'll Be Seeing You

ACT II I Get Ideas
Ain't Misbehavin'
Operator
Dream
Beat Me, Daddy, Eight to the Bar
A Fine Romance
Tuxedo Junction
Juke Box Saturday Night
As Time Goes By
Hit That Jive, Jack
Billie's Bounce
It Don't Mean a Thing (If It Ain't Got That Swing)
Lullaby of Broadway

Licensing: Music Theatre International

Difficulties/Advantages: Requires a tenor, a baritone, a soprano, and an alto. In the original production, the slickness of the staging—four singer/dancers using four standing microphones as they would have at the time of the songs—and the performances carried the show. It's a strong collection, and if you rent the show, you don't have to get individual permission from each song's publisher, but after that, you're on your own. There are lots of possibilities to recreate an authentic feeling for the era. Or just follow the original: a stage and two sets of costumes for each of the two men and two women.

A...My Name Is Alice and A...My Name Is Still Alice

A...*My Name Is Alice* at California State University, Fullerton's Arena Theatre, Fullerton, CA.

Photo: Jim Volz

Two versions of a witty, insightful, and sometimes poignant revue about women. Both are filled with some of the best sketch and song writing on the subject of being female from many talented writers, very little of which has aged (there are still "Sensitive New Age Guys" around) and much of which is hilarious (the medical lecture on the dreaded male disease "Smallcox").

A...*My Name Is Alice*

Material by Calvin Alexander, Susan Birkenhead, Maggie Bloomfield, David Crane, David Evans, Carol Hall, Cheryl Hardwick, Georgia Bogardus Holof, Winnie Holzman, Doug Katsaros, Marta Kauffman, Richard LaGravenese, Stephen Lawrence, Amanda McBroom, Anne Meara, Cassandra Medley, David Mettee, Art Murray, Susan Rice, Glen Roven, Mark Saltzman, James Shorter, June Siegel, Lucy Simon, Michael Skloff, Steve Tesich, Don Rucker, and David Zippel

Top of the (Village) Gate; February 24, 1984; 353 performances.

Conceived and directed by Joan Micklin Silver and Julianne Boyd. Choreographed by Edward Love.

Original Cast:

Roo Brown   Randy Graff
Mary Gordon Murray   Alaina Reed
Charlaine Woodard

Musical Numbers and Scenes:

ACT I   All Girl Band
         A...My Name Is Alice Poems
         At My Age
         Trash
         For Women Only Poems
         Good Thing I Learned to Dance
         Welcome to Kindergarten, Mrs. Johnson
         I Sure Like the Boys
         Ms. Mae
         Good Sports
         Detroit Persons
         Educated Feet
         The Portrait
         Bluer Than You
ACT II   Pretty Young Men
         Demigod
         The French Monologue
         The French Song
         Pay Them No Mind
         Hot Lunch
         Emily the M.B.A.
         Sisters
         Honeypot
         Friends
         All Girl Band (reprise)

A...My Name Is Still Alice

Material by Marion Adler, Dan Berkowitz, Douglas Bernstein, Francesca Blumenthal, Craig Carnelia, Randy Court, John Gorka, Carol Hall, George Bogardus Holof, Doug Katsaros, Christine Lavin, Lisa Loomer, Michael John LaChuisa, Denis Markell, Amanda McBroom, David Mettee, Lynn Nottage, Mary Bracken Phillips, Jimmy Roberts, Mark Saltzman, Kate Shein, June Siegel, Carolyn Sloan, Mark St. Germain, and Steve Tesich

Second Stage Theatre; October 13, 1992; 84 performances.

Conceived by Joan Micklin Silver and Julianne Boyd.

Original Cast:

Roo Brown   Laura Dean
Cleo King   K. T. Sullivan
Nancy Ticotin

Musical Numbers and Scenes:

ACT I   Two Steps Forward
It Ain't Over
Non-Bridaled Passion
Once and Only Thing
Cover-Up #1
Why Doesn't She Call Me?
Juanita Craiga
So Much Rain
The Group
Ida Mae Cole Takes a Stance
Cover-Up #2
Wheels
The Sorghum Sisters

ACT II   Painted Ladies
Sensitive New Age Guys
A Lovely Little Life
Play Nice
Gross Anatomy Lecture
Hard Hat Woman
Cover-Up #3
Baby
Women Behind Desks
What Did I Do Right?
Lifelines
Two Steps Forward (reprise)

Licensing: Samuel French

Difficulties/Advantages: Although the original productions each featured five women performing all the material, there's ample scenes and songs here for more than twice that many, should everyone want to get into the act. There's even one hilarious sketch ("Hot Lunch") that could benefit from a man, instead of an actress playing a man, although perhaps that would ruin some of the symmetry of the evening. The original material combined with the sequel makes for a wonderful show called *A…My Name Will Always Be Alice,* the title of a CD recording of the material and the way most theatres are presenting the show these days.

Beehive

Music and Lyrics: Various
Created by Larry Gallagher

A tribute to the girl groups and girl singers of the 1960s—and in some cases, the girl songwriters, such as Carole King. A narrator gives us the social settings of that turbulent decade, but it's the singers moving from boyfriends to "Ball and Chain" (if that's not the same thing) that chart the rise of feminism hidden in the popular music.

Village Gate Upstairs; March 11, 1986; 600 performances.

Directed by Larry Gallagher. Choreographed by Leslie Dockery.

Photo: Ellen Jarus Hanley

Beehive at the Seven Angels Theatre, Waterbury, CT.

Original Cast:

      Pattie Darcy   Alison Fraser
      Jasmine Guy   Adriane Lenox
      Gina Taylor   Laura Theodore

Musical Numbers:

      The Name Game
      My Boyfriend's Back
      Sweet Talkin' Guy
      One Fine Day
      I Sold My Heart to the Junkman
      Academy Award
      Will You Still Love Me Tomorrow
      Give Him a Great Big Kiss
      Remember (Walking in the Sand)
      I Can Never Go Home Again
      Where Did Our Love Go?
      Come See About Me
      I Hear a Symphony
      It's My Party
      I'm Sorry
      Rockin' Around the Christmas Tree
      I Dream About Frankie
      She's a Fool
      You Don't Own Me
      Judy's Turn to Cry

Where the Boys Are
The Beehive Dance
The Beat Goes On
Downtown
To Sir with Love
Wishin' and Hopin'
Don't Sleep in the Subway
You Don't Have to Say You Love Me
A Fool in Love
River Deep Mountain High
Proud Mary
Society's Child
Respect
A Natural Woman
Do Right Woman
Piece of My Heart
Try (Just a Little Bit Harder)
Me and Bobby McGee
Ball and Chain
Make Your Own Kind of Music

Licensing: Writers and Artists Agency, 19 West 44th Street, Suite 1410, Music Library Inc., New York, New York 10036

Difficulties/Advantages: Here's a compendium of songs from the 1960s by girls and girl groups that you can't beat for a rhythm-driven, audience-pleasing show, no matter how old the audience…or the performers, almost any number of whom can comprise your cast. You can do the hair as a spoof, as did the original (fifteen cans of hair spray per week, according to the publicist) but that only distracts from the songs and performances, which need to be taken as seriously as they were then if the audience is going to follow you down memory lane. It's not a collection of "what were we thinking?" songs but of some of the best rock 'n' roll ever written. An all-girl cast, with many theatres deciding to feature imitations of the original recording artists. Hit it.

Blame It on the Movies

The Reel Music of Hollywood

Music and Lyrics By Billy Barnes
Compiled and Conceived by Ron Abel, Billy Barnes, and David Galligan

From an original idea by Franklin R. Levy.

A musical cavalcade of seventy-five songs and themes from Hollywood films. Barnes's song "Music from the Movies" bookends sequences that include tributes to the 1940s, the War years, songs from foreign films, love songs from Twentieth Century Fox, songs that never won the Oscar, a ballet based on film scores, and a finale medley, in case any songs were left out.

The original production took place in 1988 at the Coast Playhouse in Los Angeles. When the show moved to New York City, it didn't do as well.

Criterion Center, Stage Left; May 16, 1989; 12 previews, 3 performances.
Directed by David Galligan. Staged and choreographed by Larry Hyman.

Original Off-Broadway Cast:

Sandy Edgerton   Kathy Garrick
Bill Hutton   Christine Kellogg
Peter Marc   Dan O'Grady
Barbara Sharma   Patty Tiffany

Musical Numbers:

An Affair to Remember
April Love
As Time Goes By
Aurora
The Best of Everything
A Certain Smile
Dream
The Fleet's In
Full Moon and an Empty Heart
Have Yourself a Merry Little Christmas
I Get the Neck of the Chicken
I Said No
In Love in Vain
It Only Happens When I Dance with You
I've Got a Girl in Kalamazoo
Jungle Love
Laura
The Long Hot Summer
Love Is a Many Splendored Thing
Make Way for Tomorrow
A Man and a Woman
Milkman, Keep Those Bottles Quiet
The Road to Morocco
The Second Time Around
Shoo-Shoo Baby
Two for the Road
You'll Never Know
Alfie
All the Way
The Ballad of Cat Ballou
Blazing Saddles Theme
Chitty Chitty Bang Bang
Ding Dong the Witch Is Dead
Goldfinger
Gone with the Wind Theme
The Good, the Bad, and the Ugly Theme
Help!
Hi Lili Hi Lo
It's a Mad, Mad, Mad, Mad World
Jaws Theme

Let's Hear It for the Boy
Midnight Express Theme
Miss Celie's Blues
Mule Train
My Foolish Heart
On the Road Again
The Pink Panther Theme
A Place in the Sun
Psycho Theme
Rocky Theme
Something's Gotta Give
That's Amoré
Town Without Pity
Walk on the Wild Side
The Way We Were
The Way You Look Tonight
What's New Pussycat?
The Windmills of Your Mind
You Stepped Out of a Dream

Licensing: Music Theatre International

Difficulties/Advantages: Eight performers originally. You can utilize any or all of the above songs in the original format, but if you want something else, you'll have to license it from the music publisher. Film clips—which, integrated into the staging, make for an artful production—must all be licensed separately from the movie studios. As difficult as all that may sound, it would be well worth it, for this run-through of four decades of Hollywood music could be riotously entertaining if a great deal of creativity (something, alas, the original production lacked) went into the staging and design.

Blues in the Night

Conceived by Sheldon Epps
Music by Bessie Smith, Duke Ellington, Johnny Mercer, Harold Arlen, Alberta Hunter, Jimmy Cox, Ida Cox, and others

Time and Place: 1930s Chicago. Three rooms in a fleabag hotel, three women, no dialogue (and no discernible concept).

Rialto Theatre; June 2, 1982; 13 previews, 53 performances.

Directed by Sheldon Epps.

Original Cast:

Woman No. 1...Leslie Uggams   Woman No. 2...Debbie Shapiro
Woman No. 3...Jean DuShon   Saloon Singer...Charles Coleman

Musical Numbers (in alphabetical order):

Am I Blue
Baby Doll
Blue Blues
Blues in the Night

Dirty No-Gooder's Blues
Four Walls (and One Dirty Window) Blues
I Gotta Right to Sing the Blues
I'm Just A Lucky So-and-So
I've Got a Date with a Dream
It Makes My Love Come Down
Lover Man
Lush Life
New Orleans Hop Scop Blues
Nobody Knows You When You're Down and Out
Reckless Blues
Rough and Ready Man
Stompin' at the Savoy
Take Me for a Buggy Ride
Take It Right Back
Taking a Chance on Love
Wasted Life Blues
When Your Lover Has Gone
When a Woman Loves a Man
Wild Women Don't Have the Blues
Willow Weep for Me

Licensing: Music Theatre International

Difficulties/Advantages: Unit set, very flexible, but if you don't know three women who can sing the blues, forget it. If you do, you'll still need a new approach to the material, because the original production on Broadway managed to make twenty-five of America's greatest blues songs boring, even with three talented women singing them.

Diamonds

Book by Bud Abbott, Ralph G. Allen, Roy Blount Jr., Richard Camp, Lou Costello, Lee Eisenberg, Sean Kelly, John Lahr, Arthur Masella, Harry Stein, Jim Wann, John Weidman, and Alan Zweibel

Music by Gerard Alessandrini, Craig Carnelia, Cy Coleman, Larry Grossman, John Kander, Doug Katsaros, Alan Menken, Jonathan Sheffer, Lynn Udall, Albert Von Tilzer, and Jim Wann

Lyrics by Gerard Alessandrini, Howard Ashman, Craig Carnelia, Betty Comden, Fred Ebb, Ellen Fitzhugh, Adolph Green, Karl Kennett, Jack Norworth, Jim Wann, and David Zippel

A revue about baseball, notable originally for the environmental approach to the staging, in which the audience was surrounded by a grassy playing field, and just beyond home plate was a dugout and the band.

Time and Place: Contemporary. Various parts of a baseball diamond, as well as the stands, a bar, and the announcer's desk.

Synopsis: This revue features a variety of sketches and songs inspired by baseball, unconnected, but a few running bits: fans in the stands and announcer Warner (Boom!) Wolf relating the history of war in the twentieth century in his unique vernacular.

Circle in the Square (Downtown); December 16, 1984; 122 performances.

Directed by Harold Prince. Choreographed by Theodore Pappas.

Original Cast:

Starting Line-up...Loni Ackerman, Susan Bigelow, Jackee Harry, Scott Holmes, Dick Latessa, Swayne Markee, Wade Raley, Larry Riley, Nestor Serrano, Chip Zien
Stadium Announcer...Bill McComb

Musical Numbers:

ACT I   Winter in New York
In the Cards
Favorite Sons
Song for a Pinch Hitter
Vendors
What You'd Call a Dream
Escorte-Moi
He Threw Out the Ball
Hundreds of Hats
1919

ACT II   Let's Play Ball
Vendors
The Boys of Summer
Song for a Hunter College Graduate
Stay in Your Own Back Yard
Ka-Razy
Diamonds Are Forever

Licensing: Samuel French

Difficulties/Advantages: Eclectic, to say the least. Each song has its own inimitable style, from ragtime to gospel to classic Kander and Ebb. The sketches range too, from vaudeville to a Kabuki version of "Casey at the Bat." The show's best sketch is the classic Abbott and Costello vaudeville routine "Who's on First?" Unfortunately, that routine puts all the original stuff in the shade. When you think of all the great sports writing that has crossed the plate since newspapers followed the game, *Diamonds* doesn't sparkle...until the narrative sequence (and film clips of the players) about the Negro leagues, which is brilliant, historical, and touching. Any number can play, but nine seems about right.

Doctor! Doctor!

A Medical Musical Comedy Revue

Music and Lyrics by Peter Ekstroom
Additional Lyrics and Material by David DeBoy

A collection of songs, with a few brief sketches, on the general themes of health, medicine, and related subjects. Mostly comical ("HMO's will sell you doctors in their plan / But they will not tell you / That these doctors trained in Pakistan"), a few quite serious ("I Loved My Father More Than He Knew"), most tuneful but silly.

Time and Place: Generally, neither, but the vague definitions of a doctor's office might be one place to start.

Player's Theatre; March 26, 1997; 31 performances.

Directed by Richard Rose. Choreographed by Amanda Aldridge.

Original Cast:

Jay...Buddy Crutchfield	Audrey...Jill Geddes
Gloria...Nancy Johnston	William...James Weatherstone
Receptionist...Albert Ahronheim	

Musical Numbers:

ACT I
The Human Body...Company
Consummate Picture...Gloria
Oh, Boy! How I Love My Cigarettes!...Jay, Audrey
I'm a Well-Known, Respected Practitioner...William
Tomorrow...Audrey, Company
World of My Own...Gloria
And Yet, I Lived On...Company
Willie...Gloria
The Right Hand Song...The Receptionist
Please, Doctor Fletcher...Audrey, Company
Take It Off, Tammy!...William
It's My Fat...Jay
Nine Long Months Ago...The Company

ACT II
Hymn...Company
Medicine Man Blues...Gloria
Private Practice...William
Nurse's Care...Audrey, Company
I'm Sure of It...William, Audrey
I Loved My Father More Than He Knew...Jay
Jesus Is My Doctor...Gloria, Company
Bing Bang Boom...Jay, Audrey
Eighty-Thousand Orgasms...Gloria, Jay
Good Ole Days (of Sex)...Audrey, William
Do I Still Have You?...William
I Hope I Never Get...Jay, Company
The Human Body (reprise)...Company

Licensing: Samuel French

Difficulties/Advantages: A note from the script, one that might be just as appropriate in most revues: "This material has been performed in every conceivable arena from a simple cabaret setting with a few singers around a piano, to a complex off-Broadway revue with every production element that the imagination (and budget) would allow." And this too, the essence of the off-Broadway movement: "As always, imagination is the most economical means to transport an audience to wherever you wish to take them." I couldn't have said it better myself.

El Grande de Coca-Cola

By Ron House, Alan Shearman, John Neville-Andrews, Diz White, and Sally Willis
From an idea by Ron House and Diz White.

A revue developed by a comedy troupe called the Low Moan Spectacular. Hilarious as a show can only be when it gestates over an eighteen-month period touring Europe and the British Isles.

Time and Place: The present. A nightclub in a run-down section of Trujillo, Honduras.

Synopsis: Senor Don Pepe Hernandez is putting on a star-studded show with money borrowed from his uncle, who owns the local Coca-Cola bottling plant, but when the stars don't show, his relatives must go on. Of course everything goes hysterically awry: a tango that ends in chaos, a blind jazz singer/guitarist who stumbles around the stage, acrobatics that cause a hernia, and hilarious scenes from Toulouse Lautrec trying to paint "Les Boobes Formidable!" to a wedding reduced to a Mack Sennet battle. All in strangely comprehensible Spanish and French.

Mercer Arts Center; February 13, 1973; 1,114 performances.

Choreographed by Anna Nygh.

Original Cast:

Señor Don Pepe Hernandez (El Compere Extraordinario)…Ron House
Miguel Hernandez (His Nephew)…Alan Shearman
Juan Rodriguez (His Cousin)…John Neville-Andrews
Consuela Hernandez (His Step-Daughter)…Diz White
Maria Hernandez (His Daughter)…Sally Willis

Licensing: Samuel French

Difficulties/Advantages: If you've got a handful of truly zany actors who are able to improvise raucous comedy and speak in comic accents, here's great material. Following the script carefully, however, will only get you halfway there, as it's the "acts" that convulse the audience, and the script is only a blueprint, call it a launching pad, for your comedians.

Five Guys Named Moe

Book by Clarke Peters
Music and Lyrics by Louis Jordan (in fact, a compilation of songs "made famous" by the alto sax bandleader Louis Jordan [1908–1975])

Uncovered at the tiny Theatre Royal Stratford in London's Fringe East End by Cameron Mackintosh, this swingin' revue opened in London's West End, was a smash, and then came to Broadway, where the producers broke through the wall of the theatre to the bar next door in order to serve drinks (at "Moe's") before, during, and after the musical.

Synopsis: The thin "book" has a sad, lovesick man serenaded by five "Moes" when they burst out of his radio in a puff of smoke.

West End production: Lyric Theatre, December 14, 1991; Broadway: Eugene O'Neill Theater, April 18, 1992; 464 performances.

Directed and choreographed by Charles Augins.

Original New York Cast:

Nomax...Jerry Dixon
Four-Eyed Moe...Milton Craig Nealy
Eat Moe...Jeffrey D. Sams

Big Moe...Doug Eskew
No Moe...Kevin Ramsey
Little Moe...Glenn Turner

Musical Numbers:

Early in the Morning
Five Guys Named Moe
Brother Beware
I Like Them Fat Like That
Messy Bessy
Pettin' and Pokin'/Life Is So Peculiar
I Know What I've Got/Azure-Te
Safe, Sane, and Single
Push Ka Pi She Pie
Saturday Night Fish Fry
What's the Use Of Gettin' Sober/If I Had Any Sense I'd Go Home
Dad Gum Your Hide Boy
The Cabaret: Five Guys (reprise)/Let The Good Times Roll/Reet, Petite, and Gone
Ain't Nobody Here but Us Chickens
Don't Let The Sun Catch You Crying
Choo Choo Ch'Boogie
Look Out Sister
Is You Is or Is You Ain't My Baby?

Licensing: Music Theatre International

Difficulties/Advantages: The imported-to-Broadway production had a British feel to it—as opposed to the uptown-in-Harlem ambiance expressed by the many black American revues, from *Sophisticated Ladies* and *Bubbling Brown Sugar* to *Eubie* and *Ain't Misbehavin'*—but local productions can find their own style, as long as it swings. All that is necessary here is a unit set, a small band, and five show-stopping men—although the fifty top-ten songs can probably be handled by any combination of good musical performers, and a rethinking of the cast might give the material more variety. Though few are alive who even remember the era, Louis Jordan's hot sax and strong rhythms formed a bridge between 1930s jazz and the soon-to-be popular rock 'n' roll, so today's performers shouldn't need too much explanation to get hip. One warning: the original performing styles were described by the *Times*'s Frank Rich felt as "racial stereotyping." But then, how many black musicals—and white for that matter—don't depend on stereotyping?

Forever Plaid

Photo: Roger S. Berlanger

Forever Plaid at the Little Theatre of Fall River, MA.

Book by Stuart Ross
Music and Lyrics: Various

There is a plot: A boy group from the 1950's—no baggy pants, no acne, no crotch-grabbing choreography, just tight harmony and matching tuxedos—returns from the dead for a concert they missed the night their car crashed into a bus while headed for the 1964 Ed Sullivan Show debut of the Beatles. (Small metaphor for the death of American pop music?) But this show is really a revue of classic songs from the post-swing, pre–rock 'n' roll era, when pop was very white, very tight, and very harmonic. According to the story, the boys weren't very good and will spend eternity trying to shake their nerves and perform that one great concert. But that's exactly what they do very shortly.

May 20, 1990; Steve McGraw's; 1,811 performances.

Directed and choreographed by Stuart Ross.

Original Cast:

Jason Graae   David Engel
Guy Stroman   Stan Chandler

Musical Numbers:

Three Coins in the Fountain
Gotta' Be This or That
Undecided

Moments to Remember
Crazy 'Bout Ya' Baby
No Not Much
Perfidia
Cry
Sixteen Tons
Chain Gang
Sing to Me Mr. C.
Dream Along with Me
Catch a Falling Star
Kingston Market
Jamaica Farewell
Matilda, Matilda
Heart and Soul
Lady of Spain
Scotland the Brave
Shangri-La
Rags to Riches
Love Is a Many Splendored Thing

Licensing: Music Theatre International

Difficulties/Advantages: Close four-part harmony makes these melodic songs not easy to sing, but if you've got four men who want to try to recreate the era of the Four Tops, the Four Freshmen, the Four Lads, the Four Aces, and the Four Many Others, this is the material to do it with. If the structure—an inept and amateur singing group becomes an outstanding one in under two hours—makes no sense, it nevertheless allows for a slow build to crescendo that a revue, particularly of this kind of music, wouldn't ordinarily have.

Free to Be…You and Me

Conceived by Marlo Thomas
Adapted for the Stage by Douglas Love and Regina Safran
Contributions by Judy Blume, Dan Greenberg, Carol Hall, Sheldon Harnick, Bruce Hart, Edward Kleban, Elaine Laron, Stephen Lawrence, Betty Miles, Shelley Miller, Carl Reiner, Mary Rodgers, Shel Silverstein, Peter Stone, and C. Zolotow

From the book *Free to Be…You and Me.*

A musical revue (from the popular book compiled by "That Girl") that beautifully illustrates for children more possibilities in life than Ozzie and Harriet ever dreamed of.

First came the book, then the album, then the show.

Television/Recording Cast:

Alan Alda	Harry Belafonte
Mel Brooks	Jack Cassidy
Dick Cavett	Carol Channing
Rosey Grier	Shirley Jones

Robert Morse	Diana Ross
Diana Sands	Tom Smothers
Marlo Thomas	Billy De Wolfe

Musical Numbers:

> Let's Hear It for Baby
> When We Grow Up
> The Sports Swing
> William's Doll
> Parents Are People
> The Spaceship Shuffle
> Glad to Have a Friend Like You
> The Tigerland Twist
> Girl Land
> It's All Right to Cry
> When We Grow Up (reprise)
> Free to Be…You and Me

Licensing: Rodgers and Hammerstein Theatre Library

Difficulties/Advantages: Minimum two males, two females (could be adults or kids) or more as desired. A great show for kids to do and to see, if they're not too jaded and cynical yet. Even then, perhaps with strong contemporary accompaniment, you can win them over too.

Greenwich Village, U.S.A.

Music by Jeanne Bargy
Lyrics by Jeanne Bargy, Frank Gehrecke, and Herb Corey
Sketches by Frank Gehrecke

Before the Village was gay, even before it was hip, it was beat. This revue celebrated that Village with a clever collection of material, now venerably historical. Dig those bongo orchestrations on songs such as "Ladies of the House" (the Greenwich Village house of detention, that is), "Miss Hi-Fi" (that's high fidelity to those who think music was always on little discs), and "Tea Party" (you don't drink it, you inhale it).

One Sheridan Square; September 28, 1960; 87 performances.

Sketches directed by Burke McHugh and Allen Hodshire. Musical numbers directed and choreographed by Jim Russell.

Original Cast:

Jack Betts	Saralou Cooper
Pat Finley	Judy Guyll
Dawn Hampton	James Harwood
Jane A. Johnston	Burke McHugh
James Pompeii	Ken Urmston

Sketches and Musical Numbers:

> Greenwich Village, U.S.A.
> It's a Nice Place to Visit

Ladies of the House
How Can Anyone So Sweet
Sunday Brunch
Love Me
How About Last Nite
Brownstone
BLT
That's How You Get Your Kicks
Miss Hi-FIE
Living Pictures
N.Y.U.
Off Broadway Broads
Shopkeepers Trio
Baby You Bore Me
Birth of a Beatnik
Espresso House
Weekend Shopping
Tea Party
What Do They Know About Love Uptown
It Pays to Advertise
We Got Love
When the Village Goes to Sleep
Save the Village (finale)

Licensing: Not in a catalogue, but the Sunbeam Music Corporation is listed as copyright owner

Difficulties/Advantages: Might be difficult to get hold of this material, but it's included here because the two-record set presents a lively collection that seems like it would make a great recreation of the beat era, a nice introduction to that prehippie, existentialist, antiestablishment movement. And better than that, the songs really swing!

Hello Muddah, Hello Fadduh!

The Allan Sherman Musical

Conceived and Written by Douglas Bernstein and Rob Krausz

Allan Sherman was a hilarious comedy-folksinger who wrote his own lyrics to classic, popular, and in rare cases Albert Hague's or his own, music. (Example: to the tune of "Down by the Riverside"—"When you go to the delicatessen store / Don't buy the liverwurst!") This revue is chock full of those songs, the most famous of which, still played on the radio today, is the title tune. Although the writers have put together a nice little "plot" to hang them all on—the birth, life, and retirement of one Barry Bockman—that hardly makes this compilation a "musical." Much of it is Jewish humor. You don't have to know that *hadassah* is Hebrew for "let's have a luncheon" or *liverwurst* is "a cold cut that's been around forever but nobody seems to eat," but it helps.

Circle in the Square Theatre; December 5, 1992; 9 previews, 235 performances.

Entire production directed and choreographed by Michael Leeds.

Hello Muddah, Hello Fadduh! at William Paterson University, Wayne, NJ.

Original Cast:

Stephen Beger   Tovah Feldshuh
Jason Graae   Paul Kreppel
Mary Testa

Musical Numbers:

ACT I   Opening Goulash
         Barry
         Sarah Jackman
         Won't You Come Home, Disraeli?
         Sir Greenbaum's Madrigal
         Good Advice
         I Can't Dance
         Kiss of Jyer
         Hello Muddah, Hello Fadduh!
         No One's Perfect
         One Hippopotami
         Phil Medley
         Harvey and Sheila
ACT II   Robbie
         Shake Hands with Your Uncle Max
         Here's to the Crabgrass
         Shine On, Harvey Bloom
         Mexican Hat Dance

Grow, Mrs. Goldfarb
Jump Down, Spin Around
Crazy Downtown
Did I Ever Really Live? (Music by Albert Hague)
Hello Muddah, Hello Fadduh!
Like Yours (Music by Albert Hague)
Down the Drain (Music by Albert Hague)
The Ballad of Harry Lewis
They Medley

Licensing: Samuel French

Difficulties/Advantages: Three men and two women can handle all the sketches, but if you have a larger group, there are plenty of roles to spread around, from kids to *alter kockers*. A community theatre in a Florida retirement community ought to sell out with this one.

Is There Life After High School?

Is There Life After High School? at the Summit Playhouse, Summit, NJ.

Book by Jeffrey Kindley
Music and Lyrics by Craig Carnelia

Suggested by the book by Ralph Keyes.

A montage of one-liners, monologues, and songs about high school delivered by a cast of thirtysomethings as thought-backs, delivered straight to the audience for the most part.

Time and Place: It's now, in the high school of your memory.

Synopsis: Nothing happens. The material is grouped by subject (e.g., "revenge") and the songs are self-contained ideas. There are no consistent roles; the actors just take on a character that might have those particular thoughts.

Ethel Barrymore Theatre; May 7, 1982; 48 previews, 12 performances.

Entire production staged by Robert Nigro. Assistant Choreographer: Gerald R. Teijelo Jr. Drum major choreography by Harry Groener and Gerald R. Teijelo Jr.

Original Cast:

Woman 1…Alma Cuervo	Woman 2…Cynthia Carle
Woman 3…Maureen Siliman	Woman 4…Sandy Faison
Man 1…Philip Hoffman	Man 2…David Patrick Kelly
Man 3…Raymond Baker	Man 4…James Widdoes
Man 5…Harry Groener	

Musical Numbers:

ACT I   The Kid Inside…All
Things I Learned in High School…Man 5
Second Thoughts…All
Nothing Really Happened…The Women
Beer…Man 2, 3, and 5
For Them…All
Diary of a Homecoming Queen…Woman 3

ACT II   Thousands of Trumpets…All
Reunion…All
High School All Over Again…Man 2
Fran and Janie…Woman 3 and 4
I'm Glad You Didn't Know Me…Woman 2, Man 1
Reunion (reprise)…All

Licensing: Samuel French

Difficulties/Advantages: Unit set (a high school) and contemporary costumes for adult actors who are looking back on high school. The ideas are pretty generic, nearly cliché. Moreover, there's a general theme that everyone had a pretty bad time in high school, and by the end of the show, you'll just want to say, "Get over it already."

I Love You, You're Perfect, Now Change

A Two-Act Musical Revue for Hopeful Heterosexuals

Book and Lyrics by Joe DiPietro
Music by Jimmy Roberts

A revue about relationships. Love the advert: "The musical revue about heterosexual love. They're here. They're straight. Get used to it." Apparently forty-eight men have gone on stage to propose to their girlfriends during the show, and according to the press office, none have been declined.

Synopsis: Act 1 limns that familiar madness leading up to marriage, act 2 the madness of marriage.

Photo: Stephanie Ferguson

I Love You, You're Perfect, Now Change at the Winter Park Playhouse, FL.

Westside Upstairs; August 1, 1996; 20 previews, 3,500 performances and still going at press time, making this the longest-running show in town, now that *The Fantasticks* has closed.

Directed by Joel Bishoff.

Original Cast:

Danny Burstein   Robert Roznowski
Jennifer Simard   Melissa Weil

Musical Numbers:

Cantata for a First Date
A Stud and a Babe
Single Man Drought
Why? 'Cause I'm a Guy
Tear Jerk
I Will Be Loved Tonight
Hey There, Single Gal/Guy
He Called Me
Wedding Vows
Always a Bridesmaid
The Baby Song
Marriage Tango
On The Highway of Love
Waiting Trio
Shouldn't I Be Less in Love with You?
I Can Live with That
I Love You, You're Perfect, Now Change

Licensing: Rodgers and Hammerstein Theatre Library

Difficulties/Advantages: If you're looking for a versatile structure, four actors playing fifty different roles in sketches and songs can't be beat. And you can't beat this one for popularity, with 150 productions around the world already. Apparently it's achieved a reputation as a great date night, a surefire draw.

Lovesong

Music by Michael Valenti
Lyrics and Book: Various, including Sir Walter Raleigh, A. E. Housman, and Elsa Rael
Original idea conceived by Henry Comor.

Just like it says: love songs.

Top of the Village Gate; October 5, 1976; 23 performances.

Musical numbers staged by John Montgomery.

Original Cast:

Melanie Chartoff	Sigrid Heath
Ty McConnell	Jess Richards

Musical Numbers:

What Is Love?
Did Not
When I Was One-and-Twenty
Bid Me Love
A Birthday
Sophia
Many a Fairer Face
Maryann
When We're Married
To My Dear and Loving Husband
I Remember
April Child
Song
What Is a Woman Like?
Let the Toast Pass
Echo
Open All Night
A Rondelay
Just Suppose
Unhappy Bela
Young I Was
Jenny Kiss'd Me
Indian Summer
The Fair Dissenter Lass
Blood Red Roses
So, We'll Go No More A-Roving
An Epitaph

Licensing: Samuel French

The Mad Show

A Musical Revue Based on *Mad* Magazine

Book by Larry Siegel and Stan Hart
Lyrics by Marshall Barer, Larry Siegel, and Steven Vinaver
Music by Mary Rodgers

We hear the orchestra warming up. Then a rattle of machine gun fire. Then the conductor appears, bandaged and bloodied. The curtain rises part way, revealing five pairs of legs, then the curtain *and the legs* rise the rest of the way, revealing the set. This two-joke opening, followed by an opening song with lyrics so nonsensical they drive an usher screaming out of the theatre, gives a hint of the kind of existential humor that has made *Mad* magazine popular for many generations. Unfortunately, the longer format of skits and songs doesn't hold up as well today, and the material would seem awfully thin in a theatre. Perhaps it would work better in a lunchtime cabaret.

Directed by Steven Vinaver.

New Theater; January 9, 1966; 871 performances.

Original Cast:

Linda Lavin   Macintyre Dixon
Dick Libertini   Paul Sand
Jo Ann Worley

Musical Numbers:

ACT I   Opening
           You Never Can Tell
           Eccch!
           Well It Ain't
           Misery Is
           Hate Song
ACT II   Looking for Someone
           The Gift of Maggie
           The Boy from…

Licensing: Samuel French

Difficulties/Advantages: Although the original production featured five performers, productions have been mounted with as many as twenty-five. If *Mad* magazine has a cult following, it's a very large one. Then there's the opportunity to introduce the uninitiated into *Mad* humor.

The Me Nobody Knows

Music by Gary William Friedman
Lyrics by Will Holt

Based on the book *The Me Nobody Knows*, written by children from seven to eighteen years old attending New York City public schools, edited by Stephen M. Joseph.

Original idea by Herb Schapiro.

The genesis of this dramatic revue is an anthology of heartfelt and extraordinary poems and essays by 200 children between the ages of seven and eighteen, primarily black and Puerto Rican, from New York public schools in Bedford-Stuyvesant, Harlem, Jamaica, Manhattan, and the Youth House in the Bronx. The spoken text and song lyrics are straightforward in both their view of reality—a thirteen-year-old taking his first heroin, use of the word *nigger*—and their hopes and dreams. The effect of the original was so powerful, the raw talent of the cast so representative of the rawness of the ghetto (now referred to as "the projects"), that it swept Clive Barnes, the *New York Times* theatre critic at the time, quite off his feet, and rightly so.

Orpheum Theatre; May 18, 1970; 385 performances.

Directed by Robert H. Livingston. Musical numbers staged by Patricia Birch.

Original Off-Broadway Cast:

Rhoda...Melanie Henderson
Carlos...Jose Fernandez
Benjamin...Douglas Grant
Melba...Gerri Dean
Lloyd...Northern J. Calloway
William...Kevin Lindsay

Lillian...Laura Michaels
Lillie Mae...Irene Cara
Catherine...Beverly Ann Bremers
Donald...Paul Mace
Clorox...Carl Thoma
Nell...Hattie Winston

Musical Numbers:

Dream Babies
Light Sings
This World
How I Feel
The White Horse
If I Had a Million Dollars
Sounds
The Tree
Something Beautiful
Sounds (reprise)
Black
War Babies
Let Me Come In

Licensing: Samuel French

Difficulties/Advantages: The original cast was very multiethnic, with an emphasis on minorities, especially black, but like most revues, any number of performers could be engaged, and the material can be spread among them, making it ideal for almost any school or young people's theatre group.

Bring In the Morning (a.k.a. *Me Too*)

Music by Gary William Friedman
Lyrics by Herb Schapiro
Based on the writings of young people participating in "Poets in Public Service, Inc."

A sequel to *The Me Nobody Knows* (originally titled *Me Too*), this collection of teen writing set to pop music offers more of the same from a twenty-five-years-later perspective.

Drugs, guns, sex, AIDS...what a long way we haven't come.

Variety Arts Theatre; April 23, 1994; 51 performances.

Directed by Sheldon Epps. Co-director and choreographer: Michelle Assaf.

Original Cast:

Sonya...Yassmin Alers
Judy...Imelda de los Reyes
Lakesha...Inaya Jafa'n
Alicia...Nicole Leach
Mavis...Raquel Polite
Nelson...Kevin R. Wright

Roberto...Roy Chicas
Cougar...Sean Grant
Inez...Yvette Lawrence
Jamal...Shannon Reyshard Peters
Hector...Steven X. Ward

Musical Numbers:

Come into My Jungle
Bring In the Morning
I-Rap: The Best-Kept Secret
Let It Rain
The Ghetto of My Mind
The Light of Your Love (La Luz de Tu Amor)
The Have-a-Heart-Take-a-Chance-Gimme-a-Break Blues
I'm on My Way
Never Stop Believin'
Funky Eyes
You (Tu)
Trip
The Glory of Each Morning
Deliver My Soul
I Want to Walk in a Garden

Licensing: Music Theatre International

Difficulties/Advantages: Multiracial and flexible, as is *The Me Nobody Knows.* Put the two together and you'd have one helluva history lesson on the dire effects of capitalism and the class system. Great for young casts, particularly in multiracial schools.

Nunsense

By Dan Goggin

Time and Place: The Present. Mt. Saint Helen's School Auditorium.

This "Habit Humor" revue is set up as if it were a benefit for (and starring) the Little Sisters of Hoboken, many of whom died from botulism when their cook served soup (and four are still in the kitchen freezer because the burial money ran out). Putting on the show is fun for the nuns, however, because the Mother Superior is a natural who wishes she could always be in the spotlight; and Sister Robert Anne, only an under-study, eventually gets her own number; and the cookbook they're selling to raise extra money has the tainted soup recipe in it, so that's out; and...well, what with one thing and another, they get through the evening, including the big numbers "Tackle That Temptation with a Time Step," which closes act 1, and "Nunsense Is Habit-Forming,"

Nunsense at the Venice Little Theatre, Venice, FL.

the second act curtain. "You know what I like best about this show?" Sister Amnesia says. "We haven't had to stoop to a single penguin joke!" Some may wish they had. If nuns in habits have long been an easy mark for comedians, creator Dan Groggin, himself a product of a Catholic education and discipline, has brought six of them to full, if caricatured, life and given them a revue's worth of material that seesaws between entertainingly silly and silly entertainment. The singing, tap-dancing nuns went over with enough audiences to make this off-Broadway musical a smash that induced sequels *Nunsense II, Nunsense Jamboree* and *Nuncrackers.*

Cherry Lane Theatre; December 12, 1985; 3,672 performances, including further editions.

Written and directed by Dan Goggin. Musical staging/choreography by Felton Smith.

Original Cast:

Prior to Entering the Convent:
Sister Mary Cardelia was Marilyn Farina
Sister Robert Anne was Christine Anderson
Sister Mary Leo was Suzi Winson

Sister Mary Hubert was Vicki Belonte
Sister Mary Amnesia was Semina De Laurentis

Musical Numbers and Scenes:

Act I   Welcome…Sr. Mary Cardella
Nunsense Is Habit-Forming…Cast
Opening Remarks…Srs. Cardelia and Hubert
A Difficult Transition…Cast
The Quiz…Sr. Mary Amnesia
Benedicite…Sr. Mary Leo

The Biggest Ain't the Best...Sr. Mary Hubert, Sr. Mary Leo
Playing Second Fiddle...Sr. Robert Anne
Taking Responsibility...Sr. Mary Cardelia
So You Want to Be a Nun...Sr. Mary Amnesia
A Word from the Revered Mother...Sr. Mary Cardelia
Turn up the Spotlight...Sr. Mary Cardelia
Lilacs Bring Back Memories...Srs. Cardelia, Hubert, Leo, and Amnesia
An Unexpected Discovery...Sr. Mary Cardelia
Tackle That Temptation with a Time Step...Cast

ACT II
Robert to the Rescue...Sr. Robert Anne
Growing Up Catholic...Srs. Robert Anne, Leo, Hubert, and Amnesia
We've Got to Clean Out the Freezer...Cast
A Minor Catastrophe...Cast
Just a Coupl'a Sisters...Srs. Cardelia and Hubert
Soup's On (The Dying Nun Ballet)...Sr. Mary Leo
Baking with the BVM...Sr. Julia, Child of God
Playing Second Fiddle (reprise)...Sr. Robert Anne
I Just Want to Be a Star...Sr. Robert Anne
The Drive In...Srs. Robert Anne, Amnesia, and Leo
A Home Movie...Cast
I Could've Gone to Nashville...Sr. Mary Amnesia
Gloria in Excelsis Deo...Cast
Closing Remarks...Sr. Mary Cardelia, Cast
Holier Than Thou...Sr. Mary Hubert, Cast
Nunsense Is Habit-Forming (reprise)...Cast

Licensing: Samuel French

Difficulties/Advantages: A note from the author: "The script indicates that the sisters are performing on the set of the eighth-grade production of *Grease,* and they are accompanied by a band. However, it should be noted that the sisters could just as easily present their benefit in a church basement with an old upright piano and no set at all. *Nunsense* is a musical comedy for everyone—everywhere!" But especially Catholic schools with a minimum of five girls anxious to put on the habit and shine. And by now there's any number of versions to choose from, too many to chronicle here, but you can peruse them via Samuel French.

Oh! Calcutta!

An Entertainment with Music

Devised by Kenneth Tynan

Contributors: Julian Barry, Samuel Beckett, Jules Feiffer, Dan Greenburg, John Lennon, Jaques Levy, Pat McCormick, Leonard Melfi, David Newman and Robert Benton, Edna O'Brien, the Open Window, Sam Shepard, Kenneth Tynan, and Sherman Yellen

A butt-naked erotic revue certainly not recommended for schools or community theatres, unless the community is a nudist colony. Nevertheless, it was an extraordinary show for its time, intended to be a sophisticated adult entertainment, where "a civilized man could take a civilized woman to an evening of civilized erotic stimulation"

(Kenneth Tynan). Well, "One man's art is another man's pornography" (The Supreme Court). *Oh! Calcutta!*—the title is taken from a painting by French Surrealist Clovis Trouille and is a French pun for (English translation) "Oh! What a lovely cunt you have!"—was both high- and low-brow at the same time, with comic sketches and much nudity, including a pas de deux between a naked man and woman so beautiful that one didn't even notice that old theatre adage about naked dancing: with the man, it never stops on the beat. Opening at the height of the uninhibited free-love sixties, it was a smash hit, although no one today will ever be convinced that its success was artistically and not commercially (that is, pornographically) driven. Its mounting was pretty much a pushing of the envelope by the off-Broadway avant-garde movement of the time, and its team of authors (see above) certainly gave it cachet. When it moved uptown, however, legions of foreign tourists kept the show running, but it was stripped of its Village ambiance and just seemed cheap. In hindsight, the sketches are seldom witty, more often crude and sophomoric, but the bodies were beautiful.

Eden Theatre (formerly the Phoenix); June 17, 1969; 1,316 off-Broadway. Moved to the Belasco Theatre on Broadway, where it ran for 606 performances. Reopened in 1976 at Broadway's Edison Theatre and ran 5,959 performances—to become, for a short time, the longest-running show on Broadway, inscribed right there on the bronze plaque at Sardi's along with *Man of La Mancha* and *Life with Father*.

Directed by Jacques Levy. Choreographed by Margo Sappington.

Original Cast:

Raina Barrett	Mark Dempsey
Katie Drew-Wilkinson	Boni Enten
Bill Macy	Alan Rachins
Leon Russom	Margo Sappington
Nancy Tribush	George Welbes

Musical Numbers and Sequences:

Prologue
Taking off the Robe
Dick and Jane
Suite for Five Letters
Will Answer All Sincere Replies
Jack and Jill
Delicious Indignities
Was It Good for You Too?
Much Too Soon
One on One
Rock Garden
Who: Whom
Four in Hand
Coming Together, Going Together

Licensing: None of the major agencies seem to carry this (oh, surprise), but if you can track down either producer Hillard Elkins, now in Beverly Hills, or conceiver Kenneth Tynan's estate in England, you could probably get the rights.

Difficulties/Advantages: Its time and place are gone with the wind. On the other hand, it's my guess that if you produced this show commercially in any city in the world that would allow it, you'd make a pile of money. Voyeurism just doesn't date.

One Mo' Time

One Mo' Time at the Williamstown Theatre Festival, Williamstown, MA.

Concept and Book by Vernel Bagneris
Directed by Vernel Bagneris

There's a libretto, but it's merely a slim excuse for talented performers to present these classic American songs, so I've placed this in the revue category.

Time and Place: 1926. An evening at the Lyric Theatre.

Synopsis: Edna's in jail and Agie took the $100 Bertha gave him to bail her out and skedaddled. That leaves just four to carry the show. But that's enough to make *Bertha Williams and Company*'s two-hour tour de force of New Orleans jazz songs and dances a real roof raiser.

We're onstage and backstage at the Lyric, a theatre on the infamous T.O.B.A. (a.k.a. "Tough On Black Asses" or "Chitlun") circuit in the pre-Depression heyday of ragtimes, Charlestons, and black bottoms. Ma Rainey, Bessie Smith, Ethel Waters, and Bill "Bojangles" Robinson aren't impersonated here, but their music and their heyday are, from "Tiger Rag" and "Muskrat Ramble" to "After You've Gone" and "You've Got the Right Key but the Wrong Keyhole." Any performance of this material will be "A Hot Time in the Old Town Tonight." The backstage "book" isn't much more than arguing among the three women, but its spot-on in the minstrel style that blackout sketches used to be, gives the cast time to change costumes more often than Cher, and helps pace the fabulous standards and not-so-standard selections that are brilliantly chosen and sequenced.

Village Gate; October 22, 1979; 1,372 performances.

Original Cast:

Bertha...Sylvia "Kuumba" Williams   Ma Reed...Thais Clark
Thelma...Topsy Chapman   Papa Du...Vernel Bagneris
Theatre Owner...John Stell

Musical Numbers:

Darktown Strutters Ball
Honky Tonk Town
Kiss Me Sweet
Don't Turn Your Back on Me
Jenny's Ball
Cake Walkin' Babies from Home
I've Got What It Takes
See See Rider
He's in the Jailhouse Now
He's Funny That Way
Tiger Rag
Kitchen Man
Shake That Thing
Wait Till You See My Baby Do the Charleston
Muskrat Ramble
Black Bottom
Take It on Outta Here
Hop Scop Blues
Hindustan
What It Takes to Bring You Back
Everybody Loves My Baby
You've Got the Right Key but the Wrong Keyhole
After You've Gone
My Man Blues
Papa De-Da-Da
Muddy Waters
Hot Times in the Ole Town Tonight

Licensing: Samuel French

Difficulties/Advantages: As with all revues, the cast size is flexible, but the offstage material needs to be hewn to pretty tightly. Three women and one man—plus the theatre owner—have short scenes. The musicians can't be timid either. They're on stage, and they have plenty of scats and solos to show off their chops too. It's a collection of great American songs that will have your audience standing at the curtain.

And if your audience still isn't satisfied, you can produce ...

Further Mo'

Conceived by Vernel Bagneris

Once more in the Lyric Theatre in New Orleans, the backstage antics are clever and limited, in favor of a second collection of the great jazz melodies.

Personals

A Musical Revue

Book and Lyrics by David Crane, Seth Friedman, and Marta Kauffman
Music by William K. Dreskin, Joel Phillip Friedman, Seth Friedman, Alan Menken,
   Stephen Schwartz, and Michael Skloff

Scenes and songs on finding a mate. The act curtain is a newspaper personals column,
with the first ad reading, "Real fine lookin' one-legged lady wishes to know tight one-
legged man. Box 619," and you know right away there's going to be some fun made
of singles on the make. A revue about men looking for women and women looking
for men, how they do it—in this case, primarily through the "personals" column—
and what happens when they do. Various sequences—some individual, some running
gags—cover meetings, the arc of relationships, and the desperation, but conclude on
an up note: "Some Things Don't End."

Time and Place: Contemporary. Unit set.

Minetta Lane Theatre; November 24, 1985; 19 previews, 265 performances.

Directed by Paul Lazarus. Choreographed by D. J. Giagni.

Original Cast:

Louis and Others...Jason Alexander
Claire and Others...Dee Hoty
Louise and Others...Nancy Opel

Kim and Others...Laura Dean
Sam and Others...Jeff Keller
Typesetter and Others...Trey Wilson

Musical Numbers:

Act I Nothing to Do with Love...Company
       After School Special...Jason, Company
       A Night Alone...Dee, Laura, Trey, Company
       Second Grade...Jeff, Jason, Trey, Company
       Imagine My Surprise...Dee
       I'd Rather Dance Alone...Company
Act II Moving in with Linda...Jeff, Company
       A Little Happiness...Trey
       I Could Always Go to You...Dee, Nancy
       The Guy I Love...Nancy, Jason
       Michael...Laura
       Picking Up the Pieces...Jason, Trey
       Some Things Don't End...Company

Licensing: Samuel French

Difficulties/Advantages: One of the many revues that draw humor—and sometimes blood—from
       relationships, but this one is a bit wittier and stronger than most and has a nice center:
       the descriptions we have to create of ourselves and the mates we're looking for in per-
       sonal columns and video-match programs. The classic "three men and three women"
       formed the original, but there are several scenes and over a dozen songs to distribute as
       you like.

Quilters

Quilters at the Little Country Theatre, North Dakota State University, Fargo, ND.

By Molly Newman and Barbara Damashek
Music and Lyrics by Barbara Damashek

Based on *The Quilters: Women and Domestic Art* by Patricia Cooper and Norma Bradley Allen.

A revue—a mosaic, really—of pioneer-women stories, elegantly blended with a score in the folk-song style. Mostly narration using story-theatre techniques, with pantomime and the girls playing everything from sheep to men. All built around the ancient art of quilting, their panels created to commemorate events in the lives of our ancestors who settled this country, under—if you didn't know this, you will after seeing this musical—horrific difficulties, from prairie fires to very large families.

Jack Lawrence Theater; September 25, 1984; 5 previews, 24 performances.

Directed by Barbara Damashek.

Original Cast:
Sarah...Lenka Peterson
The Daughters...Evalyn Baron, Marjorie Berman, Alma Cuervo, Lynn Lobban, Rosemary McNamara, Jennifer Parsons
Musicians, Daughters, and Sons...Emily Knapp Chatfield, Melanie Sue Harby, John S. Lionarons, Joseph A. Waterkotte, Catherine Way

Musical Numbers:
ACT I   Pieces of Lives
              Rocky Road

Little Babes That Sleep All Night
Thread the Needle
Cornelia
The Windmill Song
Are You Washed in the Blood of the Lamb (by E. A. Hoffman)
The Butterfly
Pieces of Lives (reprise)
Green, Green, Green
The Needle's Eye

ACT II Hoedown (traditional)
Quiltin' and Dreamin'
Pieces of Lives (reprise)
Every Log in My House
Land Where We'll Never Grow Old (by J. C. Moore)
Who Will Count the Stitches?
The Lord Don't Rain Down Manna
Dandelion (lyrics by Clara J. Denton)
Everything Has a Time
Hands Around

Licensing: Dramatists Play Service

Difficulties/Advantages: An all-female cast, although there are some men's roles that could be played by men or women.

Scrambled Feet

Book, Music, and Lyrics by John Driver and Jeffrey Haddow

A kind of "National Lampoon Goes to the Theatre." Sketches and songs about life in the theatre that drew plenty of knowing laughs in New York—and a fair number of groans too, which is part of the fun here. Best sketch: Elizabethan Dinner Theater, in which a waiter and a diner banter in Elizabethan puns.

The Village Gate; June 11, 1979; 831 performances.

Directed by John Driver.

Original Cast:

Evalyn Baron   John Driver
Jeffrey Haddow   Roger Neil
Hermione (a Duck)

Musical Numbers:

Haven't We Met?
Making the Rounds
Composer/Hungup Tango
British
Good Connections
Theater Party Ladies
Love in the Wings
Only One Dance

Child Star
Have You Ever Been Onstage…
Advice to Producers
One Happy Family

Licensing: Samuel French

Difficulties/Advantages: The original featured three men, a woman, and a duck, which is probably enough, as you wouldn't want to outweigh the very light and "in" material. Avid theatregoers should love this revue, but then, who else would turn up in the audience?

Songbook, a.k.a. *The Moony Shapiro Songbook*

Music by Monty Norman
Lyrics by Julian More
Book by Monty Norman and Julian More

"The life and times of songwriter Moony Shapiro." By the time you get to his song "Nazi Party Pooper," you'll probably catch on to the fact that there is no Moony Shapiro in ASCAP. A takeoff on composer revues.

Time and Place: 1926–1977 (the years of Moony's songwriting). America.

Synopsis: One of the actors narrates the story of "a Liverpool Irish orphan with American citizenship and a Jewish surname." His biography goes something like this: Born an orphan, illegal immigrant to Manhattan, sponsored by wealthy Jewish couple, accepted into the company of Tin Pan Alley greats, falls in love with Hollywood Star, spends her money, bankrupts in the depression, returns to New York, hit song, penthouse, Paris in its heyday, marries a socialist socialite, writes a song for Hitler's Olympics, atones with an anti-Nazi piece, joins the communist party, joins the war effort, blacklisted by Hollywood, writes the Broadway musical "Happy Hickory," a big hit. Then a dry spell: Dylan refuses to sing his protest song, the Beatles turn down his Liverpool sound, he promotes/falls for a hip chick singer, but she leaves him for California. His wife, however, is loyal, and they enjoy his golden years when his songs are successfully covered by young groups. Finally he is found dead, electrified by his new synthesizer.

Morosco Theatre; May 3, 1981; 15 previews, 1 performance.

Directed by Jonathan Lynn. Musical staging by George Faison.

Broadway Cast (three males and two females play over 100 roles):

Gary Beach
Tompthy Jerome
Annie McGreevey

Jeff Goldblum
Judy Kaye

Musical Numbers:

Aᴄᴛ I Songbook (from movie *Baltimore Ballyhoo*)
East River Rhapsody (from revue *Feldman Follies of 1926*)
Talking Picture Show (from movie *Evermore*)
Meg (trunk song)
Mister Destiny (recording)
Your Time Is Different from Mine (recording)

Pretty Face (from movie *Pretty Faces of 1934*)
Je Vous Aime, Milady (recording)
Les Halles (cabaret song)
Olympics Song (recording)
Nazi Party Pooper (trunk song)
I'm Gonna Taker Her Home to Momma (recording)
War Songs:
    Bumpity-Bump
    The Girl in the Window (Das Mädchen am Fenster)
    Victory V
Hollywood Evergreens:
    April in Wisconsin (from movie *A Yank at the Vatican*)
    It's Only a Show (from movie *Let's Do the Show Right Here*)
    Bring Back Tomorrow (from movie *Bring Back Tomorrow*)
Songbook (reprise)

ACT II   Happy Hickory (title song of musical)
Happy Hickory Rejects (trunk songs)
    Climbin'
    Don't Play That Lovesong Any More
Vocal Gems from Happy Hickory (from the musical)
    Happy Hickory
    Lovely Sunday Mornin'
    Rusty's Dream Ballet
    A Storm in My Heart
    The Pokenhatchit Public Protest Committee
    Happy Hickory (reprise)
    Happy Hickory (from Tel Aviv and Moscow productions)
I Accuse (from musical *Red, White and Black*)
Messages I (trunk song)
Messages II (version for Bob Dylan)
I Found Love (recording)
Don't Play That Lovesong Any More (trunk song)
Golden Oldie (trunk song)
Climbin' (recording)
Nostalgia (trunk song)
Don't Play That Lovesong Any More (reprise)
Songbook (reprise)

Licensing: Samuel French

Difficulties/Advantages: "Moony found himself in the Tombs prison among petty thieves, alcoholics, drug addicts, male prostitutes, pimps. It was like Hollywood—without the swimming pools." This is the sort of narration the role of "Storyteller" brings us, intermixed with the cast acting out Moony's story, authentically tongue-in-cheek. The songs—some of the silliest you've never heard—add to the festivities, which was a big enough hit in England to bring to Broadway...for one performance, after which the theatre was demolished! Broadway and London productions featured rather elaborate sets, projections, a grand and an upright piano on stage, drops and props. Yet the script says: "The production benefits from being simple and inventive." Maybe that's what went wrong. In other words, as with almost all the revues catalogued here, be creative, but about the material, not the sets.

Songs for a New World

Photo: Alan Headland

Songs for a New World, an Operating Theatre Production, UK.

A Musical Revue in Two Acts

Music and Lyrics by Jason Robert Brown

Exactly what it says: a musical revue in two acts. About? Well, does every revue have to be about something? This one by rights belongs in the composer's compendium category. Except that this composer/lyricist—who went on to bigger things, including a Tony Award—didn't yet have a large enough portfolio. These songs are the result of his first few years trying to crack the business. They range from slightly comical—Mrs. Santa Claus has had enough of being left behind—to a lullaby, to the usual yearning, sad, rock ballads today's generation of writers find de rigueur. In spite of a spiffy first production, there's plenty of rhyme but no reason, just songs the writer hopes Barbara Streisand will record.

WPA Theatre; October 11, 1995; 15 previews, 12 performances.

Conceived and directed by Daisy Prince. Choreographed by Michael Arnold.

Original Cast:

Jessica Molaskey	Andrea Burns
Billy Porter	Brooks Ashmanskas

Musical Numbers:

ACT I   Opening: The New World
On the Deck of a Spanish Sailing Ship, 1492
Just One Step

I'm Not Afraid of Anything
The River Won't Flow
Stars and the Moon
She Cries
The Steam Train
The World Was Dancing
ACT II   Surabaya-Santa
Christmas Lullaby
King of the World
I'd Give It All for You
The Flagmaker, 1775
Flying Home
Hear My Song

Licensing: Music Theatre International

Difficulties/Advantages: Any number can play; the original featured four. Probably best in a cabaret setting, with a group of singers whose passion is evident, since the basically pop lyrics are the kind that seem to convey a good deal in performance, and later you say, "Huh?"

Swingtime Canteen

Book by Thorsen Bond, William Repicci, and Charles Busch
Songs: Various, authentic 1940s

A slightly tongue-in-cheek take on the revues sent to soldiers overseas during World War II, this one performed by all women from Hollywood, a disparate bunch that some dialogue helps define. But the real songs are the real thing, and great songs they were and still are.

Time and Place: 1944. A stage at a concert for the Eighth U.S. Air Force in London.

Synopsis: When the girls aren't talking to the audience, they're talking to each other, but they get along better with the audience. A few "stories" develop slightly—our emcee is a "washed up" Hollywood star whose recent flop movie earns her an Academy Award nomination before the show is over, two of them get a bit catty with each other, the emcee's niece reveals that she married a soldier she'd only known for twelve hours before he went overseas—but, aside from dialogue that moves the show along nicely, this one is all about the songs.

Blue Angel Theatre; March 14, 1995; 294 performances.

Directed by Kenneth Elliott. Choreographed by Barry McNabb.

Original Cast:

Marian Ames...Alison Fraser
Jo Sterling...Marcy McGuigan
Katie Gammersflugel...Emily Loesser

Lilly McBain...Jackie Sanders
Topeka Abotelli...Debra Barsha

Musical Numbers:

ACT I   Bugle Call Rag...Company
Ac-cent-tchu-ate the Positive, Praise the Lord and Pass the Ammunition...Marian, Company

Hollywood Canteen...Marian, Katie, Lilly, Company
Andrews Sisters Medley:
Boogie Woogie Bugle Boy; Beat Me Daddy, Eight to the Bar, Thumboogie; Rum and
  Coca-Cola; Tico-Tico; Bei Mir Bist Du Schön; Hold Tight, Hold Tight; Three Little
  Fishes; Pennsylvania Polka; In the Mood; Beer Barrel Polka; Don't Sit Under the
  Apple Tree...Marian, Katie, Lilly
I Don't Want to Walk Without You...Katie
His Rocking Horse Ran Away...Topeka
Love Isn't Born, It's Made...Jo
Daddy...Lilly
A Nightingale Sang in Berkeley Square...Marian
Thank Your Lucky Stars and Stripes...Company
ACT II   Sentimental Journey...Topeka, Company
Don't Fence Me In...Marian, Company
How High the Moon...Katie
You'll Never Know...Marian
My Shining Hour...Topeka
I'll Be Seeing You...Jo, Company
Sing Sing Sing...Company
Keep the Homes Fires Burning, Pack Up Your Troubles...Lilly, Company
I'll Be with You in Apple Blossom Time...Company
Sing Sing Sing (reprise)...Company
You're Off to See the World...Company

Licensing: Samuel French

Difficulties/Advantages: In the original, several of the girls played instruments in the all-girl
orchestra, so if you've got singer/actresses who can play an instrument, you could fit
them in any which way or not at all. The unit set—a WWII U.S.O. stage—should be
easy and fun, but the costumes should be authentic, and unless you've got women who
can harmonize as well as the Andrews Sisters—one of the medleys—don't attempt this
one, because the vocals are everything.

Taking My Turn

A Musical from the Writings of People in Their Prime

Music by Gary William Friedman
Lyrics by Will Holt

A musical collage of thoughts on being old. Old jokes, such as, "If I had known I was
going to live this long, I'd have taken better care of myself," and observations, such as,
"It isn't easy watching the children go away" are about the best there is. The poetry
isn't very original or profound; the songs are tuneful but the lyrics banal when they're
not Rod McKuenesque. If "over 3,000 pieces of writing by the elderly" were the source,
it doesn't say much for senior literature. Still, a substantial run indicates that audiences
want to see their compatriots up there, and retired people are the theatre's mainstay.

Entermedia Theatre; June 9, 1983; 10 previews, 245 performances.

Conceived, adapted, and directed by Robert H. Livingston. Musical staging by
Douglas Norwick.

Original Cast:

Eric...Mace Barrett
John...Victor Griffin
Helen...Cissy Houston (yes, that's Whitney's mom.)
Charles...Tiger Haynes
Benjamin...Ted Thurston

Edna...Marni Nixon
Dorothy...Margaret Whiting
Janet...Sheila Smith

Musical Numbers:

ACT I   This Is My Song...Company
           Somebody Else, Not Me...Company
           Fine for the Shape I'm In...Dorothy, Edna, Helen
           Two of Me...Janet
           Janet Get Up...The Company
           I Like It...The Company
           I Never Made Money from Music...Charles
           Vivaldi...Edna, Company
           Do You Remember?...Ben, Company
           In April...Dorothy
           Pick More Daisies...Company

ACT II   Taking Our Turn...Company
           Sweet Longings...Janet, Company
           I Am Not Old...Helen
           Do You Remember? (reprise)...Ben, Company
           The Kite...John
           Good Luck to You...Eric, Company
           In the House...Eric
           Somebody Else (reprise)...Company
           It Still Isn't Over...Ben, Dorothy
           This Is My Song...Company

Licensing: Samuel French

Difficulties/Advantages: Four men, four women, all middle- to late-aged. The creators of *The Me Nobody Knows* tried here to do the same for senior citizens. I wonder if it's as depressing to perform as it is to watch. *Follies, Ballroom* and *70 Girls 70* all gave older performers a great chance to kick up their heels. This one, when it isn't a litany of complaints about being old, is a celebration of wisdom, although without demonstrating any.

Three to One

Sketches and Lyrics by Nancy Hamilton
Music by Morgan Lewis

This published script is a compilation of three revues that played successfully on Broadway in 1939, 1940, and 1946. There's not really a theme, although from the perspective of this century, it would certainly be a museum piece.

One for the Money

Booth Theatre; February 4, 1939; 132 performances.

Directed by John Murray Anderson. Musical staging by Robert Alton. Sketches staged by Edward Clarke Lilley.

Two for the Show

Booth Theatre; February 8, 1940; 124 performances.

Staged by John Murray Anderson. Sketches directed by Joshua Logan. Musical staging by Robert Alton.

Three to Make Ready

Adelphi Theatre; March 7, 1946 (later moved to Broadhurst Theatre; 327 performances.

Entire production devised and staged by John Murray Anderson. Sketches directed by Margaret Webster. Musical staging by Robert Sidney.

Performers in the various editions included Eve Arden, Betty Hutton, Alfred Drake, Gene Kelly, Keenan Wynn, Ray Bolger, Carleton Carpenter, Arthur Godfrey, Harold Lang, and Gordon MacRae.

Sketches and Musical Numbers:

ACT I   Ordinary Family
Parlor Game
At the Drop of a Hat
The Shoe on the Other Foot
I Only Know
The Christmas Tree Bauble
Portrait of the Artist
Clambake
All the World's Awheel
The Old Soft Shoe
The Story of the Opera
Teeter Totter Tessie

ACT II   How High the Moon
Wisconsin, or Kenosha Canoe
Calypso Joe
To a Skylark
Fool for Luck
Born for Better Things
Search Me
Little Miss Muffett
Cold Water Flat
A House with a Little Red Barn
The Yoo-Hoo Blues
The Quaint Companion
Kiss Me and We'll Both Go Home

Licensing: Samuel French

Difficulties/Advantages: "Small" revues of the period had two dozen performers, but I've
included this arcane artifact because none of the individual songs or scenes requires a
large number. The material ranges from humor that twenty-first century audiences
would stare at numbly to some very reliable comic sketches and songs. "The Old Soft
Shoe" is a classic song and dance (originally performed by Ray Bolger). "The Story of
the Opera," in which a woman tells her companion the story of Wagner's *Ring* cycle,
could be riotous with the right uber-soprano. "Wisconsin, or Kenosha Canoe" is a
hilarious spoof of the Broadway musical dramas, dominant at the time, of Rodgers and
Hammerstein—in which, after a narrator explains that "comedy" is no longer a necessary part of "musical comedy," the cast performs a musical based on Dreiser's *An
American Tragedy*, complete with spoofs of *Oklahoma!*'s dream ballet. When a woman
customer insists on trying a size 4 1/2-A shoe on a 7 1/2-C foot, the actor playing the
shoe salesman has golden opportunities for slapstick. On the other hand, you won't
want to use the little white girl who sings "The Yoo-Hoo Blues" in blackface and a pick-
aninny costume. So while I can't recommend the whole show, if you're looking for
some brief songs and sketches of World War II vintage, you'll find a handful of classic
ones here.

Tintypes

Tintypes at Amish Acres Round Barn Theatre, Nappanee, IN.

Book by Mary Kyte with Mel Marvin and Gary Pearle
Popular songs from 1890 to 1917.

Pre–World War I America is evoked in the words and music of the day, as delivered to
us by Anna Held, the beautiful music hall star; Emma Goldman, the notorious socialist;

a black domestic worker; a Chaplinesque Russian immigrant; and the outrageous Teddy Roosevelt, the youngest man ever to be elected President.

Theatre at St. Peter's Church off-Broadway, April 17, 1980, 137 performances; then moved to the John Golden Theatre on Broadway, October 23, 1980, 11 previews, 94 performances.

Original Cast:

Lynne Thigpen

Trey Wilson

Jerry Zaks

Carolyn Mignini

Mary Catherine Wright

Musical Numbers:

ACT I   Ragtime Nightingale
The Yankee Doodle Boy
Ta-Ra-Ra Boom-De-Ay!
I Don't Care
Come Take a Trip in My Airship
Kentucky Babe
A Hot Time in the Old Town Tonight
Stars and Stripes Forever
Electricity
El Capitan
Pastime Rag
Meet Me in St. Louis
Waltz Me Around Again, Willie
Wabash Cannonball
In My Merry Oldsmobile
Wayfaring Stranger
Sometimes I Feel Like a Motherless Child
Aye, Lye, Lyu Lye
I'll Take You Home Again, Kathleen
America the Beautiful
Wait for the Wagon
What It Takes to Make Me Love You—You've Got It
The Maiden with the Dreamy Eyes
If I Were on the Stage
Shortnin' Bread
Nobody
Elite Syncopations
I'm Goin' to Live Anyhow, 'Til I Die

ACT II   The Ragtime Dance
I Want What I Want When I Want It
It's Delightful to Be Married!
Fifty-Fifty
Then I'd Be Satisfied with Life
Jonah Man
When It's All Goin' Out and Nothin' Comin' In
We Shall Not Be Moved
Hello, Ma Baby
Tedda Da Roose

Bill Bailey, Won't You Please Come Home?
She's Getting More Like the White Folks Every Day
You're a Grand Old Flag
Toyland
Smiles

Licensing: Music Theatre International

Difficulties/Advantages: Like most revues, any number can play, although here the material has been wonderfully shaped around the five prototypes from the era. Amazingly entertaining for such old material and a wonderful history lesson as well.

Tuscaloosa's Calling Me (but I'm Not Going)

Written by Bill Heyer, Hank Beebe, and Sam Dann
Music by Hank Beebe
Lyrics by Bill Heyer

Another "I Love New York" musical revue. There's an endless well of themes in the Big Apple, and these songs exploit them as well as most, but if you're not living there, you won't get it.

Original Cast:

Len Gochman   Patti Perkins   Renny Temple

Top of the Gate; December 1, 1975; 429 performances.

Production staged and directed by James Hammerstein and Gui Andrisano.

Musical Numbers:

Only Right Here in New York City
I Dig Myself
Cold Cash
Things Were Out
Central Park on a Sunday Afternoon
New York from the Air
The Old Man
Backwards
Delicatessen
The Out of Towner
Everything You Hate Is Right Here
Suburban Fugue
Purse Snatch
Poor
Graffiti
Singles Bar
New York '69
Tuscaloosa's Calling Me...but I'm Not Going

Licensing: Hank Beebe Music Library, c/o Arts Conservatory Theater and Studio, 341 Cumberland Avenue, #2, Portland, Maine 04101; 207-761-2465; acts@maine.rr.com.

Difficulties/Advantages: Someday someone is going to put together all the best songs written about New York City and make one hell of a Big Apple revue. A few in the comic-relief variety might come from this show, but as far as a full revival goes, this material needs updating.

What's a Nice Country Like You Doing in a State Like This?

Devised by Ira Gasman, Cary Hoffman, and Bernie Travis
Music by Cary Hoffman
Lyrics by Ira Gasman

A "typically topical" revue (against which the audience is warned in the first number!) that has retained an extraordinary amount of its topicality and even, in some cases, become eerily prescient. A number on the decreasing separation of Church and State for example, seems right up to date in the Bush-Ashcroft era, and the "Terrorist Trio...Mohammed, Achmed, and Ali," who sing "There are no friendly skies anymore," is now very black humor indeed. It's absolutely good hearted, however; very funny; and one of the last in a long line of the kind of shows that, at the end of the golden age of nightclubs, filled Village theatres and cabarets upstairs, downstairs, and anywhere else they could find a small stage.

Upstairs at Jimmy's; April 2, 1973; 543 performances.

Directed and choreographed by Miriam Fond.

Original Cast:

Betty Lynn Buckley
Sam Freed
Bill La Vallee
Priscilla Lopez
Barry Michlin

Musical Numbers:

ACT I Get Out of Here
Church and State
I'm in Love With
Terrorist Trio
Hard to Be a Liberal
I'm in Love With (reprise)
Male Chauvinist Pig of Myself
The Liberation Tango
Changing Partners
I'm Not Taking a Chance on Love
The Last One of the Boys
I'm in Love With (reprise)
Runaways Suite (Street Suite)
  A. Runaways
  B. It's Getting Better
  C. Runaways (reprise)
  D. I Like Me

215

I'm in Love With (reprise)
There's No Such Thing as the Mafia
Farewell, First Amendment
I Just Pressed Button A
Nuclear Winter
New York Suite
    A. But I Love New York
    B. Why Do I Keep Going to the Theatre?
    C. Girl of My Dreams
    D. But I Love New York (reprise)
    E. A Mugger's Work Is Never Done
    F. But I Love New York (reprise)

ACT II   Hallelujah
Carlos, Juan and Miguel
Nicaragua
I'm Not Myself Anymore
I'm in Love With (reprise)
Keeping the Peace
I'm in Love With (reprise)
American, You're Looking Good
They Aren't There
American, You're Looking Good (reprise)
Fill-er Up
Porcupine Suite
    A. People Are Like Porcupines
    B. The Bar Scene
    C. Threesome
    D. Bedroom Scene
    E. Scale of 1 to 10
    F. People Are Like Porcupines (reprise)
Johannesburg
I'm in Love With (reprise)
Take Us Back, King George
Come On, Daisy
Finale
Also:
What the Hell
How'm I Doing (The Ed Koch Song)
Everybody Ought to Have a Gun (The Bernhard Goetz Song)
The Four R's

Licensing: Samuel French

Difficulties/Advantages: According to the authors: "The running order, costumes, musical arrangements, and size of cast are flexible. Certainly there is enough material to provide a challenge for anywhere from five to a dozen performers." And if that isn't flexible enough for your theatre, how about this: "The authors often write new songs to maintain the topicality of the show. If you wish to inquire about updated material for use in your production, please contact..." and the Samuel French edition of the script will give you the address of the authors! That material probably stems from their sequel:

216

What's a Nice Country Like You Still Doing in a State Like This?

Music by Cary Hoffman
Lyrics by Ira Gassman

American Place Theatre; October 21, 1984; 10 previews, 21 performances.

Directed and choreographed by Miriam Fond.

Original Cast:

Brent Barrett   Jackie Landron
Krista Neumann   Patrick Richwood
Diana Szlosberg

Musical Numbers:

Get Out of Here
Hello Mr. Church
I'm in Love With
What the Hell
Greatest Performance
Johannesburg
Who Put the Glitz in Fritz
It's Hard to Be a Liberal Today
Changing Partners
Male Chauvinist Pig
Street Suite
Runaways
It's Getting Better
I Like Me
Carlos, Juan and Miguel
Button A
Nuclear Winter
There's No Such Thing
New York Suite
But I Love New York
I Found the Girl of My Dreams on Broadway
A Mugger's Work Is Never Done
How'm I Doing?
Why Do I Keep Going to the Theatre?
Keeping the Peace
God Is Not Finished with Me Yet
America, You're Looking Good
They Aren't There
Farewell
I'm Not Myself Anymore
Porcupine Suite
People Are Like Porcupines
I'm Not Taking a Chance on Love
Threesome

Scale of 1 to 10
The Four R's
Take Us Back
Come on Daisy
Finale

Licensing: Samuel French

Difficulties/Advantages: Pick an evening's worth of your favorites from the two shows and the "updates," and make a political statement for your time and place.

Howard Crabtree's When Pigs Fly

Music by Dick Gallagher
Sketches and Lyrics by Mark Waldrop
Conceived by Howard Crabtree and Mark Waldrop

The suspicion that musical comedy and gay go together like a horse and surrey-with-the-fringe-on-top is brought home with unerring bravado in this revue, in which the outrageous costumes carry the musical numbers into our hearts, if the universal ideas and clever wordplay haven't already. Dream Curleys in rhinestones and spangled vinyl chaps, torch songs to the Christian Right, and other unique paeans to the intersection of song, dance, and gentlemen with a minority sexual preference make this revue wittier, funnier (no, that's not the same thing), and in one solo, more poignant, than many "straight" revues. The "Patriotic Finale" of act 1 ("You can't take *us* out of the U.S.A.") is, for example, a hilarious musical comedy anthem for gay, née civil, rights. Not for the average community theatre, unless your community is the Castro in San Francisco or Greenwich Village, Manhattan, but Bushies everywhere ought to be forced to sit through a production.

Douglas Fairbanks Theatre; August 14, 1996; 15 previews, 840 performances.

Original Cast:

Stanley Bojarski	David Pevsner
Keith Cromwell	Jay Rogers
John Treacy Egan	Michael West

Musical Numbers:

ACT I Prologue
When Pigs Fly
You've Got to Stay in the Game
Torch Song #1 (Newt)
Light in the Loafers
Coming Attractions with Carol Ann
Not All Man
Torch Song #2 (Strom)
A Patriotic Finale

ACT II Wear Your Vanity with Pride
Hawaiian Wedding Song
Cupid's Arrow
Shaft of Love

Sam and Me
Bigger Is Better
Torch Song #3 (Rush)
Laughing Matters
Miss Roundhole Returns
Over the Top

Licensing: Samuel French

Difficulties/Advantages: By Mark Waldrop, for the original cast album: "To quote a line from *When Pigs Fly*, 'Howard wears so many hats. And they're all so *big*.' Howard Crabtree did indeed wear many hats. He was a singer, dancer, all-round entertainer, and theatrical designer extraordinaire. His costumes gleefully propelled performers across boundaries of age, gender, body shape, and species. They blurred the lines between animate and inanimate, fact and fantasy. Yet somehow—amid all the tricks and gimmicks, the whirlwind quick changes, the ridiculous disguises, the four-foot wigs, the extravagant visuals spring-loaded to top themselves at the final chorus—the message was always about having the courage to be yourself. Howard died of complications due to AIDS on June 28, 1996, at age forty-one, just days after completing his work on this show. His genius is irreplaceable. But his spirit, which informs so much of this material, will be passed on to everyone who sees *Howard Crabtree's When Pigs Fly*—and hopefully to everyone who hears this recording."

The album, unfortunately, doesn't contain the bare-breasted mermaid, the Garden of Eden tableau, or Bette Davis as Baby Jane slinging a life-size Joan Crawford doll around. It does, however, continue the witty lyrics, solid accompaniment, and voices that make up in enthusiasm what they lack in timbre.

An earlier revue in the same vein is also available:

Howard Crabtree's Whoop-Dee-Doo

Conceived, Created, and Developed by Charles Catanese, Howard Crabtree, Dick Gallagher, Phillip George, Peter Morris, and Mark Waldrop

Songs and Sketches by Mr. Gallagher, Mr. Morris, and Mr. Waldrop

Additional Material by Brad Ellis, Jack Feldman, David Rambo, Bruce Sussman, and Eric Schorr

Actors Playhouse; June 16, 1993; 271 performances.

Directed by Philip George. Additional Staging and Choreography by David Lowenstein.

Original Cast:

Howard Crabtree
Tomy Femia
Peter Morris
Ron Skobel
Alan Tulin

Keith Cromwell
David Lowenstein
Jay Rogers
Richard Stegman

Musical Numbers:

Whoop-Dee-Doo!
Stuck on You
Teach It How to Dance

Elizabeth
Tough to Be a Fairy
Blue Flame
A Soldier's Musical
It's a Perfect Day
Last One Picked
As Plain as the Nose on My Face
I Was Born This Way
You Are My Idol
The Magic of Me
My Turn to Shine
Less Is More

Licensing: Samuel French

Part Three:
The Composer/Lyricist Revues

Here are the composer and lyricist compendiums, created after the original songs had their heyday in various other productions, the words and music of America's greatest songwriters. Almost all are available through the major licensing companies, all scripted, formatted, orchestrated, and ready for your theatre. The best have found strong concepts and, with or without dialogue or narration, offer a great evening of great songs. A few composers have been the subject of more than one; the Noel Coward, Cole Porter, and Stephen Sondheim catalogues all offer several versions. The great thing about these collections is that they bring back a trunk full of great American songs we aren't hearing on the radio. American music hit its stride with Irving Berlin and hasn't stopped singing since, but with our short and fickle memory, the great old tunes just don't get around much anymore.

IRVING BERLIN

Born Israel "Izzy" Balin, Berlin grew up on New York's Lower East Side uneducated and poverty stricken, was on his own by thirteen, began on the streets singing for pennies, became a singing waiter, then wrote songs without being able to read music or play the piano in more than one key. (F#, the black keys, of all things. A special piano—which was not, as legend has it, built for him but was a popular invention at the time—could shift the keys up and down over different strings so the player could change keys without changing his fingering.) He rose quickly to become America's most preeminent Tin Pan Alley songwriter. Outside of the fact that he lived to be 101 and the stories of how for the last thirty years of his life he was reclusive, refusing interviews and the use of his songs to everyone who petitioned him, the most melodramatic fact about his American-dream life is that he married a wealthy young Catholic woman who was disinherited by her family for her choice of beaus. The laugh was on the father-in-law, however, as with the wily business sense of the once nearly paranoid, he became richer than all of them, forming his own publishing and producing company and driving the hardest bargains in the business.

The Melody Lingers On

Music and Lyrics by Irving Berlin
Conceived by Karin Baker

Dialogue taken from the book *Irving Berlin: A Daughter's Memoir* by Mary Ellin Barrett.

Here, narration from a daughter's book about her eccentric, iconic father tells this Horatio Alger story, while the musical numbers introduce us to just about everything there is to know about early American popular songs, all by the man about whom Jerome Kern said, "Irving Berlin has no place in American music. He *is* American music."

Musical Numbers:

ACT I   Alexander's Ragtime Band
What'll I Do?
I Love a Piano
Everybody's Doin' It Now
The Girl on the Magazine Cover
Snooky Ookums
When I Lost You
Play a Simple Melody
Oh! How I Hate to Get Up in the Morning
You'd Be Surprised
A Pretty Girl Is Like a Melody
When the Midnight Choo Choo Leaves for Alabam'
Puttin' on the Ritz
Remember
How Deep Is the Ocean
Always
Blue Skies
Shakin' the Blues Away
Finale Act I

The Melody Lingers On: The Songs of Irving Berlin at Hofstra USA Productions, Hofstra University, Hempstead, NY.

ACT II

Marie
Say It Isn't So
Heat Wave
Suppertime
Easter Parade
Cheek to Cheek
Change Partners
Steppin' Out with my Baby
Let's Face the Music and Dance
Let Yourself Go
Let Me Sing and I'm Happy
All Alone
Count Your Blessings Instead of Sheep
White Christmas
This Is the Army, Mr. Jones
I'm Getting Tired So I Can Sleep
I've Got My Love to Keep Me Warm
God Bless America
It's a Lovely Day Today
You're Just in Love
You Can't Get a Man with a Gun
The Girl That I Marry
I Got the Sun in the Morning
They Say It's Wonderful
There's No Business Like Show Business
The Song Is Ended

Licensing: Rodgers and Hammerstein Theatre Library

Difficulties/Advantages: Although the premiere production at the Trinity School—one of Manhattan's poshest private schools with an annual musical that, in resources anyway, rivals Broadway—featured seventy performers (a part for every student!) this show has also been done with five males and five females just as, and perhaps more, effectively. It would be fair to say the music is easy to learn, but that might be misleading, as many performers today haven't an inkling how to present classic American music.

LEONARD BERNSTEIN

Bernstein came to fame at twenty-five when, as an assistant conductor, he stepped onto the podium of the New York Philharmonic on an afternoon's notice and demonstrated his charismatic conducting technique. Then he wrote the music for Jerome Robbins's first ballet, *Fancy Free*, and woke up the next morning internationally famous. Not stopping for breath, he wrote classical music, conducted orchestras worldwide, explained music to young audiences via television, authored books (*The Joy of Music* is a must-read for music lovers), and, oh yes, found time to write five Broadway musicals: *On the Town, Wonderful Town, West Side Story, Candide,* and the last-and-lamented *1600 Pennsylvania Avenue*. His wide-ranging interests and celebrity profile made him one of the most popular and controversial figures in music. For musical theatre lovers, he's left an extraordinary catalogue that has yet to be properly presented in miniature. Here's one attempt:

By Bernstein

Conceived by Betty Comden and Adolph Green with Michael Bawtree and Norman L. Berman
Music by Leonard Bernstein
Lyrics by Leonard Bernstein, Comden and Green, John Latouche, Jerry Leiber, and Stephen Sondheim
Written by Betty Comden and Adolph Green

Any show that previews longer than it runs obviously had a lot of trouble structuring an entertaining production. Bernstein's musical compositions, from classical to Broadway, are a treasure trove, but the songs here seem to be mostly from his trunk.

Westside Theatre; November 23, 1975; 40 previews, 17 performances.

Directed by Michael Bawtree.

Original Cast:

Jack Bittner		Margery Cohen
Jim Corti		Ed Dixon
Patricia Elliott	Janie Sell	Kurt Peterson

Musical Numbers:

Welcome
Gabey's Comin'
Lonely Me

Say When
Like Everybody Else
I'm Afraid It's Love
Another Love
I Know a Fellow
It's Gotta Be Bad to Be Good
Dream with Me
Ringaroundarosey
Captain Hook's Soliloquy
The Riobamba
The Intermission's Great
Story of My Life
Ain't Got No Tears Left
The Coolie's Dilemma
In There
Spring Will Come Again
Here Comes the Sun

Licensing: Probably not available as a show—no loss there—but Bernstein's songs are promoted through the Leonard Bernstein Music Publishing Company, c/o Universal Music Publishing Group, 2440 Sepulveda Blvd., Suite 100, Los Angeles, CA, 90064, and a good Bernstein revue—anywhere, anytime—could be an eyeopener.

JACQUES BREL

Jacques Brel Is Alive and Well and Living in Paris

Music and Original French lyrics by Jacques Brel
English Translations by Mort Shuman and Eric Blau

The original production featuring thirty of French songwriter Jacques Brel's songs performed consecutively without book or narration played at the Village Gate nightclub—a dim basement cabaret underneath a flophouse in the East Village, its air redolent with cigarette smoke and the smell of liquor—on a small corner stage featuring a permanent pole in the center. The whole beatnik nature of the thing was ideal for the French chansons of Brel, a form utterly foreign to pop music–driven America and thus wonderfully unique and startling to American audiences. The semi-obscure lyrics were brilliantly personalized by the original performances, creating an ambiance that, although librettoless and even characterless, was richly dramatic and vibrantly entertaining. Though few of the critics got it, audiences were entertained from the beginning, and the fortitude of the producers, relying on word of mouth, eventually turned the show into an international hit, complete with best-selling cast album and a unique film that featured Brel and needs to be brought out of the vault. A Brel revue—like one of Noël Coward, Stephen Sondheim, or Cole Porter—introduces us to the length and breadth of a unique and personal oeuvre of songs, in this case one with which few people are familiar and more should be.

Village Gate; January 22, 1968; 1,847 performances.

Directed by Moni Yakim.

225

Jacques Brel Is Alive and Well and Living in Paris at the Little Country Theatre, North Dakota State University, Fargo, ND.

Original Cast:

Mort Shuman

Shawn Elliott

Elly Stone

Alice Whitfield

Musical Numbers:

Marathon

Alone

Madeleine

I Loved

Mathilde

Bachelor's Dance

Timid Frieda

My Death

Girls and Dogs

Jackie

The Statue

The Desperate Ones

Sons of...

Amsterdam

The Bulls

The Old Folks

Marieke

Brussels

Fanette

Funeral Tango

Middle Class

No, Love, You're Not Alone

Next
Carousel
If We Only Have Love

Licensing: Music Theatre International

Difficulties/Advantages: Although the co-author's wife, Elly Stone, was considered a diva of the genre and was given all the best songs in the original staging, in fact the songs can be evenly distributed among two men and two women or, for that matter, any kind of a cast you want. Design offers a great deal for the imagination, or you can go with the plain, impressionistic background and simple velvet suits of the original. The songs themselves are best delivered presentationally. Aside from the fact that you must have outstanding singer/actors, it's a simple show to do, although an easy one to screw up if you don't give the lyrics a proper, passionate reading. Without a book, it is, among revues, about as dramatic as any in the genre. One difficulty: without the bohemian cabaret atmosphere, a great deal can be lost. To present Brel in a proscenium theatre is difficult and requires creativity by the director and designers. (Brel himself is no longer alive and well, so the title has been recently shortened.)

JOHNNY BURKE

Johnny Burke was born in 1908, grew up in Chicago, graduated from the University of Wisconsin, and went to work for the Irving Berlin Publishing Company as a song plugger. It wasn't long before he was writing his own lyrics. His career grew from the Fats Waller novelty hits "You're Not the Only Oyster in the Stew" and "My Very Good Friend the Milkman" to Hollywood, where he wrote so many hits for Bing Crosby that Crosby said, "One of the best things that ever happened to me was a 145-pound leprechaun named Johnny Burke." He dubbed Burke "The Poet." In the 1930s and 40s, Burke, usually with his longtime collaborator Jimmy Van Heusen, placed songs in forty-two motion pictures, including the great "Road" pictures starring Crosby, Bob Hope, and Dorothy Lamour, and four Broadway musicals: *Donnybrook! Carnival in Flanders, Nellie Bly,* and *Swingin' the Dream.* He died in 1964, leaving over 400 songs. At one time five of the top ten songs on the Hit Parade were his.

Swingin' on a Star

Lyrics by Johnny Burke
Music by Johnny Burke, Joe Bushkin, Erroll Garner, Robert Haggart, Arthur Johnston, James Monaco, Harold Spina, and Jimmy Van Heusen
Written by Michael Leeds

A revue built around a lyricist provides an eclectic array of tunes by a number of composers. Burke's collaborators range from Jimmy Van Heusen ("Here's That Rainy Day") to Erroll Gardner ("Misty"). The concept for this classic collection takes us from a Chicago speakeasy in the 1920s to the hit parade of the 1930s to a World War II U.S.O show, through the road movies of Bob Hope and Bing Crosby to the Starlight Supper Club in Manhattan, but it's all just a great excuse to sing songs—from "Dr. Rhythm" to "Personality"; from "One, Two, Button Your Shoe" to "If Love Ain't There, It Ain't There"; from "Pennies from Heaven" to the title tune, which was a number-one hit and an Academy Award winner for Crosby, for whom Burke wrote over seventy-five songs. Burke was a "Hollywood" lyricist, so don't expect the pithy sentiments of theatre musicals, but you can still bask in the glow of romance and novelty and a satchel full of American classics.

Music Box on Broadway; October 22, 1995; 19 previews, 97 performances.

Directed by Michael Leeds. Choreographed by Kathleen Marshall.

Original Cast:

Terry Burrell
Denise Faye
Eugene Fleming
Michael McGrath

Lewis Cleale
Kathy Fitzgerald
Alvaleta Guess

Musical Numbers:

You're Not the Only Oyster in the Stew
Chicago Style
Ain't It a Shame About Mame
What's New
Dr. Rhythm
Pennies from Heaven
When Stanislaus Got Married
His Rocking Horse Ran Away
Annie Doesn't Live Here Anymore
Scatterbrain
One, Two, Button Your Shoe
Whoopsie Daisy Day
What Does It Take to Make You Take to Me?
Irresistible
An Apple for the Teacher
Thank Your Lucky Stars and Stripes
Personality
There's Always the Blues
Polka Dots and Moonbeams
Swinging on a Star
Don't Let That Moon Get Away
All You Want to Do Is Dance
You Danced with Dynamite
Imagination
It Could Happen to You
Road to Morocco
Apalachicola
Ain't Got a Dime to My Name
You Don't Have to Know the Language
Going My Way
Shadows on the Swanee
Pakistan
But Beautiful
Like Someone in Love
Moonlight Becomes You
If Love Ain't There

Sunday Monday or Always
Misty
Here's That Rainy Day

Licensing: Dramatists Play Service

Difficulties/Advantages: Seven characters in the original, but over forty songs to do with what you will. The only difficulty: finding a man who can croon like Der Bingle.

NOËL COWARD

Coward was born outside London in 1899 and appeared in public for the last time—with Marlene Dietrich on his arm—when he attended a performance of the review *Oh, Coward!* in 1973. Author of too many plays, musicals, songs, diaries, short stories, and films to list here, he was also a prolific performer, a star of London's West End Theatre and New York's Broadway. He leapt to prominence by writing, directing, and starring in *The Vortex* in 1924, and knocked Las Vegas audiences dead with his songs and patter as late as the 1960s. Honored on both sides of the Atlantic for a brilliant life in the theatre, Coward can best be captured by his own advice: "Work hard, do the best you can, don't ever lose faith in yourself, and take no notice of what other people say about you."

Like those of many of his contemporaries, the songs of Noel Coward are extremely presentable out of context, and dozens of Coward revues have been staged. Nevertheless, if you don't have the time to canvass his entire life's work and put together your own show, a formidable task, here are three available compilations:

Oh, Coward!

Music and Lyrics by Noël Coward

Two men and a woman performed this collection in an upscale (tuxedos and gowns) music-hall style. Songs are mostly collected by subject matter—England, Family Album, Travel, Theatre, Love, Women—and performed presentationally. No awkward attempt to create a "book" or a "concept," just the master's songs in an intimate theatre setting. Coward's lyrics are so much like dialogue—particularly the witty, rhythmic dialogue of his own plays—that the actors are literally talking to the audience. Oh, to be at such a marvelous party once again.

New Theatre; October 4, 1972; 294 performances.

Devised and directed by Roderick Cook.

Original Off-Broadway Cast:

Roderick Cook	Jamie Ross	Barbara Cason

Musical Numbers:
Something to Do with Spring
Bright Young People
Poor Little Rich Girl
Ziegeuner
Let's Say Goodbye

Photo: Larry Levenson

Oh, Coward! at the Quality Hill Playhouse, Kansas City, MO.

This Is a Changing World
We Were Dancing
Dance Little Lady
Room with a View
Sail Away
The End of the News
The Stately Homes of England
London Pride
Uncle Harry
Chase Me Charlie
Saturday Night at the Rose and Crown
Island of Bolamazoo
What Ho Mrs. Brisket!
Has Anybody Seen Our Ship
Why Do the Wrong People Travel
The Passenger's Always Right
Mrs. Worthington
Mad Dogs and Englishmen
Dance Little Lady
You Were There
Mad About the Boy
Mrs. Wentworth-Brewster
Let's Do It
Where Are the Songs We Sung?
Someday I'll Find You
I'll Follow My Secret Heart
If Love Were All
Play Orchestra Play
I'll See You Again

Licensing: Music Theatre International

Cowardy Custard

An Entertainment Devised by Gerald Frow, Alan Strachan, and Wendy Toye
Featuring the Words and Music of Noël Coward

From England, this one features not just his songs but brief sequences from his plays, material from his autobiographies, and some unpublished material, providing a wonderful portrait of the man himself.

Mermaid Theatre (London); July 10, 1972.

Original London Cast:

Patricia Routledge	Peter Gale
Anna Sharkey	Derek Waring
Elaine Delmar	Laurel Ford
John Moffatt	Una Stubbs
Geoffrey Burridge	Olivia Breeze
Jonathan Cecil	Tudor Davies

Musical Numbers:

ACT I If Love Were All/I'll See You Again/Time and Again/Has Anybody Seen Our Ship?/Try To Learn To Love/Kiss Me/Go Slow, Johnny/Tokay/Dearest Love/Could You Please Oblige Us With a Bren Gun?/Come the Wild, Wild Weather/Spinning Song/Parisian Pierrot
Play, Orchestra, Play
You Were There
Any Little Fish
In a Boat, on a Lake, with My Darling
A Room with a View
When You Want Me
Specially for You
Beatnik Love Affair
I'm Mad About You
Poor Little Rich Girl
Louisa
Mad About the Boy
The Stately Homes of England
I've Been to a Marvelous Party
Mrs. Worthington
Why Must the Show Go On?

ACT II London Pride
London Is a Little Bit of All Right
What Ho, Mrs. Brisket!
Don't Take Our Charlie for the Army
Saturday Night at the Rose and Crown
London at Night
There Are Bad Times Just Around the Corner
Alice Is at It Again
The Passenger's Always Right
Useless Useful Phrases

Mad Dogs and Englishmen
Nina
I Like America
Bronxville Darby and Joan
I Wonder What Happened to Him?
Twentieth Century Blues
Let's Do It
Touring Days/Nothing Can Last Forever/Would You Like to Stick a Pin in My
    Balloon?/Dance, Little Lady/Men About Town/Sigh No More/Younger
    Generation/I'll Follow My Secret Heart/If Love Were All

Licensing: Samuel French

Difficulties/Advantages: Just looking at those titles brings a smile to the lips, but being able to sing isn't enough for Coward; there is that inimitable insouciance to provide as well.

Noël and Gertie

Noël and Gertie at the Bristol Riverside Theatre, Bucks County, PA.

Photo: Mierly Davis

An Entertainment Devised by Sheridan Morley
With the Words and Music of Noël Coward

Morley, a biographer of both Noël (Coward) and Gertie (Lawrence) has compiled a neat group of Coward songs and scenes, and woven them among biographical tidbits—how the two radiant stars of the 1930s West End theatre met (at ten years old), their great successes appearing together in his plays (one of which was a sequence of nine one-acts played over two evenings and a matinee!), and their lifelong friendship, cut short by Lawrence's death at fifty-three when she was enjoying her most recent and possibly greatest success, Anna in Rodgers and Hammerstein's *The King and I* (for which Coward had been asked to play the King but had to decline, and the producers instead uncovered a young unknown actor and singer of folk songs named Yul Brynner). This two-act evening adds up to a rich portrait of a wonderful, theatrical relationship; an unusual love story; and most of all, a re-creation of a bygone era of romantic comedy stage style of which they were the preeminent creators.

Donmar Warehouse (London); August 26, 1986.

Original London Cast:

Noël...Lewis Fiander   Gertie...Patricia Hodge

St. Peter's (off-Broadway); November 24, 1993; 28 performances.

Original Off-Broadway Cast:

Noël...Michael Zaslow   Gertie...Jane Summerhays

Off-Broadway revival; Lucille Lortel Theatre; July, 1998.

Noël...Harry Groener   Gertie...Twiggy

Musical Numbers:

Someday I'll Find You
Mrs. Worthington
Touring Days
Parisian Pierrot
Dance, Little Lady
Play, Orchestra, Play
We Were Dancing
You Were There
Has Anybody Seen Our Ship?
Men About Town
I Travel Alone
Sail Away
Why Must the Show Go On?
Come the Wild, Wild Weather
I'll Remember Her
I'll See You Again

Licensing: Samuel French in the United States, Curtis Brown in England

Difficulties/Advantages: It is difficult to capture the onstage presence of two such unique individuals, but the iridescent material—scenes from *Blithe Spirit, Red Peppers,* and *Private Lives,* and songs such as "Don't Put Your Daughter on the Stage, Mrs. Worthington" and "If Love Were All"—can make nearly anyone appear suave, sophisticated, and chuckling-to-hysterically funny.

E. Y. "YIP" HARBURG

Born Isidore Hochberg to Jewish immigrant parents on the Lower East Side of New York City in 1898, "Yip"—a shortened version of a Yiddish nickname that grew out of his boundless energy—held many youthful jobs, from selling newspapers to putting pickles in jars. He attended high school at an experimental school for talented children, where he worked on the newspaper, and City College of New York. He worked as a journalist in South America and as coproprietor of an electrical appliance company that went out of business with the 1929 stock-market crash. In a twist that even O. Henry wouldn't think of, the Depression forced him from business into writing to earn a living, and with the encouragement of his boyhood friend Ira Gershwin, he supplied lyrics for several revues. In 1932 he wrote the lyric that has been called "the anthem of the Depression": "Brother, Can You Spare a Dime?" Considered by Republicans to be anticapitalist propaganda, attempts were made to ban it from the radio.

His passion for social justice never abated. He wrote songs with Harold Arlen, Vernon Duke, Jerome Kern, Jule Styne, and Burton Lane, among others. With Arlen he wrote the score for the film *The Wizard of Oz*, which Harburg said he approached as a Depression fantasy. With Burton he wrote the great Broadway musical *Finian's Rainbow*, which dealt with racial prejudice (and Leprechauns looking for pots of gold at the end of the rainbow). Although Harburg never officially joined the Communist party, he had been a member of several organizations devoted to the rights of labor and was blacklisted by the film industry and had his passport revoked by the State Department—another silver lining, because it drove him back to Broadway and stage musicals, including *Darling of the Day, The Happiest Girl in the World, Finian's Rainbow, Jamaica, Flahooley* (which parodied the hysteria of the Communist witch hunting in the 1950s), and *Bloomer Girl* (with a feminist theme). Harburg and Arlen wrote the title song for Judy Garland's last movie, *I Could Go On Singing*. And he could have, but Harburg died in a car accident in Los Angeles in 1981.

Someone Sort of Grandish

A musical tribute to the lyricist, featuring fifty-nine of his 537 lyrics, with composers Burton Lane, Jay Gorney, Vernon Duke, Harold Arlen, Sammy Fain, and Jule Styne. With ballads such as "April in Paris" and "It's Only a Paper Moon," comedy such as "Lydia, the Tattooed Lady" and "When I'm Not Near the Girl I Love (I Love the Girl I'm Near)," and the classic "Over the Rainbow," any overview of his work has to be first rate.

All Souls Unitarian Church; January 22, 1976; 6 performances.

Original Cast:

Dana Coen	Hester Lewellen
Kirby Lewellen	Linda Lipson
Dick Pohlers	Tran William Rhodes
Kathleen Roche-Zujko	Monoma Rossol
Allan Smith	Tina Tymus
Gyle Waddy	Roger Whitmarsh

Licensing: The Harburg Foundation, 225 Lafayette Street, Room 813, New York, New York 10012

Difficulties/Advantages: Neither this particular "tribute" nor several other revues that have popped up over the years, particularly on Harburg's birthday centennial in 1996, have ever quite caught on as the definitive version, perhaps because his wide range of composer collaborators and projects resists a strong central concept. Nevertheless, an evening of his songs would be both highly entertaining and, for many audiences, eye-opening. Songs such as "Brother, Can You Spare a Dime" and "When the Idle Poor Become the Idle Rich" are rich in social politics. If there's a theme to be mined in Harburg, it's in his great passion for social justice.

JERRY HERMAN

Jerry Herman was born in New York City and educated at the University of Miami and Parsons School of Design (hence his hobby of buying, redecorating, and selling homes at a prolific rate). A revue he wrote in college moved to off-Broadway; his second revue, *Nightcap*, managed 400 performances there; and his first two Broadway book musicals—*Milk and Honey* and *Madame Aphrodite*—were, respectively, successful and unsuccessful. Then, with his score for a musical version of Thornton Wilder's *The Matchmaker*—for which he auditioned songs for producer David Merrick—he became one of the most successful songwriters in Broadway history. *Hello, Dolly!* ran 2,844 performances, not counting countless tours and revivals, to grab the long-run record, and featured in various companies Carol Channing (the original), Mary Martin (London and Vietnam), Phyliss Diller, Ethel Merman (who had been asked to star in the original but declined, and finally joined the company with two new songs written for her by Herman), Pearl Bailey (in a sizzling all-black production invented by Merrick and redesigned for the cast), Barbra Streisand (the film), Danny LaRue (a female impersonator), Ginger Rogers, Yvonne DeCarlo, and countless other women in the decades since.

    Dolly created Herman's reputation for writing great shows for women, and he capitalized upon this by next writing *Mame*, starring Angela Lansbury; *Dear World*, also starring Angela Lansbury; and *La Cage aux Folles*, for, okay, two men, but one of them spends much of the show in drag. No wonder, then, that the first attempt to compile his catalogue was called…

Jerry's Girls

Music and Lyrics by Jerry Herman

A compilation of songs, from *Hello, Dolly* to *La Cage aux Folles*, by the youngest of the old-fashioned songwriters in the popular category.

Onstage Theatre off-Broadway; August 17, 1981; 101 performances.

Staged and directed by Larry Alfod. Choreographed by Sharon Halley.

St. James Theatre off-Broadway; December 18, 1985; 14 previews, 139 performances.

Staged and directed by Larry Alford. Choreographed by Wayne Cilento.

Original Broadway Cast:

Dorothy Loudon	Chita Rivera	Leslie Uggams

Musical Numbers:

Jerry's Girls
It Takes a Woman
Put on Your Sunday Clothes
It Only Takes a Moment
Wherever He Ain't
We Need a Little Christmas
I Won't Send Roses
Tap Your Troubles Away
Two-a-Day

Bosom Buddies
The Man in the Moon
So Long Dearie
Take It All Off
Shalom
Milk and Honey
Show Tune
If He Walked into My Life
Hello, Dolly!
Just Go to the Movies
Movies Were Movies
Look What Happened to Mabel
Nelson
Time Heals Everything
It's Today
Mame
Kiss Her Now
That's How Young I Feel
Gooch's Song
Before the Parade Passes By
I Don't Want to Know
Jerry's New Girl
La Cage aux Folles
Song on the Sand
I Am What I Am
The Best of Times
Jerry's Turn

Licensing: Samuel French

Difficulties/Advantages: Three leading ladies—one who sang, one who danced, and one who attacked the material in her own inimitable way—buttressed by eight chorus girls performed their way through the Jerry Herman catalogue, butchering many of the songs and misinterpreting others. It's a collection, however, that can be done in more imaginative ways, by both men and women, and deserves to be. A better compilation is:

Showtune

Celebrating the Words and Music of Jerry Herman
Composer/Lyricist: Jerry Herman
Conceived by Paul Gilger

This one features forty songs from *Milk and Honey, Hello, Dolly! Mame, Dear World, Mack and Mabel, The Grand Tour, A Day in Hollywood,* and *La Cage aux Folles.*

Licensing: Music Theatre International

Difficulties/Advantages: This is an outstanding collection of songs that can work well on their own, outside the dramatic context of the librettos for which they were written, as Herman is a songwriter more in the Irving Berlin than the Stephen Sondheim tradition, and the arranger here has done an excellent job. Unfortunately, the original production (playing San Francisco, New York and Los Angeles) was utterly without direction,

Showtune at the Livestock Players Musical Theatre, Greensboro, NC.

choreography, or creativity, and left a handful of talented singers to keep up their—and our—spirits as they did their best without physical or emotional support from a concept. Or perhaps we should say fortunately, as that leaves the field wide open for you to bring your own creativity to the collection. Both one-act and two-act versions are available from the licensing company. Because of the nature of his songs—most can be taken out of context quite easily—Herman is a natural for a revue, and surely many more will be attempted in the years to come.

JONES (TOM) AND SCHMIDT (HARVEY)

Tom Jones (book and lyrics) and Harvey Schmidt (music) met at the University of Texas in 1950 on a show called *Hipsy-Boo!* a revue of American theatre music from 1900 to 1950 directed by fellow student Word Baker. Jones wrote sketches and Schmidt was the musical director. Neither, at the time, considered his future to be songwriting. Jones wanted to be a theatre director and Schmidt, a commercial artist. *Hipsy-Boo!* however was probably too much fun, and Jones and Schmidt began to collaborate on songs and, ultimately, a book musical. They graduated, served in the Army, continued to collaborate by mail, and upon mustering out of the service, took a flat in Manhattan (with fellow University of Texas alumni Robert Benton, later to become the Academy Award—winning film writer/director).

Their first years were a struggle, although Schmidt earned a decent living as a graphic artist and freelance illustrator. (His wonderful designs grace the album cover of every one of Ben Bagley's Painted Smiles recordings, and he designed the typeface that is *The Fantasticks* title.) They contributed material to Julius Monk's *Upstairs at the Downstairs* revues and Ben Bagley's *Shoestring Revues*, and then worked on a full-scale Broadway musical based on a slight, late nineteenth-century French play that spoofed

Romeo and Juliet by having two fathers fake a family feud in order to encourage a romance between their children. The play (called *The Fantasticks* in an English-language translation by a woman writing under the name George Fleming) had been introduced to them by their college professor, B. Iden Payne, who had directed it in London in 1909 with Mrs. Patrick Campbell as "The Boy" in a pants part. They embarked on turning it into a full-scale musical called *Joy Comes to Deadhorse*. Following the history recounted above, all hands agreed to return to the original title.

Although it would be difficult to live up to one of the great scores of the American theatre, Jones and Schmidt did so with Broadway scores for *110 in the Shade* and *I Do! I Do!* where they encountered the irascible David Merrick and the man Merrick dubbed the "Presbyterian Hitler," Gower Champion. Those experiences convinced them to abandon Broadway and start a theatre of their own.

With money rolling in from their Broadway and off-Broadway shows in the late 1960s, Jones and Schmidt rented a brownstone just steps west of the Broadway theatre district and there created a cozy theatre with four floors of costumes, props, and musical instruments, then hermited themselves and actors away for six years. The result, in addition to a load of experimental work and a lot of wine drinking and meaning-of-life talk, was four eccentric, experimental musicals that a few lucky New Yorkers saw: *Philemon, Celebration, Ratfink,* and *The Bone Room*.

Their next epoch revolved around the famous author, actress, music-hall performer, and lesbian, Colette. They wrote incidental music and songs for a play starring Zoe Caldwell, then turned it into a full-scale musical. Starring Diana Rigg, it toured but never made it in. Several workshops later, the project metamorphosed into *Collette Collage* and has been recorded.

They created a musical version of *Our Town*—a splendid idea for their particular talents—and worked on it for three months at a small theatre in Chicago; but clumsy producing, the lack of a male star, the substitution of a female star (Mary Martin as the Stage Manager), and her cancellation due to cancer at the last minute all conspired to keep the show from going on, until the Thornton Wilder estate withdrew the rights. They created a musical of the classic children's book *Mirette,* which had a successful tryout at Goodspeed's smaller theatre, but the producers—ignoring the rule "if it's not broken, don't fix it"—fired the director and mounted a full-size production that went in an entirely different, and wrong, direction. They finished a musical they had begun in the 1950s in Texas called *Roadside* and have shepherded it through several productions there. They were inducted into the Theatre Hall of Fame on February 1, 1999. They've created a show they star in, a revue of their theatre songs called *The Show Goes On*. And at this writing, theirs still does, somewhere in the world, every night—thank goodness for the American book musical, for no one should grow up without seeing a live production of the seminal small musical *The Fantasticks*.

Their words and music will—because they are most often unattached to time and place—live forever, and forever enchant audiences of theatre songs.

The Show Goes On

A Portfolio of Theatre Songs

This compilation was put together—and featured—the authors themselves.

St. Peter's; December 10, 1997; 88 performances.

Directed and staged by Drew Scott Harris. Choreographed by Janet Watson.

Original Cast:

Jo Ann Cunningham
Emma Lampert
Harvey Schmidt

Tom Jones
J. Mark McVey

Musical Numbers:

Come On Along
Try to Remember
Mr. Off-Broadway
Everyone Looks Lonely
I Know Loneliness Quite Well
Story of My Life
The Holy Man and the New Yorker
It's Gonna Be Another Hot Day
I Can Dance
Desseau Dance Hall
Flibberty-Gibbett
Melisande
Simple Little Things
I Do! I Do!
The Honeymoon Is Over
My Cup Runneth Over
Celebration
Orphan in the Storm
Survive
Under the Tree
Fifty Million Years Ago
Decorate the Human Face
Where Did It Go?
Wonderful Way to Die
The Room Is Filled with You
Time Goes By
Goodbye World
The Show Goes On

Licensing: Music Theatre International

Difficulties/Advantages: As flexible as any composer's compilation, and since you won't have Jones and Schmidt performing for you, you'll have to fill in the blanks anyway.

KANDER (JOHN) AND EBB (FRED)

In the older tradition of permanent partnerships (Rodgers and Hammerstein, Lerner and Loewe), John Kander (1927, Kansas City; Oberlin College, Columbia University, composing) and Fred Ebb (1936, Manhattan; New York University, Columbia University, English Literature) were for forty years one of the most unique songwriting teams on Broadway. Kander started in 1956 as pianist for *The Amazing Adele*, during a pre-Broadway run, and for *An Evening with Beatrice Lillie* on the road. He created the dance arrangements for the musicals *Irma la Douce* and *Gypsy*, then made his Broadway debut as a composer with *A Family Affair*, book and lyrics by James and William Goldman, directed by Harold Prince. Then his music publisher introduced him to lyricist Fred Ebb.

Ebb had been a writer of sketches and nightclub material, and contributed to the popular television show *That Was the Week That Was*. That first year of collaboration, they turned out the hit song "My Coloring Book" (Barbara Streisand), then met Liza Minnelli—whose unique voice and delivery would figure in their work many times—when they wrote *Flora, the Red Menace*, her first starring role. In 1966 they wrote the score for *Cabaret*, and the rest is Broadway history: *The Happy Time, Zorba, 70 Girls 70, Chicago* (starring Gwen Verdon and Chita Rivera), *The Act* (starring Minnelli), *The Rink* (starring Minnelli and Rivera), *Kiss of the Spider Woman* (starring Rivera), *Steel Pier, Woman of the Year*, and the film *Funny Lady*. Their title song for the film *New York, New York* (starring Minnelli and Robert De Niro), recorded by Frank Sinatra in the twilight of his career, has become an anthem for the city. Together they received the lifetime achievement award at the twenty-first Kennedy Center honors.

Of their amazing catalogue, *Chicago* is their most recent hit, because of the film version (which followed the Bob Fosse original stage version by twenty years!), but film and theatre fans will not let it replace the dazzling *Cabaret*, and lovers of romantic theatre music will put *Zorba* at the top of their list. The recent death of Fred Ebb has ended this great pairing, but their songs will "Say Yes" for a hundred years. They are unique and quintessential songwriters of the modern American book musical.

There is both an older and a more recent arrangement of their work. The older is:

2 x 5

Music by John Kander
Lyrics by Fred Ebb

Village Gate Downstairs; October 18, 1976; 57 performances.

Conceived and directed by Seth Glassman.

Original Cast:

D'Jamin Bartlett
Danny Fortus
Scott Stevensen

Kay Cummings
Shirley Lemmon

Musical Numbers:

Cabaret
Willkommen
Yes
Sing Happy
Mein Herr
Seeing Things
The World Goes Round
Love Song
The Money Song
Sign Here
My Own Best Friend
Losers
Military Man

Only Love
Why Can't I Speak?
Me and My Baby
Isn't This Better?
Home
Maybe This Time
Ring Them Bells
Mr. Cellophane
Among My Yesterdays
I Don't Remember You
Class
Broadway, My Street
New York, New York
On Stage
Ten Percent
Razzle Dazzle
A Quiet Thing
Cabaret

Licensing: Samuel French

A more recent compilation is also available:

And the World Goes 'Round

The Songs of Kander and Ebb

Music by John Kander
Lyrics by Fred Ebb
Conceived by Scott Ellis, Susan Strohman, and David Thompson

Westside Theater; March 18, 1991; 15 previews, 405 performances.

Directed by Scott Ellis. Choreographed by Susan Stroman.

Original Cast:

Bob Cuccioli   Karen Mason
Brenda Pressley   Jim Walton
Karen Ziemba

Musical Numbers:

And the World Goes 'Round
Yes
Coffee in a Cardboard Cup
The Happy Time
Colored Lights
Sara Lee
Arthur in the Afternoon
My Coloring Book
I Don't Remember You/Sometimes a Day Goes By
And All That Jazz

And the World Goes 'Round at the Polka Dot Playhouse, Bridgeport, CT.

Class
Mister Cellophane
Me and My Baby
There Goes the Ballgame
How Lucky Can You Get
The Rink
Ring Them Bells
Kiss of the Spider Woman
Only Love/Marry Me/A Quiet Thing
Pain
The Grass Is Always Greener
We Can Make It
Maybe This Time
Isn't This Better?
Trio
Money, Money
Cabaret
New York, New York

Licensing: Music Theatre International

Difficulties/Advantages: Almost everything they ever wrote sounds great when Liza Minnelli belts it out, but if you can get her clarion voice out of your head, there's a career full of great theatre songs here, many of them deeper and more interesting than the usual loud-is-good, big-is-better approach reveals. Nothing much but chutzpah holds them together in either of the two published revues, but if your audience is not standing and cheering by the time you get to "New York, New York," you just haven't rung their bells.

242

JEROME KERN

Born in 1885 in New York to a first-generation Jewish-German family, Jerome Kern had a mother who recognized his talent and encouraged him in music from an early age, while his father insisted that no son of his would ever pursue such a disreputable career as composing and required the sixteen-year-old to join him in his retail business. Upon his mistaken purchase of 200 pianos, however, Kern's father allowed him to study at the New York College of Music. He worked as a song-plugger and in-house composer for a New York publisher, but it was in London that Kern managed to first show his talents. At the turn of the century, everything important that happened in the musical theatre took place in London, so the nineteen-year-old Kern decided to cross the Atlantic and study English musical comedy and European operetta. He soon succeeded in having his own songs used in West End shows.

Back on Broadway, Kern joined forces with Guy Bolton and P. G. Wodehouse, and the trio wrote entirely new shows. Instead of royalty, clowns, and gods, in the European writing tradition, they turned to modern American life (especially new dance crazes) and believable people for inspiration. The small Princess Theatre musicals they created have since become legendary as the beginning of the integration of book, music, and lyrics and the genesis of the modern American book musical. The Broadway musical proper was beginning to evolve. With Kern and Hammerstein's *Show Boat* it would finally arrive. He went on to write *Sweet Adeline* (1929), *The Cat and the Fiddle* (1931), *Music in the Air* (1932), and *Roberta* (1933), featuring "Smoke Gets in Your Eyes." For Hollywood movie musicals, Kern won Academy Awards for his songs "The Way You Look Tonight" and "The Last Time I Saw Paris." In 1945 Kern returned to New York, intending to write the musical *Annie Oakley* with Dorothy Fields, but died of a heart attack.

Jerome Kern Goes to Hollywood

Conceived by David Kernan
Written by Dick Vosburgh
Music by Jerome Kern
Lyrics by Oscar Hammerstein II, Dorothy Fields, Ira Gershwin, Otto Harbach, Johnny Mercer, E. Y. Harburg, Jimmy McHugh, P. G. Wodehouse, Buddy DeSylva, Gus Kahn, Bernard Dougall, and Herbert Reynolds

Kernan—the Englishman who starred in *Side by Side by Sondheim*—here creates a similar four-character kaleidoscope, this one of golden age songs from the trunk of one of America's greatest Tin Pan Alley, Broadway, and Hollywood composers. Continuity is the usual biographical tidbits and comic stories; the songs are everything.

Ritz Theatre; January 23, 1986; 9 previews, 13 performances.

Directed by David Kernan. Additional staging by Irving Davies.

Original Cast:

Elaine Delmar	Scott Holmes
Liz Robertson	Elisabeth Welch

Musical Numbers:

> The Song Is You
> I've Told Every Little Star
> Let's Begin
> I Won't Dance
> Californ-i-ay
> I'll Be Hard to Handle
> Smoke Gets in Your Eyes
> Yesterdays
> Bojangles of Harlem
> I'm Old-Fashioned
> Make Believe
> Why Do I Love You?
> I Have the Room Above Her
> It Still Suits Me
> Day Dreaming
> I Dream Too Much
> Can I Forget You?
> Pick Yourself Up
> She Didn't Say Yes
> The Folks Who Live on the Hill
> Long Ago and Far Away
> The Show Must Go On
> Don't Ask Me Not to Sing
> The Way You Look Tonight
> A Fine Romance
> Lovely to Look At
> Just Let Me Look at You
> Who?
> Remind Me
> The Last Time I Saw Paris
> Ol' Man River
> Why Was I Born?
> Bill
> Can't Help Lovin' Dat Man
> All the Things You Are
> I've Told Every Little Star
> They Didn't Believe Me
> Till the Clouds Roll By
> Look for the Silver Lining
> Make Way for Tomorrow

Licensing: Music Theatre International

Difficulties/Advantages: And that list barely scratches the surface of the Kern catalogue! A success in London, the Broadway production might have done better off-Broadway or in cabaret. Its rather cliché staging—the usual tuxedos, straw hats, and stools—desperately needs your input. Give it a try.

CAROLE KING

Carole King (née Klein) was a musical prodigy, writing songs at the piano by her early teens in the mid-fifties. While a student at Queens College in New York, she plunged into the Tin Pan Alley world, recording demos, singing back-up and arranging. She and her first lyric partner (and first husband) scored big with "Will You Still Love Me Tomorrow," "Take Good Care of My Baby," and "Up on the Roof." A rich body of work in the style of the period poured forth—see the songs below—and culminated in her solo album as performer and writer, *Tapestry*, which has sold more than fifteen million copies worldwide. Her catalogue covers the greatest of rock 'n' roll epochs as well as recent, rich adult material, and is collected in:

Tapestry—The Music of Carole King

Music by Carole King
Lyrics by Carole King and Gerry Goffin

A musical journey through the career of Carole King, who wrote pop hits in the sixties and is still writing them. Her album *Tapestry* is still the best selling female vocal record of all time.

Union Square Theatre; February 19, 1993; 23 performances, 19 previews.

Directed by Jeffrey Martin. Musical staging by Ron Navarre.

Original Cast:

Lawrence Clayton	Mary Gutzi
Pattie Darcy Jones	Vanessa A. Jones
Frank Mastrone	Jim Morlino

Musical Numbers:

Music/Ride the Music
Where You Lead
Sweet Seasons/Been to Canaan
Up on the Roof
I Feel the Earth Move
Growing Away from Me/It's Gonna Take Some Time/It's Late
Where Does Love Go?
So Far Away/Home Again
Jazz Man
Chains/Don't Say Nothing Bad About My Baby/Will You Love Me
     Tomorrow?/Every Breath I Take/(Something Tells Me) I'm into Something
     Good/Take Good Care of My Baby/Go Away, Little Girl/One Fine Day/Hey
     Girl/(The) Locomotion
Looking Out for Number One
Chalis Borealis
Child of Mine/Daughter of Light/Only Love Is Real
Speeding Time
No Easy Way Down
Beautiful

Smackwater Jack
Tapestry
Will You Love Me Tomorrow?
Some Kind of Wonderful
(You Make Me Feel Like a) Natural Woman
Hi De Ho
Way Over Yonder
We Are All in This Together
You've Got a Friend

Licensing: Music Theatre International

Difficulties/Advantages: The original production of this assemblage of King's songs boasted not a whit (nor wit) of creativity, but as with most composers' revues, there's an awful lot to work with here. As rock 'n' roll has long supplanted show music at the top of the charts, and the baby boomers have plenty of money—if they haven't invested in dot-coms—a new approach could salvage this bouncy, commercial catalogue. See also *Beehive,* for a broader, theme-driven revue that includes some of her songs.

JOHN LATOUCHE

Largely unknown outside theatre circles, Latouche is considered by many as a precursor to Sondheim for his literate lyrics. He contributed words to the revues *Pins and Needles, From Vienna,* and *Sing for Your Supper.* For the latter he wrote, with Earl Robinson, "Ballad for Americans." When sung and recorded by Paul Robeson (and much later, Frank Sinatra), this song became a huge success for its lyrics, which, long before such things were popular, lauded the ethnic and cultural diversity of America. With Vernon Duke, he wrote an early black musical, *Cabin in the Sky.* There followed a series of less successful projects, including *Banjo Eyes* for Eddie Cantor, *The Lady Comes Across,* and *Beggar's Opera* with Duke Ellington, which featured the first interracial kiss in a Broadway musical and caused much commotion and many walkouts.

Latouche was blacklisted for his political beliefs and, quite possibly, for his homosexuality. Although *The Golden Apple* was not very successful, it is well known among musical-comedy fans for its wonderful score, its classic tale—it's based on Homer—and as an early all-sung musical. Serious music lovers would also know his text for the opera *The Ballad of Baby Doe,* music by Douglas Moore, and the dance piece *Ballet Ballads,* music by Jerome Moross. A few lesser projects followed, but he died at the age of forty-one, before hearing some of his lyrics in the Leonard Bernstein *Candide.*

Taking a Chance on Love

Lyrics by John Latouche
Music by Leonard Bernstein, Vernon Duke, Duke Ellington, Donald Fuller, John Latouche, Douglas Moore, Jerome Moross, Wolfgang Mozart, James Mundy, Earl Robinson, and John Strauss.
Devised by Erik Haagensen

Based on an idea by James Morgan.

Theatre at Saint Peter's/York Theatre Company; March 2, 2000.

246

Directed by James Morgan.

Original Cast:

> Terry Burrell Jerry Dixon
> Donna English Eddie Korbich

Musical Numbers:

ACT I Mr. Nobody
Nothing Ever Happens in Angel's Roost
Keep Your Nose to the Grindstone
Do What You Wanna Do
I'll Take the City
Oh, Baby
On the Waterfront
Beside the Troubled Waters of the Hudson
Not a Care in the World
The Surrealist
Cabin in the Sky
Little Papa Satan
In My Old Virginia Home
Honey in the Honeycomb
Love Turned the Light Out
Taking a Chance on Love

ACT II Four Little Misfits
Maybe I Should Change My Ways
Nail in the Horseshoe
Opening
My Yellow Flower
Ridin' on a Breeze
Rainy Day
Plain Words
Have You Met Delilah?
I'm Everybody's Baby
Windflowers
Ringaroundarosie
Lazy Afternoon
Always Through the Changing

Licensing: Rodgers and Hammerstein Theatre Library

Difficulties/Advantages: "The life and career of Broadway lyricist John Latouche have been woven together into a vibrant musical portrait of an endlessly fascinating character. As an openly gay man in the 1950s, Latouche traveled in rarified circles that included many swells of the time. *Taking a Chance on Love* weaves together his spectacular lyrical output with candid entries from his personal journals to chronicle one of the most intriguing paths ever forged in the musical theater." That's what the catalogue says. Here's what I say: This is a collection of the most literate and witty, passionate and professional lyrics you will ever hear in one revue, all to tunes by jazz masters. Streisand fans will know "Lazy Afternoon," and popmeisters will recognize the title song. Everything else is even better. The "book"—his diary entries and biographical information—is also most interesting, just spare enough not to bog the show down between songs. If you're looking for a revue with an unusual set of songs probably unknown to your average audience, this would certainly be it. Use the duel pianos of the original. Many of the songs are not easy to sing, requiring very musical performers. Sets and costumes entirely up to you.

TOM LEHRER

Tomfoolery

The Words and Music of Tom Lehrer
Adapted by Cameron Mackintosh and Robin Ray

When, early in his producing career, Cameron Mackintosh called up Tom Lehrer and asked if he could put Lehrer's canon of satirical pre-sixties songs into a compilation revue, Lehrer's response was, "It's all right with me—it's your money." That just about sums up the laid-back Lehrer, who got his mathematics degree from Harvard at eighteen but gained real fame when the little album he pressed for friends sold a million and a half units and made him the country's most popular satirist, the piano-playing equal of stand-up comedian Mort Sahl.

The three albums of songs he eventually recorded before he called it quits to return to the more exciting world of mathematics are among the most hilarious takes there are on the mores, institutions, and politicians of the 1950s, and together with Sahl's newspaper routine and Vaughn Meader's spoken album *The First Family*, they form a holy trinity of takes on the last innocent generation. And if that isn't enough, many of Lehrer's ditties—"Pollution," "The Old Dope Peddler," "Smut"—are chillingly prescient.

"I would describe myself as a liberal," Lehrer said at the late adolescent age of fifty-three, when this revue was being assembled and he hadn't written another pinprick in society in more than a decade. "One of the last. I think that the old liberal consensus has broken up, and that was one of the things that made my audience possible. There were a whole group of people who agreed on everything, like 'lynching is bad.' Issues that have come along since are a lot more complicated. So I just am not sure about where I stand about some things any more. Life was simpler then."

Top of the Gate; December 14, 1981; 27 previews, 120 performances.

Directed by Gary Pearle and Mary Kyte.

Original Cast:

MacIntyre Dixon	Joy Franz
Jonathan Hadary	Donald Corren

Musical Numbers:

Be Prepared
Poisoning Pigeons in the Park
I Wanna Go Back to Dixie
My Home Town
Pollution
Bright College Days

Fight Fiercely Harvard
The Elements
The Folk Song Army
In Old Mexico
She's My Girl
When You Are Old and Gray
Wernher Von Braun
Who's Next
I Got It from Agnes
National Brotherhood Week
So Long, Mom
Send the Marines
The Hunting Song
The Irish Ballad
Smut
New Math
Silent E
George Murphy
Oedipus Rex
I Hold Your Hand in Mine
Masochism Tango
The Old Dope Peddler
The Vatican Rag
We Will All Go Together When We Go
The Wiener Schnitzel Waltz

Licensing: Music Theatre International

Difficulties/Advantages: Four actors and a piano player did it first, but any combination could perform the simple melodies and hilarious lyrics. Some dialogue was created in the belief that modern audiences might, in some cases, not have a clue, but slides of the times and old *Life* magazine photos ought to do a better job of filling in the blanks and could make the evening more fluid. Double up with Allan Sherman's *Hello Muddah, Hello Fadduh* revue and you'd have a great belly-laughs reunion of 1950s humor.

LEIBER AND STOLLER

Smokey Joe's Cafe

The Songs of Leiber and Stoller

Music by Jerry Leiber and Mike Stoller
Lyrics by Jerry Leiber and Mike Stoller
Additional Numbers by Phil Spector ("Spanish Harlem" with Jerry Leiber), Ben E. King ("Stand By Me" with Leiber and Stoller), Doc Pomus ("Young Blood" with Leiber and Stoller), Barry Mann ("On Broadway" with Leiber and Stoller), Cynthia Weil ("On Broadway" with Leiber and Stoller), Kent Harris ("Shoppin' for Clothes"

Smokey Joe's Cafe at the Capital Playhouse, Olympia, WA.

with Leiber and Stoller), Ralph Dino ("Neighborhood" and "Pearl's a Singer" with Leiber and Stoller), John Sembello ("Neighborhood" and "Pearl's a Singer" with Leiber and Stoller), Carlo Donida ("I [Who Have Nothing]" with Leiber and Stoller), "Mogol" ("I [Who Have Nothing]" with Leiber and Stoller), Benjamin Earl Nelson ("There Goes My Baby" with Leiber and Stoller), Lover Patterson ("There Goes My Baby" with Leiber and Stoller), George Treadwell ("Dance with Me" and "There Goes My Baby" with Leiber and Stoller), Louis Lebish ("Dance with Me" with Leiber and Stoller) and Irv Nathan ("Dance with Me" with Leiber and Stoller.

A concert of bedrock songs in the fifties R&B bag, all written or co-written by the renowned team of Leiber and Stoller.

Synopsis: Nine great performers sing forty-plus great songs, one at a time.

Virginia Theatre; March 2, 1995; 25 previews, 2,036 performances.

Directed by Jerry Zaks. Musical staging by Joey McKneely.

Original Cast:

Ken Ard	Adrian Bailey
Brenda Braxton	Victor Trent Cook
B. J. Crosby	Pattie Darcy Jones
DeLee Lively	Michael Park
Frederick B. Owens	

Musical Numbers:

ACT I   Neighborhood
         Young Blood
         Falling

Ruby Baby
Dance with Me
Neighborhood (reprise)
Keep On Rollin'
Searchin'
Kansas City
Trouble
Love Me/Don't
Fools Fall in Love
Poison Ivy
Don Juan
Shoppin' for Clothes
I Keep Forgettin'
On Broadway
D. W. Washburn
Saved

ACT II
That Is Rock & Roll
Yakety Yak
Charlie Brown
Stay a While
Pearl's a Singer
Teach Me How to Shimmy
You're the Boss
Smokey Joe's Cafe
Loving You
Treat Me Nice
Hound Dog
Little Egypt
I'm a Woman
There Goes My Baby
Love Potion #9
Some Cats Know
Jailhouse Rock
Fools Fall in Love
Spanish Harlem
I (Who Have Nothing)
Stand by Me
That Is Rock & Roll

Licensing: Rodgers and Hammerstein Theatre Library

Difficulties/Advantages: I walked away calling this show nine performers and forty great songs in search of a concept, but the more I listened to the CD, the more I got it. Not every revue has to a have a "book" or even an idea. The musical style alone draws this concert evening together. It was originally performed by six black and three white (six male and three female) performers, but it seems to me that any number, race, size, or sex could play...as long as they can sing the roof down. And the lack of a concept for the original Broadway version leaves you free to inject your own creativity.

MALTBY (RICHARD) AND SHIRE (DAVID)

David Shire and Richard Maltby Jr. began collaborating on songs in the 1950s at Yale University and foresaw for themselves a career in Broadway musicals. It didn't happen. None of their half a dozen shows made it to Broadway, although one played off- (see *The Sap of Life*, below) and two played pre- (*Love Match* and *How Do You Do, I Love You*). Having finally established successful if separate careers as a film composer and theatre director, and still widely admired behind the scenes in the musical theatre community, they put together:

Starting Here, Starting Now

Music by David Shire
Lyrics by Richard Maltby Jr.

This enchanted audiences at the Manhattan Theatre Club, then at a cabaret restaurant. Indeed, the witty lyrics ("Crossword Puzzle") and dynamic music (the title song and "What About Today?" were recorded by Streisand) combine for a kind of song that is probably more useful in cabaret than within a dramatic skein, while at the same time, each of the songs in this first collection are wonderful opportunities for singers to act, as each offers a minimonologue for a strong character.

Original Cast:

Loni Ackerman	Margery Cohen	George Lee Andrews

Barbarann Theatre Restaurant; March 7, 1977; 120 performances.
Directed by Richard Maltby Jr. Choreographed by Ethel Martin.

Musical Numbers:

The Word Is Love
Starting Here, Starting Now
A Little Bit Off
I Think I May Want to Remember Today
Today Is the First Day of The Rest of My Life
Beautiful
Crossword Puzzle
Autumn
I Don't Remember Christmas
I Don't Believe It
I'm Going to Make You Beautiful
You Can't Let Down Your Fans
A Girl You Should Know
Travel
Watching the Big Parade Go By
What About Today
One Step
Barbara
Song of Me
A New Life Coming

Twelve years later—and still with not much more success at getting a show of their own mounted on Broadway—they collected a slightly larger cast and performed two dozen more of their songs:

Closer Than Ever

Closer Than Ever at the Capital Playhouse, Olympia, WA.

Music by David Shire
Lyrics by Richard Maltby Jr.
Conceived by Steven Scott Smith

Cherry Lane Theatre; November 6, 1989; 288 performances.

Co-directed by Richard Maltby Jr. and Steven Scott Smith.

Original Cast:

Brent Barrett   Sally Mayes
Richard Muenz   Lynne Wintersteller

Musical Numbers:

Doors
She Loves Me Not
You Want to Be My Friend?
What Am I Doin'?
Fandango
The Bear, the Tiger, the Hamster, and the Mole

Like a Baby
If I Sing
Miss Byrd
The Sound of Muzak
One of the Good Guys
There's Nothing Like It
Life Story
Next Time
I Wouldn't Go Back
The March of Time
Three Friends
There
Back on Base
Patterns
Another Wedding Song
Father of Fathers
It's Never That Easy/I've Been Here Before
Closer Than Ever

Licensing: Music Theatre International

Difficulties/Advantages: Between these two revues, there's a plethora of songs for the aspiring cabaret artist, and an entire evening of Maltby and Shire would be well worth a theatre's effort, if only to show Broadway producers what they were missing all those years. (Oh, and, not to worry, they finally got on the Broadway boards with *Baby*, see above, and *Big*, a musical based on the film, which got a little too big and failed, but was rewritten and sent out again.)

They also wrote a seven-character musical:

The Sap of Life

Book and Lyrics by Richard Maltby Jr.
Music by David Shire, in Collaboration with William Francisco
Sheridan Square Playhouse; October 2, 1961; 49 performances.

Original Cast:

Andrew...Kenneth Nelson
Oscar...Jack Bittner
Ruthanne...Patricia Bruder
Sally Ann...Lee Powell

Horatio...Jerry Dodge
Jessie...Dina Paisner
Dot...Lilian Fields

Musical Numbers:

Saturday Morning
Farewell Family
Charmed Life
Fill Up Your Life with Sunshine
Good Morning
Watching the Big Parade Go By
The Love of Your Life

A Her's Love
Children Have It Easy
She Loves Me Not
Mind over Matter
Time and Time Again

Difficulties/Advantages: The script will be hard to find, but if you want to revive it, check with Music Theatre International.

MITCHELL PARRISH

Stardust

Lyrics by Mitchell Parrish
Music by Hoagy Carmichael, Benny Goodman, Duke Ellington, Leroy Anderson, and Others
Based on an idea by Burton L. Litwin and Albert Harris.

Mitchell Parrish was born with the twentieth century in Louisiana; grew up in New York City, where he attended Columbia University and New York University; and began his career as a staff writer for one of the many Tin Pan Alley music publishers. When a revue is centered on a lyricist who wrote with numerous composers, it's difficult to find a central axis for so many different kinds of songs. On the other hand, artistic symmetry aside, any catalogue as large as this one boasts more than enough songs to keep lovers of American popular music happy for several hours, especially if they are as well performed as they were here by the original cast. Although presented in New York on Broadway, this Mitchell Parish revue began at Theatre Off Park and is flexible enough to be done in various venues. With a brief amount of narration about both the times and Parish, the cast takes you through the twenties, thirties, forties, and fifties, singing and dancing the hits for which Parish wrote the words, from "Stardust" (music by Hoagy Carmichael) and "Sophisticated Lady" (Duke Ellington) to novelties such as "Wealthy, Shmealthy, as Long as You're Healthy" (Sammy Fain).

Theatre Off Park, 59 performances; Biltmore Theatre on Broadway, February 19, 1987, 118 performances.

Conceived and directed by Albert Harris. Musical staging by Patrice Soriero. Tap dance by Henry LeTang.

Original Cast:

Michele Bautier   Maureen Brennan
Kim Criswell   Andre De Shields
Jason Graae   Jim Walton

Musical Numbers:

ACT I   Carolina Rolling Stone
           Riverboat Shuffle
           One Morning in May
           Sweet Lorraine

Sentimental Gentleman from Georgia
Sophisticated Lady
Dixie After Dark
Stairway to the Stars
Wealthy, Shmealthy, as Long as You're Healthy
Hands Across the Table
You're So Indiff'rent
It Happens to the Best of Friends
I Would If I Could But I Can't
Sidewalks of Cuba
Evenin'
Deep Purple
The Scat Song

ACT II   Sophisticated Swing
Midnight at the Onyx
Tell Me Why
Does Your Heart Beat for Me?
Stars Fell on Alabama
Don't Be That Way
Organ Grinder's Swing
Moonlight Serenade
Star Dust
Belle of the Ball
The Syncopated Clock
Take Me in Your Arms
Ciao, Ciao, Bambino
Sleigh Ride
Volaré
Ruby
Forgotten Dreams
Star Dust (reprise)

Licensing: Samuel French

Difficulties/Advantages: A cast of six—if you want to follow the original script of who sings what—and a piano would be plenty to present this cavalcade of songs by the author of 700. Like all revues, however, this one is plenty flexible in both cast and design.

COLE PORTER

Porter was the grandson of the richest man in Indiana, a patriarch who was glad to spoil both his daughter, Kate Cole, and Kate's son, who began writing songs at a precocious age. A popular student at Yale, he wrote not only college musicals but fight songs that are still part of the Yale tradition, leaving the school after contributing approximately 300 songs and six full-scale productions! Brief attempts at law school were quickly abandoned for a career as a songwriter. Moving to Paris in 1917, he flourished, living as a wealthy socialite. Descriptions of the parties he gave and attended in those years include "elaborate and fabulous, involving people of wealthy and political classes...marked by much gay and bisexual activity, Italian nobility, cross-dressing, international musicians, and a large surplus of recreational drugs." (No, it wasn't the sixties. It was Paris between world wars.) His lifelong marriage to an American divorcée was a convenient arrangement that allowed him the veneer of heterosexuality and gave her access to social status, but they warmly supported each other in one of the most famous friendships in theatre history.

Although he wrote "Don't Fence Me In" for the film musical *Hollywood Canteen* and songs for the Bing Crosby film *High Society*, it was his Broadway shows that gained him the status that he had always craved. With the exceptions of *Anything Goes* and *Can Can*, most of the shows themselves are long forgotten, but the songs—ideally suited to jazz and popular vocalists—have landed him in the American consciousness for all time. Sadly, in 1937 a horse riding accident fractured both his legs, and for the rest of his life, he lived in some pain, enduring many surgeries, moving from canes to crutches to a wheelchair to the amputation of one of his legs. The loss of his beloved companion and wife Linda also greatly depressed this once ebullient man.

Yet at the end of his life, he took on an assignment that resulted in one of the most enduring of all American musicals when he wrote the music and lyrics for *Kiss Me, Kate*. As a child at the Worcester Academy in Peru, Indiana, a Dr. Abercrombie taught him an important lesson about songs, which he would quote throughout his career: "Words and music must be so inseparably wedded to each other that they are like one." His are, as the samples below will well attest.

The original, and still the best, composer revue was Ben Bagley's production of:

The Decline and Fall of the Entire World as Seen Through the Eyes of Cole Porter

Music and Lyrics by Cole Porter
Continuity by Bud McCreery

Bagley collected mostly unfamiliar Porter material and set it against changing projections that, along with the performances, captured Porter's time and spirit, saving all the standards for the finale medley.

Square East Theatre; March 30, 1965; 273 performances.

Cast and material assembled and supervised by Ben Bagley. Musical numbers staged by Vernon Lusby.

Original Off-Broadway Cast:

Kaye Ballard		Harold Lang
Carmen Alvarez	William Hickey	Elmarie Wendel

Musical Numbers:

I've a Shooting Box in Scotland
I'm Unlucky at Gambling
Wake Up and Dream
You've Got That Thing
Hot House Rose
At Long Last Love
Leader of the Big Time Band

I'm a Gigolo
Red, Hot And Blue
I've Still Got My Health
Find Me a Primitive Man
I Loved Him but He Didn't Love Me
Let's Fly Away
I'm in Love Again
I Happen to Like New York
Ridin' High
The Tale of Oyster
Most Gentlemen Don't Like Love
Tomorrow
Come On In
A Little Skipper from Heaven Above
Make It Another Old Fashioned, Please
But in the Morning, No
Farming
After You, Who?
Her Heart Was in Her Work
Something for the Boys
I'm in Love with a Soldier Boy
By the Mississinewah
I Worship You
Thank You So Much, Missus Lowsborough-Goodby
Down in the Depths
When I Was a Little Cuckoo
Experiment

Licensing: Rodgers and Hammerstein Theatre Library

England collected Porter in:

Cole

Music and Lyrics by Cole Porter
Devised by Benny Green and Alan Strachan

Extracts from Scott and Zelda Fitzgerald and P. G. Wodehouse, as well as original narration, link the delicious Cole Porter songs in this fairly large-scale review and overview of Porter's life and times.

Mermaid Theatre (London); July 2, 1974.

Directed by Alan Strachan and David Toguri.

Cast:

Ray Cornell
Peter Gale
Julia McKenzie
Kenneth Nelson
Angela Richards

Lucy Fenwick
Bill Kerr
Rod McLennan
Elizabeth Power
Una Stubbs

Musical Numbers:

Wouldn't It Be Fun?
Another Opening, Another Show
The Bobolink Waltz
Bingo Eli Yale!
When the Summer Moon Comes 'Long
See America First
The Lost Liberty Blues
I Love Paris
Thank You So Much, Mrs. Lowsborough-Goodby
Dizzy Baby
You Don't Know Paree
Take Me Back to Manhattan
I Happen to Like New York
I'm a Gigolo
Love for Sale
Down in the Depths
Night and Day
Anything Goes
I Get a Kick out of You
Tomorrow
Begin the Beguine
What Is This Thing Called Love?
You Do Something to Me
You've Got That Thing
Let's Misbehave
The Laziest Gal in Town
At Long Last Love
It's De-Lovely
In the Still of the Night
I Worship You
Make It Another Old-Fashioned, Please
Most Gentlemen Don't Like Love
From This Moment On
Just One of Those Things
We Shall Never Be Younger
Be a Clown
Please Don't Monkey with Broadway
The Leader of a Big-Time Band
Brush Up Your Shakespeare
Why Can't You Behave?
Ev'ry Time We Say Goodbye

Licensing: Samuel French

A second English review has the appropriate title:

A Swell Party

Music and Lyrics by Cole Porter
Book by John Kane

Original Cast:

David Kernan   Angela Richards
Martin Smith   Anne Wood   Nickolas Grace

Musical Numbers:

I'm Throwing a Ball Tonight
I Get a Kick out of You
Anything Goes
From This Moment On
You've Got That Thing
I'm Unlucky at Gambling
I've Got You Under My Skin
Red, Hot and Blue
Love for Sale
Find Me a Primitive Man
Blow, Gabriel, Blow
Begin the Beguine
Miss Otis Regrets
Down in the Depths
Rap Tap on Wood
Night and Day
In the Still of the Night
I Concentrate on You
Who Said Gay Paree?
Always True to You in My Fashion
I Happen to Like New York
You're Sensational
Can-Can
I Gaze in Your Eyes
Let's Do It, Let's Fall in Love
You're the Top
Well, Did You Evah!
Ev'ry Time We Say Goodbye

Licensing: Warner/Chappell UK

Difficulties/Advantages: Benny Green, a writer and devotee of music and musicals, writes that there is clearly a difference between the songs of composers born in poverty (Noel Coward, Irving Berlin) and the songs of those born to middle class (Jerome Kern, Richard Rodgers). I don't hear it, but I do hear the very upper-class accents of the rich American Cole Porter, who dallied in European watering holes before becoming a substantial Broadway success at the nearly decrepit age, for an artist, of thirty-seven. The sophistication of Manhattan's nightclub age and the Côte d'Azur is difficult to duplicate, and that's only a small part of the possibilities in Porter's oeuvre. But almost any way you produce Porter can be effective, so witty are his lyrics and so beautiful his melodies. A very popular collection is:

Red Hot and Cole

Book by James Bianchi, Muriel McAuley, and Randy Strawderman
Music and Lyrics by Cole Porter
Conceived by Randy Strawderman

Mixes biography with the songs of Cole Porter.

Musical Numbers:

I'm Throwing a Ball Tonight
I'm a Gigolo
Tomorrow
I Love Paris
I'm in Love Again
Who Said Gay Paree?
Come Along with Me
Let's Misbehave
What Is This Thing Called Love
Love for Sale
I Get a Kick Out of You
You're the Top
Miss Otis Regrets
Begin the Beguine
Just One of Those Things
In The Still of the Night
Ridin' High
Red, Hot and Blue
It's De-Lovely
Let's Do It
The Physician
Don't Fence Me In
Ca, C'est l'Amour
Friendship
My Heart Belongs to Daddy
I'm in Love with a Soldier Boy
Ours
Kiss Me, Kate
Bull Dog
Every Time We Say Goodbye
True Love
Wake Up and Dream

Licensing: Music Theatre International

Unsung Cole (and Classics Too)

A "Musical Entertainment" in Two Acts with Songs by Cole Porter
Arranged by Norman L. Berman

Finally, this compilation of a few of Porter's hits and a number of his more obscure but no less wonderful songs has been very successful, so if your audience has heard all the standards, take a look at this.

Circle Repertory Theatre; June 23, 1977; 78 performances.

Conceived and directed by Norman L. Berman. Choreographed by Dennis Grimaldi.

Original Cast:

Gene Lindsey
Maureen Moore
John Sloman

Mary Louise
Anita Morris

Musical Numbers:

Abracadabra
After You, Who?
Almiro
Dancin' to a Jungle Drum
Down in the Depths
Farming
Friendship
Give Me the Land
Good-Bye, Little Dream, Good-Bye
The Great Indoors
I Happen to Like New York
I'm Getting Myself Ready for You
If Ever Married, I'm
I've Got Some Unfinished Business with You
Just Another Page in Your Diary
Kate the Great
A Lady Needs a Rest
The Lost Liberty Blues
Love for Sale
Nobody's Chasing Me
Olga (Come Back to the Volga)
Ours
Pick Me Up and Lay Me Down
Poor Young Millionaire
The Queen of Terre Haute
Red, Hot and Blue
Sing to Me Guitar
Swingin' the Jinx Away
Take Me Back to Manhattan
The Tale of an Oyster
Thank You So Much, Mrs. Lowsborough-Goodby
That's Why I Love You
When the Hen Stops Laying
Why Don't We Try Staying Home

Licensing: Samuel French

Difficulties/Advantages: The Porter estate seems quite happy to have his songs played and replayed (unlike the Gershwin heirs and Irving Berlin's daughters, who seem to go to great lengths to keep their legacies out of the limelight), which is why they've become so much a part of American musical culture. All these reviews are a great starting place. Or should you want to organize your own Cole Porter review, the licensing for Cole Porter is: The Cole Porter Musical and Literary Property Trusts, 1285 Avenue of the Americas, 31st Floor, New York, NY 10019.

RODGERS (RICHARD) AND HART (LORENZ)

Rodgers's New York City public school was eventually renamed in his honor, but he abandoned Columbia University after writing several "varsity" shows with two older upperclassmen: Oscar Hammerstein II and Lorenz Hart. He teamed up with Hart, and their partnership produced numerous song hits in a multitude of shows, from *Garrick Gaieties* to *Pal Joey*. It was possibly the most historic—and interesting—partnership in the American musical theatre: they met when Rodgers was sixteen, Hart twenty-three. Richard Rodgers: "I left Hart's house having acquired in one afternoon a career, a partner, a best friend, and a source of permanent irritation." Rodgers dropped out of Columbia ("Wrote two varsity shows and considered myself eligible for graduation"). First hit song: 1925, "I'll Take Manhattan," from *Garrick Gaieties*. In the next twenty-four years, Rodgers and Hart wrote thirty Broadway shows and nine Hollywood scores.

Hart, unfortunately, was, to put it bluntly, short, homely, and homosexual, which may have led to the alcoholism that eventually killed him. In the meantime, his quick wit—he is rumored to have once written a great set of lyrics to a Rodgers melody on the back of an envelope borrowed from a chorus girl in the middle of a rehearsal in approximately fifteen minutes—great insights in euphonic prose ("I'm wild again / beguiled again / a simpering, whimpering child again…"), humor ("Horizontally speaking / he's at his very best") and fiercely unrequited love songs ("Unrequited love's a bore / And I've got it pretty bad / But for someone you adore / It's a pleasure to be sad") are a huge compendium of delightful songs. There isn't a great revue in the catalogue yet, but here's a start:

Rodgers and Hart: A Celebration

Music by Richard Rodgers
Lyrics by Lorenz Hart
Concept by Richard Lewine and John Fearnley

There are two ways to do composer revues. Either you choose an evening's worth of songs and present each one with a strong concept and musical setting, or you go for the short chorus and medley approach, jamming in everything you can. This revue, with sixty songs (a bare third of their published material), obviously takes the latter course. The first act is chock-full of their romantic songs; the second, as Hart's alcoholism and insecurity increased, their more cynical ideas. A little bit of narration gives the audience some background, but it's the songs that are everything, here defined best by an Irving Berlin quotation: "Tuneful and tasty / Schmaltzy and smart / Music by Rodgers / Lyrics by Hart."

Helen Hayes Theater; May 13, 1975; 22 previews, 108 performances.

Directed by Burt Shevelove. Choreographed by Donald Saddler.

Original Cast:

Barbara Andes
Wayne Bryan
Jamie Donnelly
May Sue Finnerty
Stephen Lehew
Virginia Sandifur

Jimmy Brennon
David-James Carroll
Tovah Felshuh
Laurence Guittard
Jim Litten
Rebecca York

Musical Numbers:

Jupiter Forbid
Falling in Love with Love
Thou Swell
The Girl Friend
Where or When
To Keep My Love Alive
With a Song in My Heart
Ev'rything I've Got
This Can't Be Love
Wait Till You See Her
My Heart Stood Still
Isn't It Romantic?
Here in My Arms
My Romance
Glad to Be Unhappy
I Wish I Were in Love Again
It Never Entered My Mind
Happy Hunting Horn
How About It?
Love Me Tonight
Mountain Greenery
A Lovely Day for a Murder
Little Girl Blue
Mimi
Prayer
The Bad in Every Man
Manhattan Melodrama
Blue Moon
Johnny One Note
Way Out West
Give It Back to the Indians
I Gotta Get Back to New York
Manhattan
Any Old Place with You
On a Desert Isle with Thee
The Most Beautiful Girl in the World
Great Big Town (Chicago)
That's the Song of Paree
Ten Cents a Dance
Sing for Your Supper
I've Got Five Dollars

She Could Shake the Maracas
I Didn't Know What Time It Was
You Took Advantage of Me
You Mustn't Kick It Around
Dancing on the Ceiling
It's Got to Be Love
He and She
Blue Room
I Could Write a Book
A Ship Without a Sail
Nobody's Heart
Spring Is Here
You're Nearer
There's a Small Hotel
This Is My Night to Howl
Bewitched, Bothered and Bewildered
I Married an Angel
The Lady Is a Tramp
Have You Met Miss Jones
Lover

Licensing: Rodgers and Hammerstein Theatre Library

Difficulties/Advantages: This one opened on Broadway with twelve in the cast, on a beige set with beige costumes, beige staging, and beige performances. There's so much more there for an imaginative director. Much better is this one:

Beguiled Again

The Songs of Rodgers and Hart

Music by Richard Rodgers
Lyrics by Lorenz Hart
Conceived by J. Barry Lewis, Lynnette Barkley, and Craig D. James

This one has neither linear plot nor biographical narrative but combines various songs in theatrical groupings, including a sequence invoking the frenzy of Hollywood film-making (about which they would know a good deal, having written the score for an ahead-of-its-time film musical, *Love Me Tonight*), a live radio show, and a nicely comic running gag describing the creative process: a series of lyrics being written to a recurring tune, variously entitled "Manhattan Melodrama," "The Bad in Every Man" and "Prayer," which culminates in a eureka moment when the company launches into the standard that finally became known as "Blue Moon."

Musical Numbers:

Bewitched, Bothered and Bewildered
The Lady Is a Tramp
Thou Swell
This Can't Be Love

That Terrific Rainbow
Johnny One Note
Manhattan Melodrama (first "Blue Moon")
The Girl Friend
You Mustn't Kick It Around
A Ship Without a Sail
'Cause We Got Cake
The Bad in Every Man (second "Blue Moon")
Sing for Your Supper
With a Song in My Heart
This Is My Night to Howl
Manhattan
Mountain Greenery
Prayer (third "Blue Moon")
My Heart Stood Still
Ten Cents a Dance
Any Old Place with You
Song of Paree
Dear Old Syracuse
Great Big Town (Chicago)
She Could Shake the Maracas
I Gotta Get Back to New York
My Funny Valentine
Blue Moon
Zip
I've Got Five Dollars
You Took Advantage Of Me
My Romance
The Most Beautiful Girl in the World
It Never Entered My Mind
Little Girl Blue
Nobody's Heart
Where or When
Isn't It Romantic?
Why Can't I?
A Lovely Day for a Murder
To Keep My Love Alive
Ev'rything I've Got
Have You Met Miss Jones?
I Wish I Were in Love Again
There's a Small Hotel
Glad to Be Unhappy
Ten Cents a Dance
Falling in Love with Love

Licensing: Rodgers and Hammerstein Theatre Library

RODGERS (RICHARD) AND HAMMERSTEIN (OSCAR)

Stephen Sondheim once remarked that Rodgers was a man of infinite talent and limited soul, while Hammerstein was a man of infinite soul and limited talent. Their partnership made theatrical history right out of the gate, when Rodgers asked Lorenz Hart, with whom he had already written nearly thirty Broadway shows, if he wanted to write a musical version of the folk play *Green Grow the Lilacs*. Knowing full well that the forty-eight-year-old Hart would beg off due to illness brought on by extreme alcoholism, Rodgers had already lined up Hammerstein, and that production, which was eventually titled *Oklahoma!* ran for 2,212 performances. (A suspect figure, as there was a special ninth weekly performance given free to servicemen for a period during World War II, which historians are not sure is included in the final count.)

Oscar Hammerstein II had grown up around musicals, with his father, uncle, and grandfather all in the business. Working as an assistant stage manager and having his uncle produce his first play (unsuccessful) taught him a good deal, and while Rodgers spent two decades writing with Hart, Hammerstein wrote book and lyrics to successful operettas, including *Rose Marie, The Desert Song, The New Moon*, and many others, culminating in the quasi operetta, musical comedy *Show Boat*, with music by Jerome Kern.

As Rodgers and Hammerstein, the team followed *Oklahoma!* with *Carousel, Allegro, South Pacific, The King and I, Me and Juliet, Pipe Dream, Flower Drum Song*, and *The Sound of Music*. This extraordinary catalogue of songs for musicals has been shrunk into:

A Grand Night for Singing

A Grand Night for Singing at the Amish Acres Round Barn Theatre, Nappanee, IN.

Music and Lyrics by Rodgers and Hammerstein
Conceived by Walter Bobbie

Assiduously avoiding the sentiment so closely associated with Rodgers and Hammerstein, this successful revue revises the characters and circumstances within which the songs were originally sung, inventing its own. Cleverest example: a short man takes a ballroom lesson from a tall woman while singing "Shall We Dance." While all the songs would be well known to musical theatre fans, possibly a quarter of them wouldn't be to the average audience, and the rest form a great selection of songs from Broadway's most famous, most successful, and most indelible songwriting.

Roundabout Theatre; November 17, 1993; 41 previews, 52 performances.

Directed by Walter Bobbie. Additional staging by Pamela Sousa.

Original Cast:

Jason Graae
Alyson Reed
Martin Vidnovic

Victoria Clark
Lynne Wintersteller

Musical Numbers:

The Carousel Waltz
So Far
It's a Grand Night for Singing
The Surrey with the Fringe on Top
Stepsisters' Lament
We Kiss in a Shadow
A Wonderful Guy
I Cain't Say No
Maria
Do I Love You Because You're Beautiful?
Honey Bun
The Gentleman Is a Dope
Don't Marry Me
Many a New Day
I'm Gonna Wash That Man Right Outta My Hair
If I Loved You
Shall We Dance?
That's the Way It Happens
All at Once You Love Her
Some Enchanted Evening
Oh, What a Beautiful Mornin'
To Have and to Hold
Wish Them Well
The Man I Used to Be
It Might as Well Be Spring
Kansas City
A Hundred Million Miracles
When the Children Are Asleep
I Know It Can Happen
Soliloquy
It's Me
Love, Look Away

When You're Driving Through the Moonlight
A Lovely Night
Something Wonderful
This Nearly Was Mine
Impossible
I Have Dreamed

Licensing: Rodgers and Hammerstein Theatre Library

Difficulties/Advantages: Lots of possibilities for extending the size of the cast and lots for reimagining the interpretations, too, as only some of the creative stagings worked in the original.

Here's a more obscure compilation of the lyrics of Hammerstein:

All Kinds of People

Music by Richard Rodgers and Jerome Kern
Lyrics by Oscar Hammerstein II
Conceived by Michael Presser and the Midtown Management Group, Inc.
Written by Bruce D. Taylor

A special one-hour revue of lyrics by Oscar Hammerstein, devoted to songs that exploited his own liberal, very humanitarian feelings. Created particularly with schools in mind and never produced commercially off-Broadway, this is a great opportunity for young people, particularly audiences, to experience the most melodic tunesmiths of Broadway, and an even better way to be prompted to think about racism, anti-Semitism, and any other bigotries, all of which Hammerstein was eloquently against. When Hammerstein was informed that Paul Robeson altered the lyrics of "Ol' Man River" to make them more applicable to the current African-American status for use in his concerts, he responded: "As the author of these words, I have no intention of changing them or permitting anyone else to change them. I further suggest that Paul write his own songs and leave mine alone." He then went on to say, "Well, if I were a tall, handsome man, member of the All-American football team, Phi Beta Kappa from Rutgers University, a world-famous actor and concert singer, and I couldn't get a hotel room in Detroit, I don't really know what I'd do."

Musical Numbers:

All Kinds of People
The Other Generation
There is Nothin' Like a Dame
You've Got to Be Carefully Taught
Ol' Man River
Two Little People
Make Believe
Climb Ev'ry Mountain
You'll Never Walk Alone

Licensing: Rogers and Hammerstein Theatre Library

Difficulties/Advantages: Investigating the social consciousness of one of the American theatre's great lyricists (and inventor of the staging concept of "continuous action") could be a wonderful experience. Perhaps one day someone will combine the Hammerstein songs with those of Yip Harburg to produce a powerful left-wing cantata for civil rights and the common man.

STEPHEN SONDHEIM

When Stephen Sondheim was in high school, he wanted to write Broadway musicals. So he wrote one. Convinced it would be produced immediately by the preeminent producing team on Broadway at the time—the Rodgers and Hammerstein Organization— he walked over to his neighbor's house and presented it. His neighbor was Oscar Hammerstein, and the rest is very well-known musical-comedy history. For would-be playwrights who haven't heard the story and want the lesson, however, here it is: Hammerstein read it, called Sondheim in the next day, and told him it was awful...but not without talent. "If you want to learn to write a musical," Hammerstein said, "I'll help you," whereupon he gave Sondheim three consecutive, increasingly difficult assignments: one, to write a musical based on a play; two, to write a musical based on a book; three, to write an original. In the several years that followed, Sondheim did just that, and each time Hammerstein carefully went over his work with him. Though Sondheim went on to write musicals in forms and styles Hammerstein never dreamed of, it was a very sound beginning and a great education.

Sondheim's first optioned work was *Saturday Night*, but when the producer died, that musical was shelved for thirty years. He accepted a job writing scripts for the 1950s television show *Topper*; then, when Comden and Green weren't available, he was enlisted to write the lyrics to Bernstein's already burgeoning score for *West Side Story*. The rest really is history: *Gypsy*, music by Jule Styne; Do *I Hear a Waltz?* music by Richard Rodgers (whereupon he swore never to write lyrics for another composer again...hmmm); and music and lyrics for *A Funny Thing Happened on the Way to the Forum, Anyone Can Whistle, Company, Follies, Frogs, A Little Night Music, Pacific Overtures, Sweeney Todd, Merrily We Roll Along, Sunday in the Park with George, Into the Woods, Assassins, Passion,* and *Bounce.*

From that body of work have come an enormous number of concerts and revues, and every time he adds another show, there's more for the compiler to choose from.

There are a number of established Sondheim revues, although probably any theatre could obtain permission to perform their own selection of numbers from his vast and widely admired catalogue. One great obstacle, however, is that Sondheim is the quintessential theatre songwriter. Unlike Cole Porter, Rodgers and Hart, and the rest of the Tin Pan Alley greats, his songs don't easily stand alone. That is their strength, not their weakness. He once said that asked to write a love song, he's completely baffled, but asked to write a song for a woman on a barstool wearing a red dress and waiting for a man to arrive who's already half an hour late, he's off and running. That's the difference between theatre lyrics and pop lyrics. It makes for great theatre but makes a composer's compilation difficult. You need too much back story.

On the other hand, his songs are highly dramatic, emotionally rich, singularly unique, and often little playlets on their own, with the heart of an interesting character shining through, which makes for the best of revues if you can find a format to pull them all together.

The first and still best of the Sondheim revues is *Side by Side by Sondheim*, which was created in England, where he is as rare and interesting a bird as Noël Coward is to us. English audiences were unfamiliar with the majority of his work at the time and were suddenly confronted with selections from his earliest work through *Pacific Overtures.* According to its author, *"Side by Side by Sondheim* is a celebration of the work of Stephen Sondheim from a British point of view. We may not be able to write good musicals in this country, but we do know how to enjoy them." A narrator introduces each song with droll witticisms that set the stage, and great performances by the original English cast helped, but for musical-theatre lovers who had seen, say, Elaine Stritch in full character, in that bold chiaroscuro dress, sing "The Ladies Who Lunch" to a Jonathan Tunick orchestration, no cabaret-style delivery will ever live up to the moment.

Still, not every town is going to see a full-fledged performance of *Company,* least of all his even larger musicals, and his songs do stand on their own if the issue is simply the sheer brilliance of the lyrics and the emotional power of the music.

Side by Side by Sondheim

Photo: Nicholas Toyne

Side by Side by Sondheim by the Northcott Theatre Company in Exeter Cathedral, UK.

Lyrics by Stephen Sondheim
Music by Stephen Sondheim (also Leonard Bernstein, Jule Styne, Richard Rodgers, and Mary Rodgers)
Continuity by Ned Sherrin

London premiere at the Mermaid Theatre, London, May 4, 1976; Broadway premiere at the Music Box Theatre, April 18, 1977, 390 performances.

Directed by Ned Sherrin. Musical staging by Bob Howe.

Original Broadway Cast:

Millicent Martin
David Kernan

Julia McKenzie
Ned Sherrin

Musical Numbers:

Comedy Tonight
Love Is in the Air
Pretty Lady
You Must Meet My Wife
Send in the Clowns
Another Hundred People
Company
Barcelona
A Boy Like That
Tonight
Gee Officer Krupke
Beautiful Girls
Ah, Paris!
Broadway Baby
Could I Leave You?
I'm Still Here
The Little Things You Do Together
Marry Me a Little
I Have a Love
I Feel Pretty
One Hand, One Heart
America
Maria
I Never Do Anything Twice
We're Gonna Be Alright
Do I Hear a Waltz?
The Boy from…
If Momma Was Married
You Gotta Get a Gimmick
Anyone Can Whistle
Everybody Says Don't
You Could Drive a Person Crazy
Side by Side by Side
Somewhere
I Remember
Getting Married Today

You're Gonna Love Tomorrow

Continuity by Paul Lazarus
Music and Lyrics by Stephen Sondheim

A wonderful concert—a CD is available—that originally featured some songs that hadn't yet been heard in New York City. If they're all familiar to Sondheim fans now, it's still a terrific collection.

Sotheby Auction Hall, Whitney Museum of American Art in New York; March 3, 1983; benefit performance.

Original Cast:

George Hearn
Liz Callaway
Bob Gunton
Angela Lansbury

Cris Groenendaal
Judy Kaye
Victoria Mallory
Stephen Sondheim

Musical Numbers:

Invocation and Instructions to the Audience
It's That Kind of a Neighborhood
Saturday Night
Isn't It?
Poems
What More Do I Need?
Another Hundred People
With So Little to Be Sure Of
Pretty Little Picture
The House of Marcus Lycus
The Echo Song
There's Something About a War
Fear No More
Being Alive
You're Gonna Love Tomorrow
Love Will See Us Through
The Miller's Son
Johanna
Not a Day Goes By
Someone in a Tree
Old Friends
Send in the Clowns

Licensing: Music Theatre International

Marry Me a Little

Songs by Stephen Sondheim

Conceived and Developed by Craig Lucas and Norman René

A number of Sondheim's trunk songs—some from unproduced musicals, some from the tryout floor—were collected here for a revue, which eventually had a "book" of sorts, although no dialogue. A young man and a young woman are each moving into their own respective apartments (which is, for theatrical effect, the same apartment), where both are alone on a Saturday night in New York. Creating a book around a set of already existing songs is difficult and usually results in a jerry-rigged libretto. Any collection of Stephen Sondheim songs would be a delightful evening, and this one, especially for an audience that might not be aware of just how wonderful some of his rejects are, is very educational, although only as entertaining as two performers and a piano player can make it. (The recording is rather limp and the accompaniment muddy.)

Marry Me A Little, an Operating Theatre in Association with Musicworks Production, UK.

Though ranging from his less mature work ("Saturday Night") to extreme sophistication ("Uptown, Downtown") to the harsh number that almost became *Company*'s finale ("Marry Me a Little"), this collection is probably the weakest of the Sondheim revues.

Actor's Playhouse; March 12, 1981; 96 performances.

Directed by Norman René.

Original Off-Broadway Cast:

Suzanne Henry   Craig Lucas

Musical Numbers:

Two Fairy Tales
Saturday Night
All Things Bright and Beautiful
Bang!
The Girls of Summer
Uptown, Downtown
So Many People
Your Eyes Are Blue
A Moment with You
Marry Me a Little
Happily Ever After
Pour le Sport
Silly People
There Won't Be Trumpets
It Wasn't Meant to Happen

Putting It Together

A Musical Review

Book, Music, and Lyrics by Stephen Sondheim
Concept by Stephen Sondheim and Julia McKenzie

This one has a long and interesting history:

Old Fire Station, Oxford, England; January 27, 1992; 24 performances.
Directed by Julia McKenzie.

Cast:

Diana Rigg	Clive Carter
Claire Moore	Clarke Peters
Kit Hesketh-Harvey	

City Center Theater; April 1, 1993; 37 previews, 59 performances.
Directed by Julia McKenzie. Musical staging by Bob Avian.

Cast:

Julie Andrews	Stephen Collins
Christopher Durang	Michael Rupert (replaced by Patrick Quinn)
Rachel York	

Mark Taper Forum, Los Angeles; October 22, 1998.
Directed by Eric D. Schaeffer. Musical staging by Bob Avian.

Cast:

The Younger Man...John Barrowman	Amy, the Wife...Carol Burnett
Charles, the Husband...George Hearn	Julie, the Younger Woman...Ruthie
The Observer...Bronson Pinchot	Henshall

And finally:

Ethel Barrymore Theatre; November 21, 1999; 22 previews, 101 performances.
Directed by Eric D. Schaeffer. Musical staging by Bob Avian.

Cast:

The Younger Man...John Barrowman	Amy, the Wife...Carol Burnett
Charles, the Husband...George Hearn	Julie, the Younger Woman...Ruthie
The Observer...Bronson Pinchot	Henshall

Musical Numbers (when the show finally arrived on Broadway):

ACT I   Invocations and Instructions to the Audience
Putting It Together
Rich and Happy
Do I Hear a Waltz?
Merrily We Roll Along #1/Lovely
Hello, Little Girl
My Husband the Pig/Every Day a Little Death
Everybody Ought to Have a Maid
Have I Got a Girl for You!
Pretty Women

Licensing for Stephen Sondheim revues: Music Theatre International

Difficulties/Advantages: So many Sondheim revues to choose from! But beware the usually misguided attempt to "create" a new story from old songs. Either produce a Sondheim musical or present his songs in a reasonable concert setting.

CHARLES STROUSE

Charles Strouse began attending Broadway shows with his parents at an early age and remembers being awestruck by the glamour. He received a degree in composition from the Eastman School of Music, then studied with Aaron Copeland and Nadia Boulanger. But classical music was only one of his interests. Teaming up with lyricist Lee Adams, he wrote special material for nightclub acts, revues, and the famous Green Mansions summer resort, where they met librettist Michael Stewart and joined up to write *Bye Bye Birdie,* an enormous success and still playing in high schools throughout the world. This led them on to *All American, Golden Boy, It's a Bird, It's a Plane...It's Superman, Applause,* and *I and Albert* in London, before Strouse accepted an assignment to write the music to Martin Charnin's lyrics for *Annie.* If since then Strouse hasn't had much luck writing with Alan J. Lerner, Stephen Schwartz, or Richard Maltby Jr., he and Adams could surely retire on the song "Those Were the Days," which they wrote as the opening theme for Norman Lear's 1970s TV sitcom *All in the Family.*

By Strouse

Music by Charles Strouse
Lyrics by Lee Adams, Martin Charnin, Fred Tobias, David Rogers, and Charles Strouse

Originally done off-Broadway with five performers, including a child (for *Annie*, of course), this revue moved to a nightclub, where it had to give up the child but ran just as successfully. A handsome compendium from the pre-1980 work of one of Broadway's greatest—if lesser known by the public—golden age composers, with forty-six of his tunes from a dozen shows. No book, no concept even, but well paced and very, very tuneful.

Manhattan Theatre Club; 1978; 156 performances.

Licensing: Samuel French

Six

Music and Lyrics by Charles Strouse

A collection of original songs, with Strouse writing his own lyrics instead of with his usual partner Lee Adams. Strouse, who had a serious composer's education before winding his way from pianist-for-hire to Broadway with *Bye Bye Birdie*, here writes nearly two hours of first-class material. I hate to call them art songs, because that will surely drive the customers away, and perhaps it was because they fell into the chasm between that and musical comedy that the critics didn't get it. Although lacking any central concept or overall dramatic idea, this collection displays a real talent for dramatic songwriting and gives three men and three women a chance to display strong legit voices. Although the production was a quick el foldo, it deserves a fresh look, by both a creative director and an audience.

Cricket Playhouse; April 12, 1971; 8 performances.

Directed by Peter Coe.

Original Cast:

Johanna Albrecht	Lee Beery
Alvin Ing	Gail Nelson
Gilbert Price	Hal Watters

Musical Numbers:

What Is There to Sing About?
The Garden
Love Song
Six
Coming Attractions
The Invisible Man
The Critic
Trip
What Is There to Sing About? (reprise)
The Beginning
The Dream

Licensing: Helene Blue Musique Ltd., 421 Seventh Avenue, #901, New York, New York 10001

FATS WALLER

Thomas "Fats" Waller was born in Harlem in 1904, the son of the minister at the Abyssinian Baptist Church, where his mother taught him to sing and play the organ. Lessons from famous pianist James P. Johnson led to his becoming a professional by age fifteen, playing rent parties and the organ at movie theatres and accompanying vaudeville acts, including Bessie Smith. He began recording in 1922 and wrote tunes for the 1927 Broadway show *Keep Shufflin'* and the score for the 1929 Broadway musical *Hot Chocolates*. In 1934 he performed at a party given by George Gershwin, where an executive from Victor Records spotted him and signed him to a recording contract, under which he recorded many now classic songs, becoming a star of the nascent radio business—where he was known as "Radio's Harmful Little Armful"—and in night-clubs in London, Paris, Berlin, and Vienna. A star "personality" whose comic persona made him millions of fans, music lovers know him for his "stride" piano style—a pounding left hand—and his extension of the Johnson boogie style with jazz. Though not of his own composition, his biggest hit was the shallow "I'm Gonna Sit Right Down and Write Myself a Letter," but his signature song, performed by Louis Armstrong when he wrote it, is still "Ain't Misbehavin'." He died unexpectedly of pneumonia in 1943, leaving a legacy aptly presented in this musical revue.

Ain't Misbehavin'

The Fats Waller Musical Show

Based on an idea by Murray Horwiz and Richard Maltby Jr.

Developed off-Broadway, the roof-raising performances by the original cast of this rollicking collection of thirty songs associated with stride pianist Fats Waller—most with music by Waller, some written by others which he recorded—were so powerful it jumped right to Broadway, where it received gorgeous sets, costumes and lights, and a six piece band, and quickly became a smash hit. Tours followed—one featuring the Pointer Sisters, another featuring Patti LaBelle—and it ought to be one of those shows that is always playing somewhere in the world. *Ain't Misbehavin'* (a misnomer title if ever there was one) recreates the ambiance of a Harlem night club in the 1930s, not the ones run for the entertainment of slumming whites but the real thing, up from the juke joints of the South. A fluid series of songs—including the black blues classics "Lookin' Good but Feelin' Bad" and "'T Ain't Nobody's Biz-ness If I Do," the hip "The Reefer Song," the sly "When the Nylons Bloom Again," the misogynist "Your Feet's Too Big" and "Fat and Greasy," and the classic Negro lyric "Black and Blue"—all underscored with a jumpin' stride piano-based jazz band led on Broadway by Luther Henderson, are beautifully paced (not as easy as you'd think). Without a book but with remarkable dramatic flair, *Ain't Misbehavin'* is the rare revue that really burnishes a composer's reputation. This one also evokes his personality, as well as that of the whole Harlem Renaissance culture.

Longacre Theatre; May 9, 1978; 1604 performances.

Conceived and directed by Richard Maltby Jr. Musical numbers staged by Arthur Faria.

Original Cast:

Nell Carter
Armelia McQueen
Charlaine Woodard

Andre De Shields
Ken Page

Musical Numbers:

Ain't Misbehavin'
Lookin' Good but Feelin' Bad
'T Ain't Nobody's Biz-ness If I Do
Honeysuckle Rose
Squeeze Me
Handful of Keys
I've Got a Feeling I'm Falling
How Ya Baby
The Jitterbug Waltz
The Ladies Who Sing with the Band
Yacht Club Swing
When the Nylons Bloom Again
Cash for Your Trash
Off-Time
The Joint Is Jumpin'
Spreadin' Rhythm Around
Lounging at the Waldorf
The Viper's Drag
The Reefer Song
Mean to Me
Your Feet's Too Big
That Ain't Right
Keepin' Out of Mischief Now
Find Out What They Like
Fat and Greasy
Black and Blue
I'm Gonna Sit Right Down and Write Myself a Letter
Two Sleepy People
I've Got My Fingers Crossed
I Can't Give You Anything but Love
It's a Sin to Tell a Lie

Licensing: Music Theatre International

Difficulties/Advantages: Requires a stage full of African-American talent, as well as the proper interpretation of both music and an era long gone. Well worth the effort. But please don't "color blind" your casting. This is one era that needs authenticity.

KURT WEILL

Born in Germany in 1900, his father a cantor, Kurt Weill escaped the Nazis to become one of the Broadway musical's principal composers, contributing great scores in unique styles, working on serious and significant stories, and expanding the form itself from the original musical comedies of the twenties. From 1937 to 1950, Weill's musical plays were virtually the only musicals not following the Rodgers and Hammerstein formula.

A musical prodigy, Weill supported himself by playing piano and organ everywhere from synagogues to rathskellers. By the age of nineteen, he was convinced that he should write for the theatre, and by 1925 he was well established as a leading modern composer, heavily influenced by American dance music of the Big Band era, which he combined with the dissonance of modernists Paul Hindemith and Ernst Krenek. In what would become a lifelong attempt to find strong librettos for his work, Weill teamed with Bertholt Brecht. Their first collaboration, the 1927 songspiel *Mahagonny*, led to the full-length work *The Rise and Fall of the City of Mahagonny* in 1930 and 1929's *Happy End* (that other musical about gangsters and the Salvation Army, taking place in Chicago in 1919). But their greatest, most universal and long-lasting work was *The Threepenny Opera* (1928). Shortly after his productive "Berlin period," Weill became uncomfortable with Brecht's increasingly polemical texts and was censored by the Nazis. He immigrated to America in 1935, where he eventually became a citizen. There he composed a series of "Broadway musicals" that combined the commercial with the artistic.

Always looking for talented playwrights, he collaborated with Paul Green for a Group Theater production of the vehemently antiwar *Johnny Johnson* (1936); with Maxwell Anderson for *Knickerbocker Holiday* (1938), for which he wrote the eternal standard "September Song"; with Moss Hart and Ira Gershwin (in Ira's first work without his brother) for *Lady in the Dark* (1941), in which the musical numbers were all dream sequences launched by the psychological counseling of the leading lady; with S. J. Perleman and Ogden Nash for the Mary Martin showcase *One Touch of Venus* (1943); with Gershwin again on *The Firebrand of Florence* (1944), about the Italian artist Benvenuto Cellini; with Elmer Rice and Langston Hughes for *Street Scene* (1947), the first "opera" to follow *Porgy and Bess* on Broadway; with Alan Jay Lerner for the long-lost *Love Life* (1948), which follows a never-aging couple through 150 years of American history, an early "concept" musical; and the "musical tragedy" *Lost in the Stars* (1949), again with Anderson, based on the Alan Paton novel about blacks in South Africa, *Cry, the Beloved Country*.

Weill died in 1950, having completed some songs for a musical version of Mark Twain's *Huckleberry Finn*. Although some of his musicals were more successful than others, every one is of profound interest to the musical theatre lover, and every one boasts unique songs that could only have been written by Weill. He always insisted that there was no difference between popular music and serious music, only between good music and bad music. Virgil Thompson wrote of Weill that he was "the most original single workman in the whole musical theater…during the last quarter century.…Every work was a new model, a new shape, a new solution to dramatic problems."

"September Song," "Mack the Knife," and "Speak Low" are standards, but the songs an audience is less familiar with make an equal impression, often even more stunning for their unfamiliarity. There have been any number of Kurt Weill reviews, and a creative director probably ought to make up his or her own, since the wealth of music Weill created (from Berlin in the 1930s to Broadway in the 1950s, with a few stopovers in Hollywood, notably for the film musical *Where Do We Go from Here?* with Ira Gershwin) is a bursting treasure trove of unique theatre songs. But if you don't have the time or inclination to invent one, this is the best of the breed, a chronological jaunt through Weill's catalogue, mostly grouped by show:

Berlin to Broadway with Kurt Weill

A Musical Voyage

Berlin to Broadway with Kurt Weill at the Howard County Center for the Arts, Elliot City, MD.

Music by Kurt Weill
Lyrics by Maxwell Anderson, Marc Blitzstein, Bertolt Brecht, Jacques Deval, Michael
    Feingold, Ira Gershwin, Paul Green, Langston Hughes, Alan Jay Lerner, Ogden
    Nash, George Tabori, and Arnold Weinstein
Text and Format by Gene Lerner

Theatre De Lys; October 1, 1972; 152 performances.
Staged by Donald Saddler.

Original Cast:

Margery Cohen   Ken Kecheval
Judy Lander   Jerry Lanning
Hal Watters

Musical Numbers:

Threepenny Opera
Morning Anthem
Mack the Knife
Jealousy Duet
Tango Ballad
Love Duet
Barbara Song

Useless Song
How to Survive
Pirate Jenny
Happy Ending
Bilboa Song
Surabaya Johnny
Sailor Tango
Alabama Song
Deep in Alaska
Oh, Heavenly Salvation
As You Make Your Bed
Marie Galante
I Want for a Ship
Songs of Peace and War
Song of the Guns
Hymn to Peace
Johnny's Song
How Can You Tell an American?
September Song
My Ship
Girl of the Moment
The Saga of Jenny
One Touch of Venus
That's Him
Speak Low
Progress
Love Song
Moon-Faced, Starry-Eyed
Ain't It Awful, the Heat?
Lonely House
Lullaby
Train to Johannesburg
Trouble Man
Cry, the Beloved Country
Lost in the Stars

Licensing: Music Theatre International

Difficulties/Advantages: More of Weill's shows—from *Threepenny Opera* to *Street Scene* to *Lost in the Stars*—need to be resurrected by opera companies or in Broadway revivals. But for little theatres, this revue has it all, needing only two men, two women, and a non-singing "Guide." The songs are for real singers, to be sure, and the sentiments require strong presentations.

VINCENT YOUMANS

Private schools and piano lessons led Youmans to Yale, where he majored in engineering but quit in favor of a job on Wall Street as a clerk. He served in the Navy during World War I organizing shows, and would write some of the songs. When he mustered out, he embarked on a career in music, starting at Harms, where the famous Max Dreyfuss, a friend to many young composers, hired him as a staff pianist and song plugger. By the early 1920s, he was an established Broadway composer. With titles such as *Two Little Girls in Blue, Wildflower, Mary Jane McKane, Lollipop, Hit the Deck, Rainbow, Great Day,* and *A Night in Venice,* its not likely you're familiar with Youman's shows. Only *No, No, Nanette,* because it was successfully revived in the 1970s, is familiar to today's audiences. Yet Youmans was always pushing the boundaries of musical theatre, and *Rainbow* was an early attempt to integrate songs into the dramatic text. Today his most famous credit is probably the songs for the Hollywood film *Flying Down to Rio,* the film that partnered Fred Astaire and Ginger Rogers for the first time. In 1933 he contracted tuberculosis, and ill health forced him into semi-retirement. Ten years later, he returned to New York, where wealthy benefactor Doris Duke promoted *The Vincent Youmans Ballet Revue,* featuring modern and classical ballet, puppets, serious music, and elaborate costuming. It closed in Boston and never reached Broadway. Ahead of his time, he died at the age of forty-eight, leaving a trunkful of songs that are tuneful and the epitome of the roaring twenties.

Oh Me, Oh My, Oh Youmans

Conceived by Darwin Knight and Tom Taylor
Staged by Darwin Knight
Wonderhorse Theatre; January 4, 1981; 20 performances.

Original Cast:

Jo Ann Cunningham	Todd Taylor
Sally Woodson	Ronald Young

Musical Numbers:

Two Little Girls in Blue
Wildflower
Mary Jane McKane
A Night Out
No, No, Nanette
Oh Please
Hit the Deck
Rainbow
Great Day
Smiles
Through the Years
Take a Chance
Flying Down to Rio

Licensing: Contact the American Society of Composers, Authors and Publishers

Difficulties/Advantages: With only twenty performances, this revue hasn't gone far, but Youmans is well worth looking into if you're a fan of the early musicals.

Contact Information
for Licensing Organizations

Broadway Play Publishing

    56 East 81st Street
    New York, New York 10028-0202
    phone: 212-772-8334
    fax: 212-772-8358
    website: broadwayplaypubl.com

Dramatists Play Service

    440 Park Avenue South
    New York, New York 10016
    phone: 212-683-8960
    fax: 212-213-1539
    website: dramatists.com

Samuel French

    45 West 25th Street
    New York, New York 10010
    phone: 212-206-8990
    fax: 212-206-1429
    musical department: 212-206-8125
    website: samuelfrench.com

Music Theatre International

    421 West 54th Street
    New York, New York 10019
    phone: 212-541-4684
    fax: 212-397-4684
    website: mtishows.com

Rodgers and Hammerstein Theatre Library

    229 West 28th Street, 11th Floor
    New York, New York 10001
    phone: (800) 400-8160
    fax: 212-268-1245
    website: rnh.com

Tams-Witmark

    560 Lexington Avenue
    New York, New York 10022
    phone: 212-688-9191
    fax: 212-688-5656
    website: tams-witmark.com

Contact Information for Authors, Composers, and Lyricists

The Dramatists Guild

> 1501 Broadway, Suite 701
> New York, New York 10036
> phone: 212-398-9366
> fax: 212-944-0420
> website: dramaguild.com

American Society of Composers, Authors and Publishers

> One Lincoln Plaza
> New York, New York 10023
> phone: 212-621-6000
> fax: 212-724-9064
> website: ascap.com

Broadcast Music Inc.

> 320 West 57th Street
> New York, New York 10019
> phone: 212-586-2000
> website: bmi.com

Index of Titles

About the Author

DENNY MARTIN FLINN grew up in San Francisco and Los Angeles, majored in theatre at San Francisco State College, and then traveled to New York. There, for two decades, he worked as a dancer in American musicals on Broadway, off-Broadway, in stock and national tours, and in nightclubs, on television, and at Radio City Music Hall. He danced for famed choreographers Jerome Robbins, Gower Champion, Michael Kidd, Michael Bennett, and many others. He retired from dancing after spending two and a half years in Michael Bennett's *A Chorus Line* as Greg and Zach.

In various theatres across the country, he has directed and choreographed versions of the musicals *Grease, Godspell, The Boy Friend, Carnival, How to Succeed in Business Without Really Trying, Company, You're a Good Man, Charlie Brown*, and *Sugar*, starring Robert Morse, Larry Kert, and Cyril Ritchard. He wrote and directed the musical *Groucho* starring Lewis J. Stadlen, which played off-Broadway and toured the country for two years. He has choreographed rock-video sequences for the soap operas *Another World* and *Search for Tomorrow*, a ballroom sequence for the feature film *The Deceivers*, and *Grease* and *Damn Yankees* for the Sierra Canyon Middle School drama class!

His first book was *What They Did for Love*, the story of the making of the Broadway musical *A Chorus Line*. He followed that with two mystery novels, *San Francisco Kills* and *Killer Finish*, featuring the grandson of Sherlock Holmes. He co-authored with Nicholas Meyer the screenplay for *Star Trek VI: The Undiscovered Country* and two radio plays for the BBC: *Don Quixote,* which won a Writers' Guild of Great Britain nomination, and an adaptation of Meyer's *The Seven-Per-Cent Solution*. Returning to books, he wrote the Star Trek novel *The Fearful Summons* and *Musical! A Grand Tour—the Rise, Glory and Fall of an American Institution,* which won an ASCAP/Deems Taylor Award for popular-music writing. His most recent books are *How Not to Write a Screenplay* and *How Not to Audition.*